"国家中等职业教育改革发展示范学校建设计划"项目教材

中等职业教育"十三五"规划教材·国际贸易系列

常用国际商务单证制作习题集

主编／徐菊红　章忻雯

副主编／谢富敏

参编／林　炜　李小成

主审／傅　蕾

立信会计出版社

LIXIN ACCOUNTING PUBLISHING HOUSE

图书在版编目(CIP)数据

常用国际商务单证制作习题集 / 徐菊红,章忻雯主编. —上海:立信会计出版社,2015.9
ISBN 978-7-5429-4623-2

Ⅰ.①常… Ⅱ.①徐… ②章… Ⅲ.①国际贸易—票据—中等专业学校—习题集 Ⅳ.①F740.44-44

中国版本图书馆 CIP 数据核字(2015)第 237510 号

策划编辑　　陈　瑶
责任编辑　　陈　昕
封面设计　　周崇文

常用国际商务单证制作习题集

出版发行	立信会计出版社			
地　址	上海市中山西路 2230 号	邮政编码	200235	
电　话	(021)64411389	传　真	(021)64411325	
网　址	www.lixinaph.com	电子邮箱	lxaph@sh163.net	
网上书店	www.shlx.net	电　话	(021)64411071	
经　销	各地新华书店			
印　刷	常熟市梅李印刷有限公司			
开　本	787 毫米×1092 毫米　　　1/16			
印　张	6			
字　数	125 千字			
版　次	2015 年 9 月第 1 版			
印　次	2015 年 9 月第 1 次			
印　数	1—3 100			
书　号	ISBN 978-7-5429-4623-2/F			
定　价	30.00 元(含习题集)			

如有印订差错,请与本社联系调换

目录

第一部分　专业基础知识 ·· 1
 项目一　认识国际商务单证工作 ··· 1
 项目二　审核信用证 ··· 4
 项目三　缮制商业发票和装箱单 ··· 11
 项目四　办理出口货物的产地证书和运输 ······························· 14
 项目五　办理出口货物的保险和报检 ···································· 19
 项目六　办理出口货物的报关和出运 ···································· 23
 项目七　办理出口货物的结汇 ··· 26

第二部分　专业技能练习 ·· 30
 项目一　审核信用证 ··· 30
 项目二　缮制信用证项下 FOB 术语出口单据 ·························· 32
 项目三　缮制信用证项下 CFR 术语出口单据 ·························· 39
 项目四　缮制信用证项下 CIF 术语出口单据 ··························· 48
 项目五　缮制电汇项下 CIF 术语出口单据 ······························ 65
 项目六　缮制托收项下 CFR 术语出口单据 ···························· 77
 项目七　缮制开证申请书 ·· 87

第一部分

专业基础知识

项目一 认识国际商务单证工作

一、请将下列英语词组翻译成中文并抄写

1. SALES CONFIRMATION _____
2. TIME OF SHIPMENT _____
3. SALES CONTRACT _____
4. NAME OF COMMODITY AND SPECIFICATION _____
5. QUANTITY _____
6. UNIT PRICE _____
7. AMOUNT _____
8. TERMS OF PAYMENT _____
9. SHIPPING MARKS _____
10. PORT OF LOADING _____
11. PORT OF DESTINATION _____
12. PARTIAL SHIPMENTS _____
13. TRANSSHIPMENT _____
14. B/L DATE _____
15. INSURANCE _____

二、单项选择题

(   ) 1. 单证缮制必须做到正确、完整、及时、简明和整洁,其中单证工作的前提是_____。
    A. 及时 B. 完整 C. 正确 D. 简明

(   ) 2. 在信用证支付方式下,银行处理的是_____。
    A. 服务 B. 货物 C. 单据 D. 其他行为

(   ) 3. 按照单证形式,国际贸易单证分为_____。
    A. 金融单据和商业单据 B. 纸面单证和电子单证
    C. 基本单据和附属单据 D. 保险单据和包装单据

(   ) 4. 狭义的单证是指_____。
    A. 单据和文件 B. 信用证和证书 C. 单据和信用证 D. 信用证和文件

(   ) 5. 根据联合国设计推荐使用的用英文字母表示的货币代码表述中,不正确的是_____。
   A. RMB 135.00   B. JPY 13 500.00   C. USD 135.00   D. CNY 135.00

(   ) 6. 信用证支付方式下,制单和审单的首要依据是_____。
   A. 信用证   B. 合同买卖
   C. 相关国际惯例   D. 有关商品的原始资料

(   ) 7. 非信用证支付方式下,制单和审单的首要依据是_____。
   A. 信用证   B. 买卖合同
   C. 相关国际惯例   D. 有关商品的原始资料

(   ) 8. 银行在处理信用证业务时,要求受益人在_____内提交有效的单据。
   A. 交单期   B. 信用证的有效期
   C. 装运期前   D. 交单期且又在信用证的有效期

(   ) 9. 单证工作不仅要制单及时,交单也要及时,银行拒收迟于装运日后_____天后提交的单据。
   A. 10   B. 15   C. 21   D. 31

(   )10. 一笔出口业务,信用证有效期是2014年4月15日,装运期为2014年4月1日,实际装运日为3月16日,交单期为装运日后15天内交单,最迟交单日为_____。
   A. 2014.3.31   B. 2014.4.1   C. 2014.4.2   D. 2014.3.30

三、多项选择题

(   ) 1. 所谓单证是指进口业务中使用的各种_____,如商业发票和提单等,买卖双方凭借这些单据来处理货物的交付、运输、保险、商检和结汇等。
   A. 单据   B. 证书
   C. 检验检疫证书   D. 保险单

(   ) 2. 外贸单证工作主要有_____等方面的内容,它贯穿于进口合同履行的全过程。
   A. 审证   B. 制单   C. 审单   D. 交单

(   ) 3. 单证缮制的具体要求有_____。
   A. 正确   B. 完整   C. 及时   D. 简明和简洁

(   ) 4. 制单中"三相符"的要求包括_____。
   A. 单证相符   B. 单单相符   C. 单货相符   D. 货同相符

(   ) 5. 运输单据包括_____。
   A. 海运提单   B. 邮政收据   C. 空运单   D. 铁路运单

(   ) 6. 下列单据中,_____是可以转让的结算单据。
   A. 提单   B. 海运单   C. 商业汇票   D. 保险单

(   ) 7. 国际贸易单证通常用于处理进出口货物的_____。
   A. 交付   B. 运输与保险

　　　　C. 报检报关　　　　　　　　　　D. 结汇
(　　) 8. 单证的完整性包括_____。
　　　　A. 单证签署的完整　　　　　　B. 单证种类的完整
　　　　C. 单证份数的完整　　　　　　D. 单证内容的完整
(　　) 9. 制单的依据包括_____。
　　　　A. 买卖合同和信用证　　　　　B. 有关商品的原始资料
　　　　C. 相关国际惯例　　　　　　　D. 相关国内管理规定
(　　)10. 国际贸易单证工作可能涉及的部门包括_____。
　　　　A. 银行　　　B. 海关　　　C. 运输　　　D. 保险
　　　　E. 检验检疫机构行政管理机构等

四、判断题

(　　) 1. 单证工作能及时反映货、船、证等业务的管理现状,为了杜绝差错事故的发生,避免带来不必要的经济损失,因此必须加强工作责任心。
(　　) 2. 外贸单证员是指外贸业务履行中,根据销售合同、信用证条款进行缮制各种单据、证书的工作人员。
(　　) 3. 广义的单证指各种文件和凭证。
(　　) 4. 在国际结算中,货物是贸易双方进行结算的基础和依据。
(　　) 5. 从商业观点来看,可以说CFR合同的目的不是货物本身,而是与货物有关的单据的买卖。
(　　) 6. 单证"三相符"中最主要的是"单货相符"。
(　　) 7. 银行在审单时,如信用证无特殊规定,都是以《跟单信用证统一惯例》作为审单的依据。
(　　) 8. 单证的完整性是指成套单证的群体的完整性。
(　　) 9. 根据《2010通则》,纸面单证和电子单证具有同等效力。
(　　)10. 根据单证的用途可划分为商业单据和银行单据。

五、解读下列合同并翻译画线部分条款

SALES CONTRACT

NO.：TSD2013065

DATE：MAY. 20. 2014

SELLER：DALIAN STATIONERY AND SPORTING GOODS IMP. AND EXP. CORP.
ADDRESS：215 NANJIN ROAD, DALIAN
BUYER：TIKE TRADE CO. LTD.，
ADDRESS：5 EAST STREET, KONG ZONE, LONDON

THIS CONTRACT IS MADE BY AND BETWEEN THE BUYERS AND THE SELLERS, WHEREBY THE BUYERS AGREE TO BUY AND THE SELLERS AGREE TO SELL THE UNDER MEN-

TIONED COMMODITY ACCORDING TO THE TERMS AND CONDITIONS STIPULATED BELOW:

NAME OF COMMODITY: LADIES DENIM SKIRT

SPECIFICATION: MODEL NO. 5

QUANTITY: 2 000 DOZENS

UNIT PRICE: CFR LONDON USD 56.00 PER DOZEN

AMOUNT: USD 112 000.00 (SAY U.S. DOLLARS ONE HUNDRED ELVEN THOUSAND ONLY)

SHIPMENT: FROMDALIAN, CHINA TO LONDON, HOLLAND NOT LATER THAN JULY 30, 2014 WITH TRANSSHIPMENT AND PARTIAL SHIPMENT NOT ALLOWED

PACKING: BY SEAWORTHY CARTONS(CTNS)

INSURANCE: TO BE COVERED BY BUYERS

TERMS OF PAYMENT: BY IRREVOCABLE LETTER OF CREDIT AT SIGHT

SHIPPING MARKS: AT SELLERS' OPTION

项目二 审核信用证

一、请将下列英语词组翻译成中文并抄写

1. IRREVOCABLE LETTER OF CREDIT _____
2. ISSUING BANK _____
3. FORM OF DOC. CREDIT _____
4. DOC CREDIT NO _____
5. DATE OF ISSUE _____
6. DATE AND PLACE OFEXPIRY _____
7. APPLICANT _____
8. BENEFICIARY _____
9. AVAILABLE WITH _____
10. DRAFTS AT _____
11. CURRENCY CODE _____
12. DRAWEE _____
13. DOCUMENTS REQUIRED _____
14. DETAILS OF CHARGES _____
15. PRESENTATION PERIOD _____

二、单项选择题

(　　) 1. 信用证的基础是买卖合同,当信用证与买卖合同规定不一致并且不能接受时,受益人应要求_____。

A. 开证行修改　　　　　　　　B. 开证申请人修改

C. 通知行修改　　　　　　　　D. 自行修改

(　　) 2. 在合同中,若约定采用信用证支付方式的,负有开立信用证的义务的是_____。
  A. 进口商　　　　　　　　　B. 出口商
  C. 开证行　　　　　　　　　D. 议付行

(　　) 3. 交易金额较大,对开证行的资信不了解时,为保证货款及时收回,卖方最好选择_____。
  A. 可撤销信用证　　　　　　B. 远期信用证
  C. 承兑交单　　　　　　　　D. 保兑信用证

(　　) 4. 信用证付款方式下,如果合同与信用证条款不相符的情况下,银行付款的前提是出口商提交的单据_____相符。
  A. 与买卖合同的规定
  B. 与信用证的规定
  C. 同时与信用证规定和买卖合同的规定
  D. 与合同规定或信用证的规定

(　　) 5. 对于不可撤销信用证开出后,对其中条款的修改,下列说法中,正确的是_____。
  A. 不容许任何形式的修改
  B. 只能在一定范围内修改
  C. 在信用证有效期内,任何一方的任何修改,都必须经买卖双方协商一致同意后,由申请人通过开证行办理修改
  D. 买卖双方都可直接要求开证行修改

(　　) 6. 根据《UCP600》的解释,信用证第一付款人是_____。
  A. 进口人　　B. 开证行　　C. 议付行　　D. 通知行

(　　) 7. 信用证经保兑后,保兑行_____。
  A. 只有在开证行没有能力付款时,才承担保证付款责任
  B. 和开证行一样,承担第一性付款责任
  C. 需和开证行商议决定双方各自的责任
  D. 只有在买方没有能力付款时,才承担付款责任

(　　) 8. 在国际贸易结算方式下,下列项目中,_____不属于商业信用。
  A. 汇付　　　B. 信用证　　C. 托收　　　D. 电汇

(　　) 9. 信用证只规定有效期,未规定装运期,该信用证称为_____。
  A. 不可撤销信用证　　　　　　B. 可转让信用证
  C. 双到期信用证　　　　　　　D. 可保兑信用证

(　　)10. 一张有效的信用证,必须规定_____。
  A. 有效期　　B. 最迟装运期　　C. 付款期　　D. 交单期

三、多项选择题

(　　) 1. 对于信用证与合同关系的表述中,正确的有_____。

A. 信用证的开立以买卖合同为依据
   B. 信用证的履行不受买卖合同的约束
   C. 有关银行只根据信用证的规定办理信用证业务
   D. 合同是审核信用证的依据
( ) 2. 按《UCP 600》规定,信用证_____。
   A. 未规定是否保兑,即为保兑信用证
   B. 未规定是否转让,即为不可转让信用证
   C. 未规定是否保兑,即为不保兑信用证
   D. 未规定是否撤销,即为不可撤销信用证
( ) 3. 在国际贸易中,常用的结算方式有_____。
   A. 预付   B. 信用证   C. 托收   D. 汇付
( ) 4. 根据《UCP600》规定,开证行可以拒付货款的理由有_____。
   A. 开证申请人破产   B. 单证不符
   C. 货物与合同不符   D. 单单不符
( ) 5. 根据《UCP600》规定,银行在处理信用证业务时应做到_____。
   A. 不管单据
   B. 不管贸易合同
   C. 不管货物
   D. 不管买卖双方是否已对合同履约

四、判断题

( ) 1. 如果受益人超过信用证有效期到银行议付,受益人只要征得开证人的同意,即可以要求付款银行付款。
( ) 2. 汇付是付款人主动通过银行或其他途径将货款交收款人的一种支付方式,所以属于商业信用,而托收通常称为银行托收,因而它属于银行信用。
( ) 3. 信用证是一种银行开立的有条件承诺付款的书面条件。
( ) 4. 在信用证业务中,信用证的开立是以买卖合同为基础的,因此,信用证条款与买卖合同条款严格相符是开证行向受益人承担付款责任的条件。
( ) 5.《UCP 600》规定,信用证的修改通知书有多项内容时,受益人可只接受同意的内容,而对不同意的内容予以拒绝即可。
( ) 6. 在审核信用证条款时,如果发现该信用证条款彼此矛盾,应提出修改信用证。
( ) 7. 跟单信用证是指结算货款时,应将所有单据随附在该信用证项下的汇票后。
( ) 8. 在信用证支付方式下,不仅单据表面与信用证条款相符合,而且要和实物相符,开证行才按规定付款。
( ) 9. 信用证的基本当事人有出口商、进口商、付款银行和开证银行。
( )10. 只要在L/C规定的交单期内,不论受益人何时向银行提交符合L/C要求

的单据,开证行一律不得拒收单据和拒付货款。

五、解读信用证并回答问题

SEQUENCE OF TOTAL	*27	1/1
FORM OF DOC. CREDIT	*40	IRREVOCABLE
DOC. CREDIT NUMBER	*20	AIB. IM06063506
DATE OF ISSUE	*31C	140624
EXPIRY	*31D	DATE 1406 PLACE CHINA
APPLICANT BANK	51A	AIBKIE2DXXX
		AIB BANK
		DUBLIN
APPLICANT	*50	BAND C CANTWELL, CC FITTINGS,
		MEADOWLANDS GRANTSTOWN CO WATERFORD
BENEFICIARY	*59	GUANGDONG TEXTILES IMPORT AND
		EXPORT COTTON MANUFACTURED GOODS CO
		14/F GUANGDONG TEXTILES MANSIONS
		168 XIAO BEI RD GUANGZHOU CHINA
AMOUNT	*32B	CURRENCY USD AMOUNT 20 060.00
AVAILABLE WITH/BY	*41A	AIB BANK BY ACCEPTANCE
DRAFTS AT …	42C	30 DAYS SIGHT
DRAWEE	42A	AIBKE2DXXX
		AIB BANK
		DUBLIN
PARTIAL SHIPMENTS	43P	PROHIBITED
TRANSSHIPMENT	43T	PERMITTED
LOADING IN CHARGE	44A	GUANGZHOU CHINA
FOR TRANSPORT TO …	44B	DUBLIN, IRELAND
DESCRIPT. OF GOODS	45A	DRAWER SLIDES AND HANDLES
		AS PER S/C NO. 89745CIF DUBLIN, IRELAND
DOCUMENTS REQUIRED	46A:	+SIGNED INVOICES IN TRIPLICATE
		+FULL SET OF CLEAN ON BOARD MARINE BILLS OF
		LADING CONSIGNED TO ORDER, BLANK ENDORSED,
		MARKED FREIGHT PREPAID AND CLAUSED
		NOTIFY APPLICANT
		+INSURANCE POLICY/CERTIFICATE BLANK
		ENDORSED COVERING ALL RISKS FOR 10 PER CENT
		ABOVE THE CIF VALUE
		+CERTIFICATE OF CHINA ORIGIN ISSUED BY A
		RELEVANT HORITY
		+PACKING LIST N TRIPLICATE

DETAILS OF CHARGES	71B	BANK CHARGES EXCLUDING ISSUING BANKS ARE FOR ACCOUNT OF BENEFICIARY
PRESENTATION PERIOD	48	DOCUMENTS TO BE PRESENTED WITHIN 21 DAYS FROM SHIPMENT DATE
CONFIRMATION	*49	WITHOUT

问题：

1. 谁是 ISSUING BANK?

2. 这是即期 L/C 还是远期 L/C? 为什么?

3. L/C 的付款方式是哪一种?

4. 装运期是何时? 为什么?

5. 保险费应该有哪一方承担? 为什么?

6. 装箱单应该提交几份?

7. 如果货物实际于 2014 年 6 月 16 日装运,按照交单期的规定,最迟应该在何时交单?

8. 银行费用由谁承担?

六、根据销售合同审核并修改信用证

（一）合同资料

SALES CONTRACT

SELLERS: NINGBO FINE CHEMICALS IMPORT 　　CONTRACT NO. PSO2005X06
　　　　 AND EXPORT CO. LTD.,　　　　　　　 DATE: APR. 22. 2014.
　　　　 22F, MAOXING RDNINGBO, P. R. CHINA SIGNED AT: NINGBO
TEL: 86-0574-58391128
BUYERS: TANWAI TRADE CORP.
ADDRESS: 1, CHANGKYO-DONG CHOONG-KU
　　　　　SEOUL, KOREA
THE SALES CONTRACT IS MADE BY AND BETWEEN THE SELLERS AND BUYERS WHEREBY THE SELLERS AGREE TO SELL AND THE BUYERS AGREE TO BUY THE UNDER-MENTIONED GOODS ACCORDING TO THE TERMS AND CONDITIONS STIPULATED BELOW:
　　DIMETHOUATE 96 PCT TECH　12MT(12 000KGS)　USD 3.00/KG　USD 36 000.00
　　PACKING:150KGS NET IN ONE IRON DRUM,　　　　CFR HAIPHONE PORT
　　80 DRUMS IN ONE 20 FEET CONTAINER,

ORIGIN CHINA

DELIVERY FROM NINGBO TO HAIPHONE PORT

SHIPPING MARKS DIMETHOATE 96PCT TECH/VIPESCO HANOI/GROSS WT. /NET. WT/DATE OF MFG. /DATE OF EXP

TIME OF SHIPMENT: MAY. 30, 2014 AFTER RECEIPT OF L/C. ALLOWING TRANSSHIPMENT AND PARTIAL SHIMPMET

TERMS OF PAYMENT: BY 100% CONFIRMED IRREVOCABLE LETTER OF CREDIT IN FAVOR OF THE SELLERS TO BE AVAILABLE BY SIGHT DRAFT TO BE OPENED AND TO REACH CHINA BEFORE MAY. 1, 2014 AND REMAIN TO VALID FOR NEGOTIATION IN CHINA UNTIL THE 15TH DAYS AFTER THE AFORESAID TIME OF SHIPMENT. L/C MUST MENTION THIS CONTRACT NUMBER, L/C ADVISED BY BANK OF CHINA NINGBO LANXI BR

INSURANCE: TO BE EFFECTED BY BUYERS

其他材料：进出口方明确出口方应提交如下单据：标明合同号码的手签的发票三份，装箱单三份，全套清洁凭越南银行指示的、通知人为申请人的提单；质检局出具的产地证一份，质量和数量证书各一份。

（二）信用证资料

ISSUING BANK:		SHINNAN BANK, SEOUL
FORM OF DOC. CREDIT	40A	IRREVOCABLE AND CONFIRMED
DOC CREDIT NO	20	W3 745603TU03402
DATE OF ISSUE	31C	140428
EXPIRY	31D	DATE 140501 PLACE IN BENE'S COUNTRY
APPLICANT	50	TANWAI TRADE CORP
		1, CHANGKYO-DONG CHOONG-KU
		SEOUL, KOREA
BENEFICIARY	59	NINGBO FINE CHEMICALS IMPORT AND EXPORT CO. ITD. ,
		22F, MAOXING RD NINGBO, P. R. CHINA
		TEL: 86-21-58391218
AMOUNT	32B	USD 36 000. 00 (SAY US DOLLARS THIRTY SIX THOUSAND ONLY)
AVAILABLE WITH / BY	41A	ANY BANK BY NEGOTIATION
DRAFTS AT	42C	30 DAYS AFTER SIGHT
PARTIAL SHIPMENTS	43P	PROHIBITED
TRANSSHIPMENT	43T	PERMITTED
LOADING IN CHARGE	44A	NINGBO PORT
FOR TRANSPORT TO	44B	HAIPHONE PORT
SHIPMENT PERIOD	44C	AT THE LATEST APR. 30, 2015
DESCRIPTOF GOODS	45A	DIMETHOATE 96 PCT TECH
		PACKING: 150KGS NET IN ONE IRON DRUM,
		80 DRUMS IN ONE 40' FEET CONTAINER,

		12MT(12 000KGS) AT USD 2.875/DRUM ORIGIN CHINA CFR HAIPHONE PORT
DOCUMENTS REQUIRED	46A	+SIGNED COMMERCIAL INVOINE IN TRIPLICATE
+PACKING LIST IN TRIPLICATE
+A COPY OF CLEAN ON BOARD MARINE BILL OF LADING MADE OUT TO ORDER OF VIETINDE BANK HANOI BRANCH, MARKED FREIGHT PREPAID AND NOTIFY BRANCH OFFICE
NO. 1 IN HANOI OF VIETNAM PESTICIDE COMPANY-802 TRIEU QUOC DAT HANOI VIETNAM
+CERTIFICATE OF ORIGIN ISSUED BY THE CHINESE CHAMBER OF COMMERCE AND INDUSTRY
+INSURANCE POLICY/CERTIFICATE COVERING ALL RISKS AND WAR RISKS OF PICC, INCLUDING WAREHOUSE TO WAREHOUSE CLAUSE UP TO FINAL DESTINATION AT HAIPHONE FOR AT LEASE 120 PCT OF CIF VALUE
+SHIPPING ADVICES MUST BE SENT TO APPLICANT WITHIN 2 DAYS AFTER SHIPMENT ADVISING NO OF PACKAGES, GROSS & NET WEIGHT, VESSEL NAME, BILL OF LADING NO. AND DATE, CONTRACT NO., VALUE
+QUAITY CERTIFICATE ISSUED BY MAKER.
+QUANTITY/WEIGHT CERTIFICATE ISSUED BY MAKER
SHIPPING MARKS: DIMETHOATE 96PCT TECH
VIPESCO HANOI
GROSS WT
NET. WT
DATE OF EXP
PRESENTATION PERIOD	48	7 DAYS AFTER ISSUANCE DATE OF SHIPPING DOCUMENT
CONFIRMATION	49	WITHOUT
INSTRUCTIONS	78	T/T REIMBURSEMENT NOT ALLOWED
UPON RECEIPT OF ALL DOCS AND DRAFTS IN CONFORMITY WITH TERMS AND CONDITIONS OF THIS CREDIT WE SHALL REMIT THE PROCEEDS TO THE BANK DESIGNATED BY NEGOTIATING BANK, THE DRAFTS MUST BE NEGOTIATED AT SIGHT BASIS SINCE ACCEPTANCE COMM AND DISCOUNT CHARGES ARE

FOR BUYER'S ACCOUNT. DOCS AND DRAFTS MUST BE COURIERED TO US IN ONE LOT.

REIMBURSEMENT IS SUBJECT TO ICC URR525

要求:请根据上述销售合同审核信用证存在的问题,并加以详细列出。

1. _____
2. _____
3. _____
4. _____
5. _____
6. _____
7. _____
8. _____
9. _____
10. _____

项目三 缮制商业发票和装箱单

一、请将下列英语词组翻译成中文并抄写

1. COMMERCIAL INVOICE _____
2. ISSUER _____
3. TRANSPORT DETAILS _____
4. TERMS OF PAYMENT _____
5. MARKS AND NUMBERS _____
6. NUMBER AND KIND OF PACKAGE _____
7. DESCRIPTION OF GOODS _____
8. INVOICE NO _____
9. PACKAGE _____
10. GROSS WEIGHT _____
11. NET WEIGHT _____
12. MEASUREMENT _____

二、单项选择题

( ) 1. _____是结汇单证中最重要的单据,其他单据都是以其为依据缮制的。
　　　A. 装箱单　　　　　　　　B. 原产地证书
　　　C. 商业发票　　　　　　　D. 运输单据

( ) 2. 发票根据作用不同,可分为商业发票、形式发票、领事发票、厂商发票、联合发票、海关发票和证实发票等,其中_____是出口业务结汇中最重要的单据之一,是出口货物的核心单据。

A. 商业发票　　　　　　　　　　B. 形式发票
C. 领事发票　　　　　　　　　　D. 海关发票

( )3. 商业发票编号由出口公司根据本公司的实际情况自行编制,是全套结汇单据的_____。
A. 佐证编号　　　　　　　　　　B. 参考编号
C. 联系编号　　　　　　　　　　D. 中心编号

( )4. 商业发票的签发日期在整套结汇单据中应_____。
A. 早于汇票的签发日期　　　　　B. 早于提单签发日期
C. 早于保险单的签发日期　　　　D. 是最早签发的单据

( )5. 目前经常使用的有_____海关发票,其他的已不多见。
A. 美国　　　B. 日本　　　C. 加拿大　　　D. 英国

( )6. 厂商发票是厂方出具给出口商的销售货物的凭证。来证要求提供厂商发票,其目的是_____。
A. 检查是否有削价倾销行为,以便确定应否征收"反倾销税"
B. 按某些国家法令规定,出口商对其国家输入货物时必须取得进口国在出口国或其邻近地区的领事签证的、作为装运单据一部分和货物进口报关的前提条件之一的特殊发票
C. 为进口商向其本国当局申请进口许可证或请求核批外汇之用
D. 作为国际商务单据中的基础单据,是缮制报关单、产地证、报检单、投保单等其他单据的依据

( )7. 发票唛头应按信用证或合同规定的填制,如没有唛头,则填写_____。
A. NO　　　B. YES　　　C. N/M　　　D. N/N

( )8. 汇丰银行东京分行开立 L/C,开证人是 YILING LTD. CO., NEW-YORK, USA, L/C 规定 INVOICE MUST OUT TO XYZ LTD. CO., TOKYO JAPAN,出口商发票的抬头人应该作成_____。
A. YILING LTD. CO., NEWYORK, USA
B. XYZ LTD. CO., TOKYO JAPAN
C. YILING LTD. CO., NEWYORK, USA AND XYZ LTD. CO., TOKYO JAPAN
D. 汇丰银行东京分行

( )9. 包装单据一般不应显示货物的_____,因为进口商把商品转售时只要交付包装单据和货物,不愿泄露其购买成本。
A. 品名、总金额　　　　　　　　B. 单价、总金额
C. 包装件数、品名　　　　　　　D. 品名、单价

( )10. 包装单据是详细反映货物数量、包装和装箱等情况的单据,它是_____的补充单据,因此往往不需要再显示货物的价格等内容。
A. 品质证书　　　　　　　　　　B. 提单
C. 产地证　　　　　　　　　　　D. 商业发票

(   )11. 信用证规定不迟于9月底装运大约8 000双皮鞋,单价为5美元,总金额4万美元,出口商最多可装运_____双皮鞋。
   A. 8 000   B. 8 800   C. 7 200   D. 7 800

三、多项选择题

(   ) 1. 商业发票(COMMERCIAL INVOICE),在实际工作中简称发票(IN-VOICE),商业发票指_____。
   A. 出口方向进口方开列发货价目清单
   B. 买卖双方记账的依据,也是进出口报关交税的总说明
   C. 它是结汇单证中最重要的单据,能让有关当事人了解一笔交易的全貌
   D. 其他单据都是以发票为依据

(   ) 2. 唛头是货物的识别标志,运输企业在装卸、搬运时,根据唛头来识别货物,作为重要的识别标志,必须在整套单据中正确显示。唛头通常包括_____。
   A. 收发货人简称   B. 合同号、件号等
   C. 目的港(地)   D. 体积和总价等

(   ) 3. 在显示发票抬头人时,必须注意的事项有_____。
   A. 抬头可以是空白的
   B. 如果信用证有指定其他抬头人的,按来证规定制单
   C. 如果该信用证已被转让,则银行也可接受由第二受益人提交的以第一受益人为抬头的发票
   D. 必须做成信用证的申请人名称、地址

(   ) 4. 下面关于海关发票描述中,正确的有_____。
   A. 出口商填写的
   B. 由进口商填写
   C. 出口人向出口地海关报关时提供的单据
   D. 是进口地海关进行估价定税,征收差别关税或反倾销税的依据

(   ) 5. 发票中的价格条件十分重要,以下说法中,正确的有_____。
   A. 因为它涉及买卖双方责任的承担、费用的负担和风险的划分问题,另外,也是进口地海关核定关税的依据
   B. 来证价格条件如与合同中规定的有出入,应及时修改信用证,如事先没有修改,还是应该照信用证规定制单,否则会造成单证不符
   C. 另外,也是进口地海关核定关税的依据
   D. 价格可以根据具体情况酌情修改

(   ) 6. 形式发票也称预开发票或开价发票,通常在未成交之前,为进口商向本国当局申请进口许可证或请求核批外汇之用,下列说法中,正确的有_____。

A. 形式发票不是一种正式发票
B. 能用于托收和议付，正式成交后不要另外重新缮制商业发票
C. 形式发票与商业发票的关系密切，信用证在货物描述后面常有"按照某月某日之形式发票"等条款
D. 假如来证附有形式发票，则形式发票构成信用证的组成部分，制单时要按形式发票内容全部打上

四、判断题

(   ) 1. 在出口发票上必须明确显示数量、单价、总值和贸易术语(价格条款)等。

(   ) 2. 如果信用证没有规定不允许，出口发票的出票日期可早于信用证的开证日期。

(   ) 3. 信用证只规定了货物的总称，发票可写详细的货名，不出现总称。

(   ) 4. 如信用证规定，发票要证实 THE CONTENTS OF INVOICE ARE TRUE AND CORRECT，制作发票时必须把这句话显示出来，并做签署。

(   ) 5. 信用证品名是 MEN'S TROUSERS，发票打 MEN'S TROUSERS AND SOCKS (FREE OF CHARGE)，单到开证行，开证行认为是不符点，这是不正确的。

(   ) 6. 如信用证总金额是按含佣金价计算的，商业发票显示总金额时应扣除佣金。

(   ) 7. 某信用证规定 CFR DUBAL LINER TERM，出口发票打 CFR DUBAL，B/L 加注 LINER TERM，开证行不能以此拒付。

(   ) 8. 信用证中注明 INVOICE IN THREE COPIES，受益人向银行交单时，提供了三张副本发票。此做法，违反了信用证的规定。

(   ) 9. 出口商出口一批布匹，信用证规定 10 000 码，金额 4 万美元，现出运了 10 500 码，发票金额 USD 42 000，导致了超装，给收汇带来了风险。

(   )10. 货物外包装上的运输标志须在有关的托运单、商业发票、装箱单、提单上显示，但指示性标志、警告标志和危险性标志无须在上述文件上显示。

项目四　办理出口货物的产地证书和运输

一、请将下列英语词组翻译成中文并抄写

1. CERTIFICATE OF ORIGIN ＿＿＿＿＿＿＿＿＿＿＿＿
2. CERTIFICATE NO ＿＿＿＿＿＿＿＿＿＿＿＿
3. EXPORTER ＿＿＿＿＿＿＿＿＿＿＿＿
4. CONSIGNEE ＿＿＿＿＿＿＿＿＿＿＿＿
5. MEANS OF TRANSPORT AND ROUTE ＿＿＿＿＿＿＿＿＿＿＿＿
6. DESTINATION PORT ＿＿＿＿＿＿＿＿＿＿＿＿

7. NUMBER AND DATE OF INVOICE _____
8. DECLARATION BY THE EXPORTER _____
9. OCEAN BILL OF LADING _____
10. B/L NO _____
11. SHIPPER _____
12. NOTIFYPARTY _____
13. VESSEL _____
14. FREIGHT AND CHARGES _____
15. PREPAID AT _____
16. FREIGHT PAYABLE AT _____
17. PLACE AND DATE OF ISSUE _____
18. NUMBER OF ORIGINAL BS/L _____

二、单项选择题

( ) 1. 原产国的基本含义是出口产品的_____。
　　A. 起运国　　B. 制造国　　C. 出口国　　D. 消费国

( ) 2. 根据我国有关规定,出口企业最迟应于货物出运前_____天,向签证机构申请办理原产地证。
　　A. 1～2　　B. 2～10　　C. 3～5　　D. 4～8

( ) 3. 在"一般原产地证书"中在商品名称栏目填完后,在下面一行加上＊＊＊＊＊表示填写_____。
　　A. 开始　　B. 连接符号　　C. 结束　　D. 无意义

( ) 4. 原产地证书中原产地标准,按货物原料进口成分的实际情况分别按比例填制。按规定用一个英文大写字母表示,_____表示完全不含进口成分,并冠以引号。
　　A. "F"　　B. "G"　　C. "P"　　D. "W"

( ) 5. 原产地证书是证明本批出口商品的生产地,并符合《中华人民共和国出口货物原产地规则》的一种文件,如果信用证或合同对签证机构未作具体规定,一般由_____签发。
　　A. 中国出入境检验检疫局　　B. 中国国际贸易促进委员会
　　C. 海关　　D. 出口商

( ) 6. G. S. P. FORM A 是一种_____的证明书。
　　A. 品质证明书　　B. 普惠制产地证明书
　　C. 重量证明书　　D. 动植物检疫证明书

( ) 7. 出口业务中,国外某客户要求我方提供"GSP产地证",在我国这种证书的签发机构是_____。
　　A. 商务部　　B. 贸促会
　　C. 出入境检验检疫局　　D. 出口商

(   ) 8. 出口商应在(   )通过传真、邮寄等方式,向进口商发出装运通知。
　　　　A. 装运前　　　　B. 装船完毕　　　C. 交单后　　　　D. 收款后

(   ) 9. 信用证规定贸易术语为 CIF 或 CFR 时,提单上"FREIGHT & CHARGE"
　　　　一栏应作_____表示。
　　　　A. FREIGHT PREPAID　　　　　B. FREIGHT PREPAYABLE
　　　　C. FREIGHT COLLECT　　　　　D. FREIGHT TO BE PREPAID

(   )10. 根据《UCP 600》的规定,海运提单的签单日期应理解为_____。
　　　　A. 货物开始装船的日期　　　　B. 货物装船完毕的日期
　　　　C. 货物装运过程中的任何一天　D. 运输合同中的装运日

(   )11. 根据《UCP 600》的解释,若信用证条款未明确规定是否"允许分期发运"
　　　　"允许转运",则应理解为_____。
　　　　A. 允许分期发运,但不允许转运　B. 允许分期发运,允许转运
　　　　C. 允许转运,但不允许分期发运　D. 不允许分期发运,不允许转运

(   )12. 海运提单的抬头是指提单的_____。
　　　　A. SHIPPER　　　　　　　　　B. CONSIGNEE
　　　　C. NOTIFY PARTY　　　　　　D. SINGER

(   )13. 根据《UCP 600》的规定,正本运输单据受益人或其他代表在不迟于发运日
　　　　之后的 21 个日历内交单,并不得迟于信用证的截止日。若发生正本提单
　　　　交银行超过提单签发日期 21 天,这时,该正本提单为_____。
　　　　A. 过期提单　　B. 倒签提单　　C. 不清洁提单　　D. 无效提单

(   )14. 以下海运提单收货人不同,提单_____需要托运人背书。
　　　　A. TO ORDER　　　　　　　　B. TO ABC COMPANY
　　　　C. TO ORDER OF ISSUING BANK　D. TO ORDER OF APPLICANT

(   )15. 在买卖合同和信用证中,一般都规定卖方须提供_____。
　　　　A. 备运提单　　　　　　　　　B. 清洁的已装船提单
　　　　C. 不清洁的已装船提单　　　　D. 记名提单

(   )16. 在信用证条件下,提单的被通知人一栏应按信用证要求填制,如信用证规
　　　　定:"NOTIFY PARTY APPLICANT",此栏填_____。
　　　　A. 开证人全称　　　　　　　　B. 开证人和开证行全称
　　　　C. 开证行全称　　　　　　　　D. 受益人全称

(   )17. 按照有关规定,托运一票货物而有不同包装种类,托运单中的件数和包装
　　　　种类应填写合计总件数,包括合计件数数字和包装种类总称,该包装种类
　　　　总称用_____。
　　　　A. CARTONS　　B. PIECES　　C. PACKAGES　　D. PALLETS

(   )18. 各种运输单据中,能同时具有货物收据、运输合同和物权凭证作用的
　　　　是_____。
　　　　A. 铁路运单　　B. 航空运单　　C. 海运提单　　D. 海运单

(   )19. 有一信用证规定货物从中国港口运至英国伦敦港,不允许分批装运。出

口商提交下列两套海运提单。第一套提单显示：
PORT OF LOADING: DALIAN, CHINA   VESSEL & VOY.: SUNSHIN V. 507
PORT OF DISCHARGE: LONDON, UK   ON BOARD DATE: MAY. 07,2014

第二套提单显示：
PORT OF LOADING: QINGDAO, CHINA   VESSEL & VOY.: SUNSHIN V. 507
PORT OF DISCHARGE: LONDON, UK   ON BOARD DATE: MAY. 09,2014

如果受益人将两份提单一起提交给银行，以下关于提单的正确理解应是_____。

A. 提单发生分批发运不予接受，因为装运港不同、装运时间不同
B. 提单未发生分批发运可接受，因为同一运输工具并经由同次航程运输至同一目的地
C. 提单发生分批发运不予接受，因为提交了两份提单
D. 提单未发生分批发运可接受，因为两套提单的目的地相同

三、多项选择题

( ) 1. 根据我国有关规定，出口企业最迟于货物出运前3天向签证机构申请办理原产地证书，并按签证机构提供的格式和填制要求，应提供已缮制的_____。
A. "一般原产地证明书申请单"
B. "中华人民共和国原产地证明书"
C. 出口商业发票
D. 装箱单

( ) 2. 原产地证明书是由出口国政府有关机构签发的一种证明货物原产地或制造地的证明文件，通常多用于不需要提供_____的国家和地区。
A. 海关发票   B. 领事发票   C. 证实发票   D. 联合发票

( ) 3. 普遍优惠制度是发达国家给予发展中国家出口的_____普遍的、非歧视性的、非互惠的一种关税制度。
A. 制成品   B. 半制成品   C. 初级产品   D. 高级产品

( ) 4. 我国出口商可以向以下三大机构_____或其下属机构申领原产地证明书。
A. 中华人民共和国海关
B. 中华人民共和国国家质量监督出入境检验检疫局
C. 中国国际贸易促进委员会
D. 中华人民共和国商务部

(　　) 5. 根据《UCP 600》的规定,在出口业务中,卖方可以凭以结汇的装运单据有_____。
   A. 提单　　　　　　　　　　B. 不可转让的海运单
   C. 租船合同提单　　　　　　D. 装货单
   E. 空运单据　　　　　　　　F. 报关单
   G. 公路、铁路和内陆水运单据

(　　) 6. 按《UCP 600》的规定,海运提单中货物的描述_____。
   A. 只要不与信用证的描述相抵触,可使用货物的统称
   B. 必须使用货物的全称
   C. 必须与商业发票的货物描述完全一致
   D. 符合信用证或合同的,与实际货物的名称、规格、型号、成分、品牌等相一致

(　　) 7. 电子托运单订舱是实现未来我国"无纸化贸易运输"项目的发展方向,电子订舱的优点主要在于_____。
   A. 订舱速度快　　　　　　　B. 形式简单
   C. 电子托运单可与纸质托运单共存　D. 差错率降低

(　　) 8. 按不同的运输方法,提单可分为_____。
   A. 直达提单　　　　　　　　B. 电放提单
   C. 转船提单　　　　　　　　D. 多式联运提单

(　　) 9. 出口货物托运人缮制"国际货物托运委托书"的依据文件有_____。
   A. 外销出仓单　　　　　　　B. 销售合同
   C. 信用证　　　　　　　　　D. 配舱回单

(　　)10. 以下指示提单中,需要背书才可以转让的提单有_____。
   A. TO ORDER
   B. TO ORDER OF SHIPPER
   C. TO APPLICANT
   D. TO ORDER OF ISSUING BANK

(　　)11. 提单的主要作用有_____。
   A. 货物收据　　　　　　　　B. 物权凭证
   C. 装船依据　　　　　　　　D. 运输合同的证明

(　　)12. 提单中的通知人一栏,根据信用证或合同要求填写通知人的全称、街名、城市、国家、联系电话和传真号,可以有_____。
   A. 进口商　　　　　　　　　B. 开证银行
   C. 开证行的代理人　　　　　D. 信用证的开证申请人

(　　)13. 根据《UCP600》的规定,通过以下_____方式表明货物已在信用证规定的装运港装上具名船只。
   A. 预先印就"已装船"文字
   B. 已装船批注注明货物的装运日期

C. 提单上加盖"已装船"戳记

D. 已装船批注注明货物的装运日期和船名

( )14. 承运人或其具名代理人签发以下_____提单是具有欺诈性的违法行为。

A. 倒签提单　　B. 电放提单　　C. 顺签提单　　D. 预借提单

( )15. 对托运人而言,选择海上货物承运人时,主要考虑的因素包括_____。

A. 运输服务的定期性　　　　　B. 运输速度

C. 运输费用　　　　　　　　　D. 运输的可靠性

四、判断题

( ) 1. "普惠制产地证书"是证明有关商品的原产地或制造地为该受惠国的专门证书,是给惠国海关凭以减免关税的重要证件。

( ) 2. "普惠制产地证书"的主要格式有:格式 A(Form A),格式 B(Form B),格式 C(Form C)和格式 59A(Form 59A),其中格式 A 使用范围较广。

( ) 3. 凡装在同一条船上或同一航班上的货物,即使装运地点不同,也不作为分批装运。

( ) 4. 所有运输单据都是承运人签发给托运人的货物收据,故都是物权凭证,都可以持单向目的地的承运人提货。

( ) 5. 全式提单是指提单上除有正面条款之外,还在背面印有承运人和托运人的权利、义务等详细内容条款。略式提单仅有提单正面内容,如船名、货号、标志、件数装运港、目的港,而略去了提单背面全部条款,但提单效力相同。

( ) 6. 提单签发日不得超过信用证规定的装运日,并在信用证的有效期内。

( ) 7. 货物装船后,托运人凭装货单(S/O)向承运人或其代理人换取提单(B/L)。

( ) 8. 对于价格术语 FOB,由买方指定承运人并安排运输,因此如果合同中未规定"装船通知"条款时,卖方在装船后允许不发装运通知给买方。

( ) 9. 海运提单与海运单都是运输契约,两者都可以通过背书转让。

( )10. 空白抬头提单是指提单收货人处空白,空白背书是指提单背面没有人背书。

项目五　办理出口货物的保险和报检

一、请将下列英语词组翻译成中文并抄写

1. INSURANCE POLICY _____
2. POLICY NO _____
3. COMMODITY AND SPECIFICATIONS _____

4. AMOUNT INSURED _____

5. TOTAL AMOUT INSURED _____

6. AS ARRANED _____

7. F. P. A _____

8. W. P. A _____

9. ALL RISKS _____

二、单项选择题

( ) 1. 在国际货物销售合同的商品检验条款中,关于检验时间与地点,目前使用最多的是_____。

    A. 在出口国检验

    B. 在进口国检验

    C. 在出口国检验,在进口国复验

    D. 在出口国检验,进口国复验,再到第三国检验

( ) 2. 对列入《法检目录》的进口商品,海关凭检验检疫签发的_____验放。

    A. "入境货物检验检疫证明"   B. "入境货物调离通知单"

    C. "入境货物通关单"   D. "品质证书"

( ) 3. 如果检验检疫机构需要对出境货物实施检验检疫时,报检员应按要求配合施检,在机构_____递交报检单和随附单据。

    A. 施检前   B. 施检时

    C. 施检后   D. 通关放行时

( ) 4. 按规定,出境货物最迟在出口报关或装运前_____天报检;输入植物、种子、种苗及其他繁殖物应在入境前_____天报检。

    A. 7~15   B. 7~7   C. 15~7   D. 15~15

( ) 5. 根据国家有关规定,以下各个项目中,不属于检验检疫机构的基本任务是_____。

    A. 法定检验   B. 公正鉴定

    C. 通关检验   D. 实施监督管理

( ) 6. "出境货物报检单"中的起运地栏目,根据规定应填报_____。

    A. 货物最后离境的口岸   B. 货物最后离境的港口

    C. 装货地   D. 原产地

( ) 7. 某货轮在航行途中,A舱失火,船长误以为B舱也同时失火,命令对两舱同时施救,A舱共有两批货物,甲批货物全部焚毁,乙批货物为棉织被单,全部遭受水浸;B舱货物也全部遭受水浸。那么_____。

    A. A舱乙批货物与B舱货物都属于单独海损

    B. A舱乙批货物与B舱货物都属于共同海损

    C. A舱乙批货物属于共同海损、B舱货物属于单独海损

    D. A舱乙批货物属于单独海损、B舱货物属于共同海损

( ) 8. 某公司以 CIF 条件与国外客户达成一笔出口交易,某公司应负责替客户投保,双方就具体险别未作明确协议,按国际惯例规定,可投保的险种是_____。
  A. 一切险加战争险   B. 一切险
  C. 平安险   D. 水渍险

( ) 9. 按中国人民保险公司海洋货物运输保险条款规定,在三种基本险别中,就保险公司承担的风险责任范围从大到小排列,在下列四种排列程序中,_____是正确的。
  A. 平安险、一切险、水渍险   B. 水渍险、一切险、平安险
  C. 一切险、水渍险、平安险   D. 一切险、平安险、水渍险

( )10. 在伦敦保险协会货物保险条款的三种主要险别中,保险人责任最低的险别有_____。
  A. A 险   B. B 险   C. C 险   D. D 险

( )11. 黑龙江某进出口公司出口大米 50 公吨,在海运途中遭受暴风雨,海水涌入舱内,致使一部分大米发霉变质,这种损失属于_____。
  A. 实际全损   B. 推定全损   C. 共同海损   D. 单独海损

( )12. 某公司出口的货物在运输途中遭遇风暴,运输船舶与货物均失踪,6 个月后依然杳无音讯。该公司损失的货物应属于_____。
  A. 部分损失   B. 全部损失   C. 共同损失   D. 共同海损

( )13. "仓至仓"条款是_____。
  A. 承运人负责运输责任起讫的条款
  B. 保险人负责保险责任起讫的条款
  C. 出口人负责交货责任起讫的条款
  D. 进口人向保险公司索赔的起讫的条款

( )14. 在进出口贸易中,按照国际惯例投保时的保险加成率一般为_____。
  A. 20%   B. 30%   C. 10%   D. 15%

三、多项选择题

( ) 1. 我国商检机构的基本任务是_____。
  A. 实施法定检验   B. 实施监督管理
  C. 办理公证鉴定业务   D. 进行对外索赔

( ) 2. 商品检验证书在国际贸易中的作用是_____。
  A. 证明卖方所交货物是否符合合同规定的依据
  B. 对外索赔的依据
  C. 仲裁机构受理案件的依据
  D. 海关通关放行的有效证件
  E. 银行付款的主要依据

( ) 3. 商品检验条款的内容包括_____。

A. 检验时间、地点　　　　　　　　B. 检验机构
C. 检验证书　　　　　　　　　　　D. 检验标准与方法
E. 复验

(　　) 4. 某市进出口公司按CIF出口一批陶瓷茶具,在运输途中的装卸、搬运过程中,致使部分货物受损。如果要得到保险公司赔偿,该公司可投保_____。
A. 平安险加破碎险　　　　　　　　B. 一切险
C. 水渍险加破碎险　　　　　　　　D. 一切险加破碎险

(　　) 5. 我国海运货物保险条款将海运货物保险险别分为_____两类。
A. 平安险　　B. 水渍险　　C. 基本险　　D. 附加险

(　　) 6. 在海洋运输货物保险业务中,海上损失按程度可分为_____。
A. 实际损失　　B. 共同损失　　C. 全部损失　　D. 部分损失

(　　) 7. 国际货物买卖合同中的保险条款内容有_____。
A. 保险金额　　　　　　　　　　　B. 投保险别
C. 保险费　　　　　　　　　　　　D. 保险单证和保险适用条款

(　　) 8. 我国对外贸易货运保险分为_____。
A. 海上运输保险　　　　　　　　　B. 陆上运输保险
C. 航空运输保险　　　　　　　　　D. 邮包运输保险

(　　) 9. 构成实际全损的情况有_____。
A. 保险标的物全部灭失
B. 保险标的物已全部丧失
C. 保险标的物已丧失商业价值或原有用途
D. 船舶失踪达到6个月以上

(　　) 10. 根据我国现行《海洋货物运输保险条款》的规定,能够独立投保的险别有_____。
A. 平安险　　B. 水渍险　　C. 一切险　　D. 战争险

(　　) 11. 根据英国的《协会货物条款》的规定,下列险别中,可以单独投保的险别有_____。
A. I.C.C.(A)　　B. I.C.C.(B)　　C. I.C.C.(C)　　D. 协会战争险

四、判断题

(　　) 1. 以装运港检验机构出具的证书为议付单据,以目的港检验结果为索赔依据,这种做法对买卖双方均有好处。

(　　) 2. 对列入《法检目录》的出口商品,除活动物由口岸检验检疫机构实施检疫外,原则上应在产地办理检验检疫手续。

(　　) 3. 对列入《法检目录》的进口商品,除了急用品允许先入境后补入境通关单外,其余商品原则上先实施检验检疫,机构对合格商品签发《入境货物通关单》,海关凭此验放。

(　　) 4. 若出口商品的木质包装已按要求实施熏蒸,机构对熏蒸后的木包装加盖了进口认可的标识,在这种情况下,出口商同意需要机构出具的《熏蒸/消毒证书》,以交进口商。

(　　) 5. 出境危险品是法定检验检疫产品,但危险品的外包装不需要检验检疫机构签发的任何证明书便可出境。

(　　) 6. 海上保险业务的意外事故,仅局限于发生在海上的意外事故。

(　　) 7. 保险利益是投保人所投保的保险标的。

(　　) 8. 计收保险费的公式为保险费=保险金额×保险费率。

(　　) 9. 托运出口玻璃制品时,被保险人在投保一切险后,还应加保破碎险。

(　　)10. 载货船舶途中搁浅,船长有意识合理地将部分货物抛入海中,使船只能继续航行至目的港,上述搁浅和抛货损失均属于共同海损。

项目六　办理出口货物的报关和出运

一、请将下列英语词组翻译成中文并抄写

1. NEW YORK _____
2. LONG BEACH _____
3. LOS ANGELES _____
4. MELBOURNE _____
5. SYDNEY _____
6. LIVERPOOL _____
7. LONDON _____
8. OSAKA _____
9. TOKYO _____
10. YOKKAICHI _____
11. BUSAN _____
12. LNCHON _____

二、单项选择题

(　　) 1. 出口商得到托运确认后,应填制_____连同发票等相关单据向海关申报出口货物。
　　　　A. 汇票　　　B. 报检单　　　C. 报关单　　　D. 装货单

(　　) 2. 根据我国《海关法》规定,进口货物的报关期限为:自运输工具申报进境之日起_____天之内申报,若进口货物的收货人或其代理人逾期申报,海关将征收滞报金,滞报金的日征收金额为进口货物到岸价的_____。
　　　　A. 14　0.05%　　B. 14　0.5%　　C. 15　0.05%　　D. 15　0.5%

(　　) 3. 除特殊货物之外,海运出口货物的发货人或其代理人根据海关规定,应当

在货物运抵海关监管区后,装船_____向海关申报货物出口。

A. 48 小时　　　B. 48 小时前　　　C. 24 小时　　　D. 24 小时前

(　　) 4. 某外商投资企业委托上海化工进出口公司进口投资设备,在进口报关单上,经营单位栏目填报_____,标记及备注栏目填报_____。

A. 外商投资公司　　上海化工进出口公司

B. 外商投资公司　　外商投资公司

C. 上海化工进出口公司　　外商公司

D. 上海化工进出口公司　　上海化工进出口公司

(　　) 5. 托运人在得到海运托运确认并办理了海关申报后,海关对放行出口货物将在配舱回单第五联上加盖_____,据此联,船公司才可以将单据上的货物装上船。

A. 监管章　　　B. 放行章　　　C. 验收章　　　D. 验讫章

(　　) 6. 上海良友(集团)进出口公司向韩国出口 600 吨散装小麦。该货分装在同一艘船的 3 个货舱内。出口报关单上的件数栏目和包装种类栏目的正确填报应是_____。

A. 600 吨　　　B. 1 船　　　C. 3 船舱　　　D. 1 散装

(　　) 7. 出口报关单上对于货物出口海运运费单价每运费吨为 600 美元的正确填报应是_____。

A. 110/600/2　　B. 502/600/1　　C. 502/600/2　　D. 502/600/3

(　　) 8. 若某货物由上海吴淞港(关区代码:2202)出运,在出口报关单上"出口口岸"栏目正确的填报应是_____。

A. 上海口岸　　　　　　　　　B. 吴淞海关 2202

C. 上海海关 2202　　　　　　　D. 吴淞口岸

(　　) 9. 出境货物通关单的编号应在出口报关单的_____栏目中显示。

A. 备案号　　　B. 随附单据　　　C. 批准文号　　　D. 海关编号

(　　)10. 在各种运输单据中,能起到货物收据、运输合同的证明和物权凭证作用的是_____。

A. 铁路运单　　B. 航空运单　　C. 海运提单　　D. 海运单

(　　)11. 海运提单的抬头通常做成_____。

A. 记名式抬头　　B. 来人抬头　　C. 指示性抬头　　D. 空白

三、多项选择题

(　　) 1. 一般货物在出境时,必须提交给海关出口货物报关单和随附单据,根据海关规定,_____的代码和编号不需要显示在报关单上"随附单据"栏目中。

A. 进料加工登记手册　　　　　B. 出境货物通关单

C. 商业发票　　　　　　　　　D. 出口许可证

(　　) 2. 目前海关电子报关申报方式有_____。

A. EDI 申报方式　B. 终端申报方式　C. 网上申报方式　D. 电子信箱

(　　) 3. 下列_____单证属于出口报关的基本单证。
　　A. 商业发票　　　　　　　　B. 出口货物报关单
　　C. 装箱单　　　　　　　　　D. 出境货物通关单

(　　) 4. 进出口货物报关单中的运输方式专门指载运货物进出关境所使用的运输工具种类,其中"其他运输"是指_____。
　　A. 江海运输　　B. 管道运输　　C. 人力扛运　　D. 电网

(　　) 5. 以下关于出口报关单"件数"和"包装种类"栏目的填报,符合海关规定的选项有_____。
　　A. 裸装货物的件数填报为"1",包装种类为"裸装"
　　B. 散货的件数填报为"1",包装种类为"散装"
　　C. 2托盘,每托盘上装10纸箱的货物,件数填报为"20",包装种类填报"件"
　　D. 2托盘,每托盘上装10纸箱的货物,件数填报为"2",包装种类填报"托盘"

(　　) 6. 以下关于进出口货物报关单缮制规范的陈述中,正确的有_____。
　　A. 一份报关单只允许填报一种贸易方式
　　B. 一份报关单只允许填报一种运输方式
　　C. 一份报关单只允许填报一份原产地证书
　　D. 一份报关单只允许填报一个集装箱箱号

(　　) 7. 申报人必须按照海关规定,对于同一批货物中,不同的_____,应分单申报。
　　A. 运输工具名称　　B. 提运单号　　C. 征免性质　　D. 许可证号

(　　) 8. 按海关规定,申报每项商品的_____栏目,应分行填报。
　　A. 项号　　　　　　　　　　B. 商品名称、规格型号
　　C. 单价　　　　　　　　　　D. 数量及单位

(　　) 9. 按海关规定,以下_____的编号应填报在报关单的"备案号"栏目内。
　　A. 加工贸易登记手册　　　　B. 减免税证明
　　C. 出口货物通关单　　　　　D. 加工贸易低值辅料

(　　)10. 按海关的相关规定,进出口货物报关单中"经营单位"栏目可以填报的选项有_____。
　　A. 执行外贸合同的企业
　　B. 签订外贸合同但不执行外贸合同的企业
　　C. 有报关权但无进出口经营权的企业
　　D. 进出口企业之间相互代理进出口情况下的代理方企业

(　　)11. 入境货物报检单上填报的货物总值应与_____上所列相应栏目一致。
　　A. 合同　　　　B. 商业发票　　　C. 装箱单　　　D. 报关单

四、判断题

( ) 1. 海关在对进口货物查验时,如果收货人或其代理人没有按照海关规定准时到场,这时,海关不能未经收货人或其代理人同意而自行开箱查验货物或者提取货样。

( ) 2. 办理进出口货物的海关申报手续,可以选择纸质报关单或电子数据报关单的形式,两种形式的报关单具有同等的法律效力。

( ) 3. 在我国,凡有进出口经营权的企业都享有进出口货物报关权。

( ) 4. 进出口货物报关单上的"商品名称、规格型号"栏目,正确的填写应该有规范的中文名称、英文名称和规格型号,缺一不可。

( ) 5. 一票出口货物有两种商品,该两种商品项下的两份原产地证明书应填制同一份出口货物报关单向海关申报。

( ) 6. 一份出口货物报关单上允许填报多个原产地证书编号,也可填报多个出口许可证编号和多个提运单号。

( ) 7. 一般出口货物申报日期不得早于运输工具进口申报日期,也不能晚于运输工具出境日期。

( ) 8. 海运托运单和海运提单都是托运人和承运人运输合同的契约,尽管形式不同,但作用是相同的。

( ) 9. 信用证规定装运港为"CHINESE PORT"(中国口岸),受益人在缮制提单时应照打"CHINESE PORT",以免单证不符。

( )10. 货物由我国大连出口至香港,提单上显示装运港"中国,大连",目的港"香港",这种表述是正确的。

( )11. 银行不接出单日期迟于装船或发运或接受监管之日的保险单,即使保险单上表明保险责任最迟于货物装船或发运或接受监管之日生效。

( )12. 提单的被通知人,若信用证无明确规定,则应填写开证申请人。

( )13. 空白抬头提单是指提单收货人处空白,空白背书是指提单背面没有人背书。

( )14. 海运提单与海运单的区别之一是,提单是物权凭证,经过背书是可以转让的;而海运单不是物权凭证,不可以转让。

( )15. 出口报关单上"集装箱箱号"一栏,此栏内只需填入同一票货物其中的一个集装箱箱号和自重,其余箱号则在备注栏内显示。

项目七　办理出口货物的结汇

一、请将下列英语词组翻译成中文并抄写

1. BILL OF EXCHANGE _____
2. BILL OF COLLECTION _____

3. AT SIGHT _____
4. AMOUNT _____
5. BRANCH _____
6. BANK _____
7. BANK OF CHINA _____
8. D/P _____
9. DRAFT _____
10. D/A _____
11. EXCHANGE _____

二、单项选择题

( ) 1. 一张商业汇票见票日为1月31日，见票后1个月付款，则到期日为_____。
  A. 2月28日 B. 3月1日 C. 3月2日 D. 3月3日

( ) 2. 汇票的收款人有三种填写方式，根据我国《票据法》的规定，其中凡签发_____汇票无效。
  A. 限制性抬头   B. 指示性抬头
  C. 持票人或来人抬头 D. 记名抬头

( ) 3. 我国《票据法》规定，即期汇票持票人对出票人和承兑人的追索权，应在出票日起算_____内行使。
  A. 3个月 B. 6个月 C. 1年 D. 2年

( ) 4. 结汇单据中的汇票，指用于托收和信用证收汇方式中，出口商向进口商或银行签发的，要求后者即期或在一个固定的日期或在可以确定的将来时间，对某人或某指定人或持票人支付一定金额的无条件的书面支付命令。大部分情况下，使用_____。
  A. 光票   B. 跟单汇票
  C. 银行汇票 D. 商业承兑汇票

( ) 5. 信用证在汇票条款中注明DRAWN ON US，出口商缮制汇票时，应将付款人做成_____。
  A. 开证行 B. 议付行 C. 开证申请人 D. 偿付行

( ) 6. 托收方式下，汇票付款人应填_____。
  A. 交单行 B. 托收行 C. 代收行 D. 进口商

( ) 7. 信用证支付方式下，汇票付款人应填_____。
  A. 开证行 B. 议付行 C. 代收行 D. 开证申请人

( ) 8. 在远期付款中，在其他条件相同的条件下，对收款人最为有利的远期汇票是_____。
  A. 出票后60天付款   B. 见票后60天付款
  C. 提单日后60天付款 D. 货物抵达目的港后60天付款

(   ) 9. 一张汇票规定见票后60天付款,而持票人于9月28日提示承兑,则付款到期日为_____。
   A. 11月28日　　　　　　　　B. 11月27日
   C. 11月26日　　　　　　　　D. 11月29日

(   )10. YIYANG TRADE COMPANY向议付行中国银行上海分行提交信用证项下全套单据。其中,汇票上显示出票人为YIYANG TRADE COMPANY,付款人为XYZ COMPANY,受款人做成TO ORDER OF YIYANG TRADE COMPANY,根据《国际银行标准实务》(ISBP),汇票到期日应该为_____。
   A. 由YIYANG TRADE COMPANY背书
   B. 由XYZ COMPANY背书
   C. 由中国银行上海分行背书
   D. 无须任何人背书

(   )11. 以下须经背书方可转让的汇票抬头是_____。
   A. 限制性抬头　　B. 指示性抬头　　C. 来人抬头　　D. 持票人抬头

(   )12. 我国《票据法》规定,不接受_____的汇票。
   A. 限制性抬头　　B. 指示性抬头　　C. 来人抬头　　D. 限定性抬头

三、多项选择题

(   ) 1. 我国《票据法》规定,汇票必须记载的,除了表明"汇票"字样、无条件支付委托和确定的金额以外,还有_____,如未记载上述规定事项之一的汇票,无效。
   A. 付款人名称　　B. 收款人名称　　C. 出票日期　　D. 出票人签章

(   ) 2. 汇票抬头具体有_____。
   A. 限制性抬头　　　　　　　　B. 指示性抬头
   C. 持票人或来人抬头　　　　　D. 记名抬头

(   ) 3. 在实际业务中,远期汇票付款时间的规定办法有_____。
   A. 见票后若干天付款　　　　　B. 出票后若干天付款
   C. 提单签发日后若干天付款　　D. 指定日期付款

(   ) 4. 汇票背书的方式主要有_____。
   A. 限制性背书　　B. 指示性背书　　C. 空白背书　　D. 记名背书

(   ) 5. 票据具有_____的特性。
   A. 流通性　　B. 金钱证券　　C. 无因证券　　D. 要式证券

四、判断题

(   ) 1. 汇票的出单日期可由交单行或托收行代填,但对外寄单时,此栏不能为空。

(   ) 2. 信用证汇票的受款人最好打上出口商名,然后由出口商背书给交单行,使交单行议付后可成为正当持票人。

( ) 3. 托收业务的汇票的出票条款处,可标明有关合约号。

( ) 4. 作为可以支取信用证金额的凭证,汇款在本质上是一种单据,而不是票据。

( ) 5. 在远期汇票中,用 60 DAYS AFTER DATE OF DRAFT 与 60 DAYS FROM DATE OF DRAFT 表达汇票期限,到期日相同。

( ) 6. 即期付款,在汇票上的付款期限处,加打"＊"或"－",如 AT＊＊＊SIGHT, AT-SIGHT。

( ) 7. 出口商可以将商业发票号作为汇票的编号。

( ) 8. 合格的汇票遭拒付时,持票人有权向背书人和出票人追索。

( ) 9. 票据是一种流通证券,所有票据的转让都必须经过背书手续。

( )10. 全套汇票的正本份数,应该是三份。

第二部分

专业技能练习

项目一 审核信用证

根据下列销售合同审核信用证。

1. 贸易合同

售货合同
SALES CONTRACT

卖方：GREAT WALL TRADING CO., LTD
Sellers：

Contract No.：GW2005X06
Date：2014.4.22
Signed at：NINGBO

地址：
Address：TM201, HUASHENG BUILDING, NINGBO,
　　　　P. R. CHINA

Fax：0574-25763368

Buyers：F. T. C. CORP
Address：AKEDSANTERINK AUTO P. O. BOX9, FINLAND

　　　　　　　　　　　　　　　　　　　　　　　Fax：＿＿＿＿＿＿＿

THIS SALES CONTRACT IS MADE BY AND BETWEEN THE SELLERS AND THE BUYERS, WHEREBY THE SELLERS AGREE TO SELL AND BUYERS AGREE TO BUY THE UNDER-MENTIONED GOODS ACCORDING TO THE TERMS AND CONDITIONS STIPULATED BELOW：

(1) 货号、品名及规格 NAME OF COMMODITY AND SPECIFICATIONS	(2) 数量 QUANTITY	(3) 单位 UNIT	(4) 单价 UNIT PRICE	(5) 金额 AMOUNT
ALOGEN FITTING W500 10% MORE OR LESS BOTH IN AMOUNT AND QUANTITY ALLOWED	9 600PCS	PC	CIFHELSINKI USD 3.80 /PC	USD 36 480.00
	TOTAL AMOUNT			USD 36 480.00

(6) PACKING：CARTON　　(7) DELIVERY FROM NINGBO TO HELSINKI　　(8) SHIPPING MARKS：N/M
(9) TIME OF SHIPMENT：WITHIN 30 DAYS AFTER RECEIPT OF L/C, ALLOWING TRANS-SHIPMENT AND PARTIAL SHIPMENT.
(10) TERMS OF PAYMENT：BY 100% CONFIRMED IRREVOCABLE LETTER OF CREDIT IN FAVOR OF THE SELLERS TO BE AVAILABLE BY SIGHT DRAFT TO BE OPENED AND TO REACH CHINA BEFORE MAY.1, 2014 AND TO REMAIN VALID FOR NEGOTIATION IN CHI-

NA UNTIL THE 15TH DAYS AFTER THE FORESAID TIME OF SHIPMENT. L/C MUST MENTION THIS CONTRACT NUMBER. 1 L/C ADVISED BY BANK OF CHINA NINGBO BRANCH. ALL BANKING CHARGES OUTSIDE CHIAN (THE MAINLAND OF CHINA) ARE FOR ACCOUNT OF THE DRAWEE.

(11) INSURANCE: TO BE EFFECTED BY SELLERS FOR 110% OF FULL INVOICE VALUE COVERING F. P. A. UP TO HELSINKI.

(12) ARBITRATION: ALL DISPUTE ARISING FROM THE EXECUTION OF OR IN CONNECTION WITH THIS CONTRACT SHALL BE SETTLED AMICABLEY NEGOTIATION. IN CASE OF SETTLEMENT CAN NOT BE REACHED THROUGH NEGOTIATION THE CASE SHALL THEN BE SUBMITTED TO CHINA INTERNATIONAL ECONOMIC & TRADE ARBITRATION COMMISION IN SHENZHEN (OR IN BEIJING) FOR ARBITRATION IN ACT WITH ITS SUE OF PROCEDURES. THE ARBITRAL AWARD IS FINAL AND BINDING UPON BOTH PARTIES FOR SETTLING THE DISPUTE. THE FEE FOR ARBITRATION SHAL BE BORNE BY THE LOSING PARTY UNLESS OTHERWISE AWARDED.

THE SELLER GREAT WALL TRADING CO., LTD.　　　　THE BUYER ALICE

马丁

2. 信用证资料

Issuing Bank:	METITA BANK LTD., FINLAND
From of Doc. Credit:	REVOCABLE
Credit Number:	LRT9802457
Date of Issue:	140428
Expiry:	Date 140416 PLACE FINLAND
Applicant:	F. T. C. CO. AKEKSANTERINK AUTO P. O. BOX9, FINLAND
Beneficiary:	GREAT WALL TRADINGCO., LTD. RM201, HUASHENG BUILDING, NINGBO, P. R. CHINA
Amount:	USD 3 648.00 (SAY U. S. DOLLARS THIRTY SIX THOUSAND FOUR HUNDERD AND EIGHT ONLY)
Available with/by:	ANY BANK IN ADVISING COUNTRY BY NEGOTIATION
Draft at...:	DRAFTS AT 20 DAYS' SIGHT FOR FULL INVOICE VALUE
Partial Shipments:	NOT ALLOWED
Transhipment	ALLOWED
Loading in Charge:	NINGBO
For transport to	HELSINKI
Shipment Period	AT THE LATEST MAY 30, 2014
Descrip. Of goods	9 600PCS OF HALOGEN FITTING W500, USD6.80 PER PC AS PER SALES CONTRACT GW2015M06 DD22, 4, 2014 CIF HESINKI
Documents required	* COMMERCIAL INVOICE 1 SIGNED ORIGINAL AND 5 COPIES * PACKING LIST IN 2 COPIES * FULL SET OF CLEAN ON BOARD MARINE BILLS OF LADING, MADE OUT TO ORDER, MARKED "FREIGHT PREPAID" AND NOTIFY APPLICANT (AS INDICATED ABOVE)

* GSP CERTIFICATE OF ORINGIN FORM A, CERTIFYING GOODS OF ORIGIN INCHINA, ISSUED BY COMPETENT AUTHORITIES
* INSURANCE POLICY/CERTIFICATE COVERING ALL RISKS AND WAR RISKS OF PICC INCLUDING WAREHOUSE TO WAREHOUSE CLAUSE UP TO FINAL DESTINATION AT HELSINKI, FOR AT LEAST 120 PCT OF CIF VALUE.
* SHIPPING ADVICES MUST BE SENT TO APPLICANT WITHIN 2 DAYS AFTER SHIPMENT ADVISING NUMBER OF PACKAGES, GROSS & NET WEIGHT, VESSEL NAME, BILL OF LADING NO. AND DATE, CONTRACT NO. , VALUE

Presentation Period: 6 DAYS AFTER ISSUANCE DATE OF SHIPPING DOCUMENT
Confirmation WITHOUT
INSTRUCTIONS: THE CEGOTIATION BANK MUST FORWARD THE DRAFTS AND A ALL DOCUMENTS BY REGISTERED AIRMAIL DIRECT TO US IN TWO CONSECUTIVE LOTS, UPON RECEIPT OF THE DRAFTS AND DICUMENTS IN ORDER, WE WILL REMIT THE PROCEEDS AS INSTRUCTED BY THE NEGOTIATING BANK.

3. 审核信用证
根据销售合同的内容审核上述信用证,找出信用证中的不符点,并详细列出:
(1) _____
(2) _____
(3) _____
(4) _____
(5) _____
(6) _____
(7) _____
(8) _____
(9) _____
(10) _____

项目二　缮制信用证项下FOB术语出口单据

资料一
ISSUING BANK: CYPRUS POPULAR BANK LTD. , LARNAKA
ADVISING BANK: BANK OF CHINA, SHANGHAI BRANCH
SEQUENCE OF TOTAL　　＊27: 1/1
FORM OF DOC. CREDIT　＊40A: IRREVOCABLE
DOC. CREDIT NUMBER　＊20: 186/04/10014
DATE OF ISSUE　　　　31C: 140105
EXPIRY　　　　　　　＊31D: DATE 140229 PLACE CHINA
APPLICANT　　　　　＊50: LAIKI PERAGORA ORPHANIDES LTD.
　　　　　　　　　　　020 STRATIGOU TIMAGIA AVE. , 6 046, LARNAKA,

	CYPRUS
BENEFICIARY	*59: SHANGHAI GARDEN PRODUCTS CO., LTD. 43 CHIFENG ROAD, SHANGHAI, CHINA
AMOUNT	*32B: CURRENCY USD AMOUNT 8,500.00
AVAILABLE WITH/BY	*41D: ANY BANK BY NEGOTIATION
DRAFT AT…	42C: AT 30 DAYS SIGHT
DRAWEE	*42D: CYPRUS POPULAR BANK LTD., LARNAKA
PARTIAL SHIPMENT	43P: ALLOWED
TRANSSHIPMENT	43T: ALLOWED
LOADING IN CHARGE	44A: SHANGHAI PORT
FOR TRANSPORT TO	44B: LIMASSOL PORT
LATESTDATE OF SHIP	44C: 140214
DESCRIPT. OF GOODS	45A: WOODEN FLOWER STANDS @USD 10.00/PC 400PCS
	WOODEN FLOWER POTS @USD 5.00/PC 900PCS
	AS PER S/C NO. TFD 236. FOB SHANGHAI PORT, INCOTERMS 2010

DOCUMENTS REQUIRED 46A:
+ COMMERCIAL INVOICE IN QUADRUPLICATE ALL STAMPED AND SIGNED BY BENEFICIARY CERTIFYING THAT THE GOODS ARE OF CHINESE ORIGIN
+ FULL SET OF CLEAN ON BOARD BILL OF LADING MADE OUT TO ORDER OF SHIPPER AND BLANK EN-DORSED, MARKED FREIGHT PREPAID AND NOTIFY APPLICANT
+ PACKING LIST IN TRIPLICATE SHOWING PACKING DETAILS SUCH AS CARTON NO. S AND CONTENTS OF EACH CARTON
+ CERTIFICATE STAMPED AND SIGNED BY BENEFICIARY STATING THAT THE ORIGIAL INVOICE AND PACKING LIST HAVE BEEN DISPATCHED TO THE APPLICANT BY COURI-ER SERVISE 2 DAYS BEFORE SHIPMENT

PRESENTATION PERIOD	48: WITHIN 15 DAYS AFTER THE DATE OF SHIPMENT BUT WITHIN THE VAUDITY OF THE CREDIT
CONFIRMATION	*49: WITHOUT

资料二

发票号码:04SHGD3029　　发票日期:2014年2月9日

提单号码:SHYZ042234　　提单日期:2014年2月12日

集装箱号码:FSCU3214999　　集装箱封号:1295312

船名:MOON RIVER　　航次:V.025W

PACKING: WOODEN FLOWER STANDS 2PCS/CTN

MEAS: 66×22×48(CM)/CTN　　G.W.　11KGS/CTN　　N.W 9KGS/CTN

H.S. CODE: 44219090.90

PACKING: WOODEN FLOWER POTS, 6PCS/CTN

MEAS: 42×42×45(CM)/CTN　　G.W.　15KGS/CTN　　N.W 13KGS/CTN

H.S. CODE: 44219090.90

要求:根据上述信用证和合同资料缮制下列有关单据,如果信用证无规定的项目可按惯例制作。

（一）商业发票

SHANGHAI GARDEN PRODUCTS CO., LTD.
43 CHIFENG ROAD, SHANGHAI, CHINA

COMMERCIAL INVOICE

TEL: 0086-21-65756156　　　　　　　　　　　　INV. No.: _____

FAX: 0086-21-65756189　　　　　　　　　　　　DATE: _____

TO: _____

FROM: _____　　TO: _____

SHIPPING MARK

DESCRIPTION	QTY(set)	UNIT PRICE	AMOUNT
TOTAL:			

TOTAL: _____

（二）装箱单

SHANGHAI GARDEN PRODUCTS CO., LTD.
43 CHIFENG ROAD, SHANGHAI, CHINA

PACKING LIST

TEL: 0086-21-65756156　　　　　　　　　　　　INV. No.: _____

FAX: 0086-21-65756189　　　　　　　　　　　　DATE: _____

TO: _____

FROM: _____　　TO: _____

SHIPPING MARK

DESCRIPTION	QTY(　)	CTNS	G. W.(　)	N. W.(　)	MEAS(　)
TOTAL:					

（三）普惠制产地证明书

普惠制产地证明书申请书

申请单位(盖章)：　　　　　　　　　　　　　　　　证书号：_____
申请人郑重证明：　　　　　　　　　　　　　　　　　注册号：_____
　　本人是被正式授权代表出口单位办理和签署本申请书的。
　　本申请书及普惠制产地证格式 A 所列内容正确无误，如发现弄虚作假，冒充格式 A 所列货物，擅改证书，自愿接受签证机关的处罚及负法律责任。现将有关情况申报如下：

申请单位		注册号	
商品名称 (中英文)		H.S.税目号 (以六位数码计)	
商品(FOB)总值 (以美元计)		发票号	
最终销售国		证书种类划"√"	加急证书　　　√普通证书
货物拟出运日期			

贸易方式和企业性质(请在适用处划"√")							
正常贸易 C	来料加工进 L	补偿贸易 B	中外合资 H	中外合作 Z	外商独资 D	零售 Y	展卖 M

包装数量或毛重或其他数量	

原产地标准：
1. 本项商品系在中国生产，完全符合该给惠国给惠方案规定，其原产地情况符合以下第(1)条：
　　(1) "P"（完全国产，未使用任何进口原材料）：
　　(2) "W"其 H.S.税目号为　_____　（含进口成分）；
　　(3) "F"（对加拿大出口产品，其进口成分不超过产品出厂价值的 40%）。
本批产品系：1. 直接运输从　_____　到　_____。
2. 转口运输从　_____　中转国(地区)　_____　到　_____。

申请人说明　　　　　　　　　　　　　　　　　领证人(签名)
　　　　　　　　　　　　　　　　　　　　　　　电话：
日期　　年　　月　　日

　　现提交中国出口商业发票副本一份，普惠制产地证明书格式 A(FORM A)一正二副，以及其他附件份，请予审核签证。
　　注：凡含有进口成分的商品，必须按要求提交《含进口成分受惠商品成本明细单》。

商　检　局　联　系　记　录

普惠制产地证明书

1. Goods consigned from (Exporter's business name, address, country)	Reference No. **GENERALIZED SYSTEM OF PREFERENCES CERTIFICA OF ORIGN** (combined declaration and certificate) FORM A LSSUED IN THE PEOPLES REPUBLIC OF CHINA (COUNTRY)			
2. Goods consigned to (Consignee's name, address, consigned)					
3. Means of transport and route (as for as know)					
	4. For official use				
5. Item number	6. Marks and numbers of packages	7. Number and kind of packages; description of goods	8. Origin criterion (see notes overleaf)	9. Gross weight or other quantity	10. Number and date of invoices
11. certification It is hereby certified, on the basis of control carried out, that the declaration by the exporter is correct	12. declaration by the exporter The undersigned hereby declares that the above details and statements are correct, that all the goods were Produced in _____CHINA_____ (country) and that they comply with the origin requirements specified for those goods, in the generalized system of preference for goods exported to .... (importing country)				
Place and date, signature and stamp of certifying authority	Place and date, signature of authorized signatory				

(四) 报关单

中华人民共和国海关出口货物报关单

预录入编号：　　　　　　　　　　　　　　　　　海关编号：

出口口岸		备案号		出口日期		申报日期	
经营单位		运输方式		运输工具名称		提运单号	
发货单位		贸易方式		征免性质		结汇方式	
许可证号		运抵国(地区)		指运港		境内货源地	
批准文号		成交方式	运费		保费		杂费
合同协议号		件数	包装种类		毛重(千克)		净重(千克)
集装箱号		随附单据				生产厂家	
标记唛码及备注							
项号　商品编号　商品名称、规格型号　数量及单位　最终目的国(地区)　单价　总价　币制　征免							
税费征收情况							
录入员　　录入单位		兹声明以上申报无讹并承担法律责任			海关审单批注及放行日期(签章)		
报关员					审单　　　审价		
单位地址		申报单位(签章)			征税　　　统计		
邮编　　　电话　　　填制日期					查验　　　放行		

(五) 汇票

BILL OF EXCHANGE

凭
Drawn _____   不可撤销信用证
                                 Irrevocable L/C NO. _____

日期
Date _____   支取 Payable with interestr @__%__按____息____付款

号码   汇票金额   大连
No _____   Exchange for _____   Dalian _____

见票   日后(本汇票之副本未付)付交
At _____ singt of this First of Exchang (Second of Exchange Being unpaid) pay
to the order of _____

金额
The sum of

此致
To

1. 请翻译上述信用证中的 46A 中的单据条款。

(1)

(2)

(3)

(4)

(5)

(6)

(7)

(8)

(9)

(10)

2. 向银行交单议付,根据信用证规定需要提交哪些单据?

项目三 缮制信用证项下 CFR 术语出口单据

根据合同资料用英文缮制单证。

信用证样本

ADVISING BANK: BANK OF COMMUNICATIONS SHANGHAI(HEAD OFFICE)

OPENING BANK: BANGKOK BANK PUBLIC COMPANY LIMITED, BANGKOK

SEQUENCE TOTAL	*27	1/1
FORM DOC CREDIT	*40A	IRREVOCABLE
DOC CREDIT NUM	*20	1411LC123756
DATE OF ISSUE	31C	141103
DATE/PLACE EXPIRY	*31D	Date 150114 Place BENEFICIARIES' COUNTRY
APPLICANT	*50	MOUN CO., LTD.
		NO. 443, 249 ROAD
		BANGKOK THAILAND
BENEFICIARY	*59	SHANGHAI FOREIGN TRADE CORP.
		700 JIAOZHOU ROAD, SHANGHAI, CHINA
CURR CODE, AMT	*32B	CODE USD AMOUNT 18 000
AVAILABLE WITH /BY	*41D	ANY BANK IN CHINA BY NEGOTIATION
DRAFTS AT	42C	SIGHT
DRAWEE	43D	ISSUING BANK
PARTIAL SHIPMENTS	43P	NOT ALLOWED
TRANSSHIPMENT	43T	ALLOWED
LOADING ON BRD	44A	CHINA MAIN PORT, CHINA
FORTRANSPORT TO	44B	BANGKOK, THAILAND
LATEST SHIPMENT	44C	141220
GOODS DESCRIPT.	45A	2 000KGS. ISONIAZID BP 98
		AT USD 9.00 PER KG. CFR BANGKOK
DOCS REQUIRED	46A	DOCUMENTS REQUIRED:

+COMMERCIAL INVOICE IN ONE ORIGINAL PLUS 5 COPIES INDICATING F.O.B. VALUE, FREIGHT CHARGES SEPARATELY AND THIS L/C NUMBER, ALL OF WHICH MUST BE MANUALLY SIGNED

+FULL SET OF 3/3 CLEAN ON BOARD OCEAN BILLS OF LADING AND TWO NON-NEGOTIABLE COPIES MADE OUT TO ORDER OF BANGKOK BANK PUBLIC COMPANY LIMITED, BANGKOK. MARKED FREIGHT PREPAID AND NOTIFY APPLICANT AND INDICATING THIS L/C NUMBER

+PACKING LIST IN ONE ORIGINAL PLUS 5 COPIDIES, ALL OF WHICH MUST BE

MANUALLY SIGNED
+ CERTIFICATE OF ANALYSIS IN ONE ORIGINAL
PLUS ONE COPY

相关资料:
发票号码:SHE 02/1845
提单号码:SCOISG7564
船名:JENNY V.03
货物装箱情况:50KGS/DRUM
集装箱:1×40′ FCL CFS/CFS
UXXU4240250 0169255

发票日期:2014年11月26日
提单日期:2014年12月19日
装运港:上海港
总毛重:2 200KGS
运费:USD 0.08/KG

根据上述资料缮制相关单据。

中华人民共和国出口货物许可证
EXPORT LICENCE THE PEOPLE'S REPUBLIC OF CHINA A 类

申领许可证单位　　　编码 Export				出口许可证编号 Licence No.		
发货单位 Consigne				许可证有效期 Validity		
贸易方式 Terms of trade				输往国家(地区) Country of destination		
合同号 Contract No.				收款方式 Terms of payment		
出运口岸 Port of shipment				运输方式 Means of transport		
唛头—包装件数 Marks & numbers—number of packages						
商品名称 Description of commodity				商品编码 Commodity No.		
商品规格型号 Specification	单位 Unit	数量 Quantity	单价( ) U/price	总值( ) Amount	总值折美元 Amount in USD	
总计 Total						
备注 Supplementary details				发证机关盖章 Issuing authority's stamp & signature 发证日期 Date		

对外经济贸易部监制　　　　　　　　　　　　　　　　　　本证不得涂改,不得转让

ISSUER		COMMERCIAL INVOICE	
TO		NO.	DATE
TRANSPORT DETAILS		S/C NO.	L/C NO.
		TERMS OF PAYMENT	
Marks and Numbers	Number and kind of package Description of goods	Quantity	Unit Price	Amount
SAY TOTAL				

ISSUER		PACKING LIST				
TO		INVOICE NO.	DATE			
Marks and Numbers	Number and kind of package Description of goods	Quantity	PACKAGE	G. W.	N. W.	MEAS.
	TOTAL					
SAY TOTAL						

一般原产地证明书/加工装配证明书
申 请 书

申请单位注册号：　　　　　　　　　　　　　　证书号：

申请人郑重申明：

　　本人被正式授权代表本企业办理和签署本申请书。

　　本申请书及一般原产地证明书/加工装配书所列内容正确无误,如发现弄虚作假,冒充证书所列货物,擅自证书,自愿接受签发机构的处罚并承担法律责任,现将有关情况申报如下：

企业名称		发票号	
商品名称		H.S.编码(六位数)	
商品FOB总值(以美元计)		最终目的地国家/地区	
拟出运日期		转口国(地区)	

贸易方式和企业性质(请在适用处画"√")					
一般贸易		三来一补		其他贸易方式	
国有企业	三资企业	国有企业	三资企业	国有企业	三资企业

包装数量或毛重或其他数量		
证书种类(画"√")	一般原产地证明书	加工装配证明书

　　现提交中国出口货物商业发票副本一份,一般原产地证明书/加工装配证明书一正三副,以及其他附件_____份,请予以审核签证。

申请单位盖章　　　　　　　　　　　　　　　申请人(签名)：
　　　　　　　　　　　　　　　　　　　　　电话：
　　　　　　　　　　　　　　　　　　　　　日期：

　商 检 局 联 系 记 录

ORIGINAL

1. Exporter (full name and address)	Certificate No.
	CERTIFICATE OF ORIGIN OF THE PEOPLE'S REPUBLIC OF CHINA
2. Consignee (full name, address, country)	
3. Means of transport and route	5. For certifying authority use only
4. Destination port	

6. Marks and numbers of packages	7. Description of goods; number and kind of packages	8. H. S. Code	9. Quantity or weight	10. Number and date of invoice

11. Declaration by the exporter The undersigned hereby declares that the above details and statements are correct; that all the goods were produced in China and that they comply with the Rules of Origin of the People's Republic of China	12. Certification It is hereby certified that the declaration by the exporter is correct
Place and date, signature and stamp of authorized signatory	Place and date, signature and stamp of certifying authority

怡祥船务有限公司
货运委托书

经营单位（托运人）			托书编号	
提单B/L项目要求	发货人： Shipper：			
	收货人： Consignee：			
	通知人： Notify Party：			
海洋运费(√) Sea freight	预付（ ）或（ ）到付 Prepaid or Collect	提单份数		提单寄送地址
起运港	目的港	可否转船		可否分批
集装箱预配数	20× 40×	装运期限		有效期限
标记唛码	件数及包装式样	中英文货号 Description of goods	毛重 (千克)	尺码 (立方米)	成交条件 (总价)
			特种货物 □ 冷藏货 □ 危险品	重件：每件重量	
内装箱(CFS)地址				大件 (长×宽×高)	
			特种集装箱：（　　　　）		
门对门装箱地址			物资备妥日期		
外币结算账号			物资进栈(√)　自送（ ）或（ ）派送		
声明事项			人民币结算单位账号		
			托运人签章		
			电　话		
			传　真		
			联系人		
			地　址		
			制单日期		

Shipper		B/L No.
		中国外运上海公司
		SINOTRANS SHANGHAI COMPANY
Consignee or order		**OCEAN BILL OF LADING**
		SHIPPED on board in apparent good order and condition (unless otherwise indicated) the goods or packages specified herein and to be discharged at the mentioned port of discharge or as near there to as the vessel may safely get and be always afloat.
Notify address		The weight, measure, marks and umbers, quality, contents and value, being particulars furnished by the Shipper, are not checked by the Carrier on loading.
Pre-carriage by	Port of loading	The Shipper Consignee and the Holder of this Bill of Lading hereby expressly accept and agree to all printed, written or stamped provisions, exceptions and conditions of this Bill of Lading, including those on the back hereof.
Vessel	Port of transshipment	IN WITNESS where of the number of original Bills of Lading stated below have been signed, one of which being accomplished, the other(s) to be void.
Port of discharge	Final destination	
Container seal No. or marks and Nos.	Number and kind of packages Description of goods	Gross weight (Kg)	Measurement (M^3)
Freight and charges	REGARDING TRANSHIPMENT INFORMATION PLEASE CONTACT		
Ex. rate	Prepaid at	Freight payable at	Place and date of issue
	Total Prepaid	Number of original Bs/L	Signed for or on behalf of the Master As Agent

报 关 委 托 书

(出口)报托 第　　号

××××公司：

我单位现委托贵公司代理货物（出口）报关

合同号：　　　　　货名：　　　　　件数：

毛重：　　　　　　净重：　　　　　价值：

我单位保证遵守《中华人民共和国海关法》及国家有关法规，保证所提供的单位与所报的货物相符，如申报货物有任何问题，责任由我单位承担。本委托书有效期至本委托书项下货物报关、缴税及退税完毕止。

委托单位:(盖章)　　　　　　　　　　代理单位:(盖章)

海关注册登记编码：　　　　　　　　　海关注册登记编码：

法定代表人姓名：　　　　　　　　　　法定代表人姓名：

联系电话：　　　　　　　　　　　　　联系电话：

经办人：　　　　　　　　　　　　　　经办人：

年　　月　　日

中华人民共和国海关出口货物报关单

预录入编号：　　　　　　　　　　　　　　　　　　　海关编号：

出口口岸		备案号		出口日期		申报日期	
经营单位		运输方式		运输工具名称		提运单号	
发货单位		贸易方式		征免性质		结汇方式	
许可证号		运抵国(地区)		指运港		境内货源地	
批准文号		成交方式		运费		保费	杂费
合同协议号		件数		包装种类	毛重(千克)		净重(千克)
集装箱号		随附单据				生产厂家	
标记码及备注							

项号	商品编号	商品名称、规格型号	数量及单位	最终目的国(地区)	单价	总价	币制	征免

税费征收情况		
录入员　　　　录入单位	兹声明以上申报无讹并承担法律责任	海关审单批注及放行日期(签章)
报关员		审单　　　　审价
单位地址	申报单位(签章)	征税　　　　统计
邮编　　　电话　　　填制日期		查验　　　　放行

汇票：

BILL OF EXCHANGE

凭
Dawn Under _____   不可撤销信用证
                                      Irrevocable   L/C No. _____

日期 _____   支取 Payable With interest @ ____ % 按 ____ 息 ____ 付款

号码 _____ 汇票金额 _____
No. _____ Exchange for _____   上海 shanghai

见票   日后（本汇票之副本未付）付交
At _____   sight of this FIRST of Exchange (Second of Exchange
Being unpaid) pay to the order of

金额
the sum of _____

此致
To _____
_____

SHIPPING ADVICE

TO:

INVOICE No.:
L/C No.:
S/C No.:

DEAR SIRS:
WE HEREBY INFORM YOU THAT THE GOODS UNDER THE ABOVE MENTIONED CREDIT HAVE BEEN SHIPPED. THE DETAILS OF THE SHIPMENT ARE STATED BELOW.
COMMODITY: _____
NUMBER OF PKGS: _____
TOTAL G. W.: _____
OCEAN VESSEL: _____
DATE OF DEPARTURE: _____
B/L No.: _____
PORT OF LOADING: _____
DESTINATION: _____
SHIPPING MARKS: _____

项目四　缮制信用证项下 CIF 术语出口单据

（一）信用证资料

SEQUENCE OF TOTAL	*27:	1/1
FORM OF DOC, CREDIT	*40A:	IRREVOCABLE TRANSFERABLE
DOC. CREDIT NUMBER	*20:	DC LCK429276
DATE OF ISSUE	31C:	140216
DATE AND PLACE OF EXPIRY	*31D:	140419 PLACE IN THE COUNTRY OF BENEFICIARY
APPLICANT	*50:	GOODWEST ENTERPRISES LTD.

		11/F., LIFUNG TOWER
		888CHEUNG SHA WAN ROAD.
		KOWLOON, HONG KONG
ISSUING BANK	52A:	HSBCHK
BENEFICIARY	*59:	SHANGHAIINTERNATIONAL IMPORT
		AND EXPORT CO., LTD.
		20A NO.1, LANE 628, ZHANGYANG RD.
		SHANGHAI,CHINA
AMOUNT	*32B:	AMOUNT USD 25 850.00
AVAILABLE WITH / BY	*41D:	ANY BANK IN CHINA BY NEGOTIATION
DRAFTS AT…	42C:	DRAFTS AT SIGHT FOR FULL INVIOCE COST
DRAWEE	42A:	ISSUING BANK
PARTIAL SHIPMENTS	43P:	PROHIBITED
TRANSSHIPMENT	43T:	PROHIBITED
LOADING ON BOARD	44A:	SHANGHAI CHINA
FOR TRANSPORTATION TO…	44B:	OSAKA JAPAN
LATEST DATE OF SHIPMENT	44C:	14APR07
DESCRIPT OF GOODS	45A:	100 PERCENT COTTON PRINTED SHEETING AS
		S/C NO 07-FGW-AEOW-0036

STYLE	COLOR	QTY (YARDS)	UNIT PRICE (USD/YD)
BTS 07			
S/4071	NIGHT OWL-WHITE	7 500	1.20
S/3094	CROSSWORD-TEAL SHADOW	7 000	1.20
S/3084	TEXT TWIST-WHITE	6 500	1.30

CIF OSAKA

DOCUMENTS REQUIRED 46A:

+SIGNED COMMERCIAL INVOICE IN DUPLICATE

+PACKING LIST IN DUPLICATE

+ORIGINAL INSPECTION CERTIFICATE ISSUED AND SIGNED BY GOODWEST ENTERPRISES LIMITED. TITLE OF THIS DOCUMENT (INSPECTION CERTIFICATE) DIFFER IS NOT ACCEPTABLE

+COPY OF CERTIFICATE OF ORIGIN

+3/3 ORIGINAL CLEAN ON BOARD OCEAN BILLS OF LADING MARKED "FREIGHT PREPAID"CONSIGNED TO ORDER, BLANK ENDORSED AND NOTIFY GOODWEST ENTERPRISES LTD., 9C, HK SPINNERS IND. CENTRE, 760-762 CHEUNG SHA WAN ROAD, LAT CHI KOK, KOWLOON, VIETNAM

+DUPLICATE OF MARINE INSURANCE POLICY IN NEGOTIABLE FORM AND BLANK ENDORSED, MENTIONING SHIPMENT DATE AND NAME OF VESSEL FOR FULL CIF VALUE PLUS 10 PERCENT COVERING INSTITUTE CARGO CLAUSES (A) INSTITUTE WAR CLAUSES (CARGO) AND INSTITUTE STRIKES CLAUSES (CARGO) EVIDENCING CLAIMS PAYABLE AT DESTINATION IN THE CURRENCY OF THE DC

+BENEFICIARY'S FAX COPY TO DC APPLICANT FOR ATTENTION OF ALEN CHAN/CAN CHU (FAX NO:852-2300 3051)ADVISING SHIPMENT DETAILS INCLUDING NAME OF VESSEL, ON BOARD DATE, ESTIMATED ARRIVAL DATE, VALUE OF GOODS, QUANTITY, COLOR BREAKDOWN, TOTAL CARTONS/ROLLS AND INCLUDING INVOCE AND PACKING LIST HAVE BEEN FAXED TO DC APPLICANT WITHIN 2 DAYS AFTER DATE OF SHIPMENT

+BENEFICIARY'S CERTIFICATE CERTIFYING THAT THE FOLLOWING DOCUMENTS HAVE BEEN SENT TO GOODWEST ENTERPRISES LTD., BY EXPRESS COURISER SERVICE WITHIN 2 DAYS AFTER SHIPMENT EFFECTED

(A) N/N COPY BILL OF LADING
(B) SIGNED COMMERCIAL INVOICE IN DUPLICATE
(C) PACKING LIST IN DUPLICATE
(D) ORIGINAL CERTIFICATE OF ORIGIN
(E) ORIGINAL MARINE INSURANCE POLICY, BLANK ENDORSED

CHARGES　　　　　　　　　　71B： ALL BANKING CHARGES OUTSIDE JAPAN ARE FOR ACCOUNT OF BENEFICIARY

PERIOD FOR PRESENTATION　　18： DOCUMENTS MUST BE PRESENTED WITHIN 15 DAYS AFTER THE DATE OF SHIPMENT BUT WITHIN THE VALIDITY OF THE CREDIT

（二）补充资料

1. INVOICE NO:XH056671
2. INVOICE DATE:FEB.25,2014
3. PACKING:PACKED IN ONE BALES OF 100 YARDS
   G.W.:30KGS/BALE　　N.W.:28KGS/BALE　　MEAS:0.4CBM/BALE
   交货方式:CFS TO CFS
   　　　　MARKS: LI&. FUNG TRADING LTD.
   　　　　07-FGW-AEOW-0036
   　　　　　　STYLE:
   　　　　　　COLOR:
   　　　　　　ROLL NO.:
   　　　　　　Q'TY: YARDS
   　　　　　　MADE IN CHINA
4. H.S. CODE:5208510092
5. VESSEL:VIKING EAGLE V.702S
6. B/L NO.:SYSHIJVE7027042
7. B/L DATE:20140314
8. POLICY NO.:SH078812
9. REFERENCE NO.:20140220
9. FREIGHT FEE:USD 1 200.00
10. INSURANCE FEE:USD 183.00
11. 注册号:7895478966
12. 证书号:580511478

13. 报检单编号:896541231
14. 报检单位登记号:1254789479
15. 生产单位注册号:12345Q
16. 投保单编号:TB0562311
17. 金发编号:JF0387124
18. 人民币账号:RMB061222   外币账号:WB68432144
19. 海关编号:外港海关 2225
20. 境内货源地:上海
21. 上海国际进出口有限公司企业代码:3122260176

要求:请根据以上信用证资料和补充资料的内容缮制下列有关单据。

中华人民共和国出口货物许可证
EXPORT LICENCE THE PEOPLE'S REPUBLIC OF CHINA A 类

申领许可证单位编码 Export		出口许可证编号 Licence No.		
发货单位 Consigne		许可证有效期 Validity		
贸易方式 Terms of trade		输往国家(地区) Country of destination		
合同号 Contract No.		收款方式 Terms of payment		
出运口岸 Port of shipment		运输方式 Means of transport		
唛头—包装件数 Marks & numbers-number of packages				
商品名称 Description of commodity		商品编码 Commodity No.		
商品规格型号 Specification	单位 Unit	数量 Quantity	单价( ) U/ price	总值( ) Amount	总值折美元 Amount in USD
总计 Total					
备注 Supplementary details		发证机关盖章 Issuing authority's stamp & signature 发证日期 Date		

对外经济贸易部监制   本证不得涂改,不得转让

上海国际进出口有限公司
SHANGHAI INTERNATIONAL IMPORT & EXPORT CO., LTD.
20A NO. 1, LANE 628, ZHANGYANG RD.
SHANGHAI, CHINA

COMMERCIAL INVOICE

TO		INVOICE NO.	
		INVOICE DATE	
		S/C NO.	
		S/C DATE	
FROM		TO	
Letter of Credit No.		Issued By	

Marks and Numbers	Number and kind of package Description of goods	Quantity	Unit Price	Amount
SAY TOTAL				

SINGED BY _____

上海国际进出口有限公司
SHANGHAI INTERNATIONAL IMPORT & EXPORT CO., LTD.
20A NO. 1, LANE 628, ZHANGYANG RD.
SHANGHAI, CHINA

PACKING LIST

TO		INVOICE NO.	
		INVOICE DATE	
		S/C NO.	
		S/C DATE	
FROM		TO	
Letter of Credit No.		Date of Shipment	
Marks and Numbers	Number and kind of package Description of goods	Quantity	PACKAGE	G. W.	N. W.	MEAs.
	Total					
SAY TOTAL						

SINGED BY _____

一般原产地证明书/加工装配证明书
申 请 书

申请单位注册号：　　　　　　　　　　　　　　　　　　　证书号：

申请人郑重申明：

　　本人被正式授权代表本企业办理和签署本申请书。

　　本申请书及一般原产地证明书/加工装配书所列内容正确无误，如发现弄虚作假，冒充证书所列货物，擅改证书，自愿接受签发机构的处罚并承担法律责任，现将有关情况申报如下：

企业名称		发票号	
商品名称		H.S.编码(六位数)	
商品FOB总值(以美元计)		最终目的地国家/地区	
拟出运日期		转口国(地区)	
贸易方式和企业性质(请在适用处画"√")			
一般贸易		三来一补		其他贸易方式	
国有企业	三资企业	国有企业	三资企业	国有企业	三资企业
包装数量或毛重或其他数量					
证书种类(画"√")	一般原产地证明书 || 加工装配证明书		

　　现提交中国出口货物商业发票副本一份，一般原产地证明书/加工装配证明书一正三副，以及其他附件　　份，请予以审核签证。

　　　　　　　　　　　　　　　　　　　　　　　　　　申请人(签名)：

申请单位盖章：　　　　　　　　　　　　　　　　　　　电话：

　　　　　　　　　　　　　　　　　　　　　　　　　　日期：

　　商 检 局 联 系 记 录

ORIGINAL

1. Exporter	Certificate No.
2. Consignee	**CERTIFICATE OF ORIGIN OF THE PEOPLE'S REPUBLIC OF CHINA**
3. Means of transport and route	5. For certifying authority use only
4. Country / region of destination	

6. Marks and numbers	7. Number and kind of packages; description of goods	8. H. S. Code	9. Quantity	10. Number and date of invoices

11. Declaration by the exporter The undersigned hereby declares that the above details and statements are correct, that all the goods were produced in China and that they comply with the Rules of Origin of the People's Republic of China Place and date, signature and stamp of authorized signatory	12. Certification It is hereby certified that the declaration by the exporter is correct Place and date, signature and stamp of certifying authority

报检委托书

_____出入境检验检疫局：

本单位将于　　　年　　　　月间出/进口如下货物：

品名：　　　　　　　　　　　　商品编码：

数(重)量：　　　　　　　　　　提单号：

合同号：　　　　　　　　　　　信用证号：

　　根据《中华人民共和国进出口商品检验法》《中华人民共和国进出境动植物检疫法》《中华人民共和国国境卫生检疫法》《中华人民共和国食品卫生法》等有关法律、法规的规定和检验检疫机构制订的各项规章制度,本委托人全权委托 _____ 公司(地址：_____ 联系电话：_____ 联系人：_____),代表委托人办理报检事宜,并承担委托范围内产生的一切相关的法律责任。请贵局按有关法律规定予以办理。

委托人名称：　　　　　　　　　　　　　　　　　　　委托人印章：

委托人地址：

邮政编码：

法人代表：

联系电话：

企业性质：

　　　　　　　　　　　　　　　　　　　　　　　　　　年　月　日

本委托书有效期至　　年　月　日

中华人民共和国出入境检验检疫出境货物报检单

报检单位(加盖公章)：　　　　　　　　　　＊编号＿＿＿＿＿＿＿＿

报检单位登记号：　　　联系人：　　　电话：　　　报检日期　年　月　日

发货人	(中文)				
	(外文)				
收货人	(中文)				
	(外文)				
货物名称(中/外文)	H.S.编码	产地	数/重量	货物总值	包装种类及数量

运输工具名称号码		贸易方式		货物存放地点	
合同号		信用证号		用途	
发货日期		输往国家(地区)		许可证/审批号	
启运地		到达口岸		生产单位注册号	
集装箱规格、数量及号码					

合同、信用证订立的检验检疫条款或特殊要求	标记及号码	随附单据(划"√"或补填)	
		□ 合同	□ 包装性能结果单
		□ 信用证	□ 许可/审批文件
		□ 发票	□
		□ 换证凭单	□
		□ 装箱单	□
		□ 厂检单	□

需要证单名称(划"√"或补填)		＊检验检疫费	
□ 品质证书　＿正＿副　□ 植物检疫证书　＿正＿副		总金额(人民币)	
□ 重量证书　＿正＿副　□ 熏蒸/消毒证书　＿正＿副			
□ 数量证书　＿正＿副　□ 出境货物换证凭单＿正＿副			
□ 兽医卫生证书　＿正＿副　□		计费人	
□ 健康证书　＿正＿副　□			
□ 卫生证书　＿正＿副　□		收费人	
□ 动物卫生证书　＿正＿副　□			

报检人郑重声明： 1. 本人被授权报检。 2. 上列填写内容正确属实,货物无伪造或冒用他人的厂名、标志、认证标志,并承担货物质量责任。 签名：	领取证单	
	日期	
	签名	

注：有"＊"号栏由出入境检验检疫机关填写。　　　　　　◆国家出入境检验检疫局制

THE PEOPLE'S INSURANCE COMPANY OF CHINA SHANGHAI BRANCH
出 口 运 输 险 投 保 单

编号 _____

兹将我处出口物资依照信用证规定拟向你处投保国外运输险计开：

被保险人 （中文）	过户		
（英文）			

标记及发票号码	件数	物资名称	保险货物金额

运输工具（及转载工具）	约于　年　月　日启运	赔款偿付地点	

运输路程	自　经　到	转载地点	

投保险别：

投保单位签章

　　　　　　　年　月　日

中 国 人 民 保 险 公 司
THE PEOPLE'S INSURANCE COMPANY OF CHINA
总 公 司 设 于 北 京　　一 九 四 九 年 创 立
Head Office：BEIJING　　Established in 1949

保险单　　　　　　　保险单号次
INSURANCE POLICY　　POLICY NO.

中国人民保险公司(以下简称本公司)
THIS POLICY OF INSURANCE WITNESSES THAT PEOPLE'S INSURANCE COMPANY OF CHINA (HEREINAFTER CALLED "THE COMPANY")

根据

AT THE REOUEST OF _____

(以下简称被保险人)的要求,由被保险人向公司缴付约

(HEREINAFTER CALLED "THE INSURED") AND IN CPMSIDERATION OF "THE AGREED PREMIUM PAD" TO THE COMPANY BY THE

定的保险费,按照本保险单承保险别和背面所载条款与下列

INSURED UNDERTAKES TO INSURE THE UNDERMENTIONED GOODS IN TRANSPORTATION SURIECT TO THE CONDITIONS OF THIS POLICY

特款承保下述货物运输保险,特立本保险单

AS PER THE CLAUSES PRINTED OVERLEAF AND OTHER SPECIAL CLAUSES ATTCHED HEREON

标记 MARKS & NOS	包装及数量 QUANTITY	保险货物项目 DESCRIPTION OF GOODS	保险金额 AMOUNT INSURED

总保险金额:

TOTAL AMOUNT INSURED _____

保费   费率   装载运输工具

PREMIUM <u>AS ARRAGED</u>   RATE <u>AS ARRAGED</u>   PER CONVEYANCE SS _____

开航日期   自   至

SLG. IN OR ABT _____   FROM _____   TO _____

承保险别

CONDITIONS _____

所保货物,如遇出险,本公司凭本保险单及其他有关证件给付赔偿。

CLAIMS IF ANY PAYABLE ON SURRENDER OF THIS POLICY TO GETHER WITH OTHER RELEVANT DOCUMENTS.

所保货物,如果发生本保险单项下负责赔偿的损失或事故,应立即通知本公司下述代理人查勘。

IN THE EVENT OF ACCIDENT WHEREBY LOSS OR DAMAGE MAY RESULT IN A CLAIM UNDER THIS POLICY IMMEDIATE NOTICE,, APPLYING FOR SURVEY MUST BE GIVEN TO THE COMPANY'S AGENT AS MENTIONED HSREUNDER.

                               中国人民保险公司上海分公司

                 THE PEOPLE'S INSURANCE CO. OF CHINA SHANGHAI BRANCH

赔款偿付地点

CLAIM PAYABLE AT /IN _____

日期

DATE _____

金发船务有限公司
货运委托书

经营单位 (托运人)				委托书 编号		
提单 B/L 项目 要求	发货人： Shipper：					
	收货人： Consignee：					
	通知人： Notify Party：					
海洋运费(√) Sea freight	预付( )或( ) 到付 Prepaid or Collect		提单份数		提单寄送 地址	
起运港		目的港		可否转船		可否分批
集装箱预配数		20× 40×		装运期限		有效期限
标记唛码	件数及包装 式样	中英文货号 Description of goods	毛重 (千克)		尺码 (立方米)	成交条件 (总价)
内装箱(CFS) 地址			特种货物 □ 冷藏货 □ 危险品		重件：每件重量 大件 (长×宽×高)	
			特种集装箱：( )			
门对门装箱地址			物资备妥日期			
外币结算账号			物资进栈(√) 自送( )或( )金发派送			
声明事项			人民币结算单位账号			
			托运人签章			
			电 话			
			传 真			
			联系人			
			地 址			
			制单日期			

Shipper		B/L No.
		中国外运上海公司 **SINOTRANS SHANGHAI COMPANY** **OCEAN BILL OF LADING** SHIPPED on board in apparent good order and condition (unless otherwise indicated) the goods or packages specified herein and to be discharged at the mentioned port of discharge or as near there to as the vessel may safely get and be always afloat. The weight, measure, marks and umbers, quality, contents and value, being particulars furnished by the Shipper, are not checked by the Carrier on loading. The Shipper Consignee and the Holder of this Bill of Lading hereby expressly accept and agree to all printed, written or stamped provisions, exceptions and conditions of this Bill of Lading, including those on the back hereof. IN WITNESS where of the number of original Bills of Lading stated below have been signed, one of which being accomplished, the other(s) to be void.
Consignee or order		
Notify address		
Pre-carriage by	Port of loading	
Vessel	Port of transshipment	
Port of discharge	Final destination	
Container seal No. or marks and Nos.	Number and kind of packages Description of goods	Gross weight (kgs)	Measurement (M³)
---	---	---	---

Freight and charges	REGARDING TRANSHIPMENT INFORMATION PLEASE CONTACT		
Ex. rate	Prepaid at	Freight payable at	Place and date of issue
	Total Prepaid	Number of original Bs/L	Signed for or on behalf of the Master As Agent

报 关 委 托 书

(出口)报托 第 号

××××公司：

我单位现委托贵公司代理货物（出口）报关

合同号： 货名： 件数：

毛重： 净重： 价值：

我单位保证遵守《中华人民共和国海关法》及国家有关法规，保证所提供的单位与所报的货物相符，如申报货物有任何问题，责任由我单位承担。本委托书有效期至本委托书项下货物报关、缴税及退税完毕止。

委托单位:(盖章)　　　　　　　　　代理单位:(盖章)

海关注册登记编码：　　　　　　　　海关注册登记编码：

法定代表人姓名：　　　　　　　　　法定代表人姓名：

联系电话：　　　　　　　　　　　　联系电话：

经办人：　　　　　　　　　　　　　经办人：

年　月　日

中华人民共和国海关出口货物报关单

预录入编号： 海关编号：

出口口岸		备案号	出口日期	申报日期
经营单位		运输方式	运输工具名称	提运单号
发货单位		贸易方式	征免性质	结汇方式
许可证号	运抵国(地区)		指运港	境内货源地
批准文号	成交方式	运费	保费	杂费
合同协议号	件数	包装种类	毛重(千克)	净重(千克)
集装箱号	随附单据		生产厂家	
标记码及备注				

项号	商品编号	商品名称、规格型号	数量及单位	最终目的国(地区)	单价	总价	币制	征免

税费征收情况

录入员　　　录入单位	兹声明以上申报无讹并承担法律责任	海关审单批注及放行日期(签章)	
报关员		审单	审价
单位地址	申报单位(签章)	征税	统计
邮编　　　电话　　　填制日期		查验	放行

SHIPPING ADVICE

TEL: INV NO.:
FAX: S/C NO.:
       L/C NO.:

TO MESSRS:

DEAR SIRS:

    WE HEREBY INFORM YOU THAT THE GOODS UNDER THE ABOVE MNTIONED CREDIT HAVE BEEN SHIPPED. THE DETAILS OF THE SHIPMENT ARE STAETD BELOW.

COMMODITY: _____   SHIPPING MARKS
MUMBER OF CTNS: _____
TOTAL G. W.: _____
OCEAN VESSEL: _____
DATE OF DEPARTURE: _____
B/L NO.: _____
PORT OF LOADING: _____
DESTINATION: _____

BILL OF EXCHANGE

凭 Drawn Under	信用证 L/C NO.
日期 Date	支取 按 息 付款 Payable With interest @ %
号码 No.	汇票金额 宁波 Exchange for Ningbo
见票 at Pay to the order of	日后(本汇票之副本未付)付交 sight of this FIRST of Excgange (Second of Exchange Being unpaid)
金额 The sum of	
此致 To	

 简答

1. 请问当这批货物出口后,应向银行提交哪些单据?

2. 请问这批货物出口时,向海关报关应提交哪些单据?

项目五 缮制电汇项下 CIF 术语出口单据

(一)销售合同书

中国宁波合作股份有限公司
CHINA NINGBO COOPERATION HOLDING LTD.

地址:中国,宁波西岗区黄河区 28 号	Tel:00-411-83780896
Address:28, Huanghe Rd, Xigang Dist,	Fax:00-411-83780892
Ningbo, China	合同号 Contract No:CDIG/T:20140701-2
	日期 Date:2014-7-1

售 货 合 同
SALES CONTRACT

购货方 Buyers:Juct Food Co., Ltd.

地址 Address:6-7, KAWARA MACH YOKOHAMA JAPAN

电话 Tel:0081-02-3456789

传真 Fax:0081-02-34565788

This Sales Contract is made by and between the sellers and the buyers, whereby the sellers agree to sell and buyers agree to buy the under-mentioned goods according to the terms and conditions stipulated below:

(1) 唛头 Marks & No	(2) 货号、品名及规格 Name of Commodity and specifications	(3) 数量 Quantity	(4) 单位 Unit	(5) 单价 Unit Price (USD/PC)	(6) 金额 Amount (USD)
JUCT FOODS	工作服 Ladies' Coats Ladies' Pants Men's Coats Men's Pants	1 050 1 075 350 275	PC PC PC PC	CIFYOKOHAMA 7.21 5.62 7.46 6.2	7 570.50 6 041.50 2 611.00 1 705.00
	Total amount:USD17 928.00				

(7) 包装 Packing:纸箱 CARTON

(8) 唛头 Shipping Marks:有

(9) 产地和制造商 Origin & Manufacture:中国

(10) 到货期 Date of Arrival:合同签订后 45 天

(11) 装运港 Ports of Shipment:中国宁波

(12) 目的港 Ports of Destination:日本横滨

(13) 保险:由售方按 110% 发票金额投保一切险和战争险

   The Sellerprocures an insurance policy against All Risks and War Risk for 110% of invoice value

(14) 付款条件 Terms of Payment：

Ⅰ．T/T 方式支付：by 30％ of invoice within 10 days after singned contract and t/t 70％ of invoice within 30 days after goods arrived.

合同签约后 10 日内付 30％定金,货到横滨 30 内付 70％货款。

Ⅱ．该信用证凭以下装运单据议付：

全套已装船清洁提单：Full set of clean on board Bills of Lading.

商业发票 3 份：Commercial Invoice.

在 CIF 条件下的保险单/保险凭证 2 份：Under the term of CIF, Insurance Policy/Insurance Certificate.

装箱单一式 2 份：Packing List.

由工厂出具的品质证明书：Quality Certificate issued by manufacture.

发货通知书 1 份：Notice of Shipment.

Ⅲ．购货方责任 Buyer's Duties：

(15) 检验与索赔 Inspection and Claims：

Ⅰ．货物在装运前,卖方有权向设在装运港的检验检疫机构申请对货物进行检验,其检验证书为最后依据。

The Seller shall have the right to apply for inspection to inspection and Quarantine government at the port of shipment before the shipment of the goods, and its Inspection Certificate are to be taken an final.

Ⅱ．买方自货抵最终目的地卸货完毕之日起 30 天内,如发现货物的质量、规格、数量等与合同规定不符,应在前述期限内向卖方索赔,卖方应赔偿买方因此受到的包括利润在内的损失。

Within 30 days from the date of the arrival of the goods at the final destination, should qulity, specification, quantity and other requirements stipulated in the Contract be found not in conformity with the stipulations of the Contract, the Buyers shall give a notice of claims to the Seller within the above mentioned time limit and have the right to lodge claims against the Seller on the strength of the inspection certificate issued by the inspection organization above mentioned. The sellwe shall compensate for damage (include profits) tothe Buyer.

(16) 品质保证 Warranty：

卖方保证其所提供的全部货物均符合本合同规定,货物的保质期为自最终目的港卸货之日起 30 天。在质量保证期内,凡因设计、制造和所用材料而产生的缺陷,卖方应自负费用进行修理或更换货物或部件。同时买方有权就前述缺陷所造成的损失向卖方要求赔偿。

The Seller shall warrant that all goods delivered by the Seller shall be in conformity to the Contract stipulations. Warranty period is within 30 days after the date of the completion of unloading of the goods at the port of destination. Within the warranty period, the Seller shall remove all defects of the foods due to design, workmanship and improper material used either by repairing or by replacing the defective parts or the goods on his own account. Meanwhile the Buyer has the right to bring the claims for their damages against the Seller.

(17) 延期和违约金 Late delivery and Penalty：

如卖方不能按合同及时交货,除不可抗力外,卖方应向买方支付违约金,违约金按每周延期货物总值的 0.1％计算,不足 1 周按 1 周计,但违约金总额不得超过延期货物总值的 1％。如延期达 1 个月,买方即可书面通知卖方解除合同,卖方应赔偿买方因此所受到的包括利润在内的的损失。

Should the Seller fail to make delivery of all or any part of the goods on time as stipulated in the Contract, with excetion of Force Majeure causes, the Seller shall pay Penalties. The rate of Penalty is charged at 0.1% of the delayed goods for every seven days, and days less than seven days should be counted as seven days, however the penalty shall not exceed 1% of the total value of the goods involved in the late delivery. In case the Seller fail to make delivery one month later than the time of shipment stipulated in the Contract, the Buyer shall inform the Seller in written to cancel the Contract, the Seller shaoo compensate for damages (include profits) to the Buyer.

(17) 不可抗力 Force Majeure：
任何一方对因下列原因导致的不能或暂不能履行全部或部分合同义务不负责任：水灾、火灾、地震、干旱、战争、内乱或其他任何在签约时不能预料、无法控制且不能避免和克服的事件，但受不可抗力影响的一方，应在事发后15日内将事发地公证机构出具的不可抗力事件的证明寄交对方。
Either Party shall not be held responsible for failure of delay to perform all or any part of the Contract due to flood, fire, earthquake, drought, war or any other events which could not be predicted at the time of the conclusion of the Contract and could not becontrolled, avoided or overcome by the parties. However, The effected by the Event of Force Majeure shall inform the other party of its coccurrence in written within 15 days after its occurrence and thereafter send a certificate of the Event issued by the native notarial office.

(18) 凡因执行本合同或与本合同有关的一切争议，双方应友好协商。协商仍不能解决争议，则应将争议提交北京中国国际经济贸易仲裁委员会仲裁解决。仲裁裁决是终局的，对双方均有约束力。
All disputes arising from the execution of or in connection with the Contract should be settled through friendly negotiations, if no settlement can be reached through negotiation, the case shall then be submitted to the China International Economic and Trade ARBITRATIONCommission (Beijing) for arbitration in accordance with its provisional rules of procedure. The award of the arbitration shall be final and binding upon both parties.

(19) 其他 Other Condition：
Ⅰ. 对本合同的任何变更，仅在以书面经双方签字后，方为有效，任何一方在未取得对方书面同意前，无权将本合同规定之义务转让给第三方。
Any alternations to the contract shall be valid only if they are made out in writing and signed by both paries. Neither party is entitled to transfer its obligation under the Contract to a third party before obtaining a written consent from the other party.

Ⅱ. 除非另有规定，"FOB""CIF""CFR"(CNF and C&F)均依国际商会制定的《国际贸易术语解释通则》(INCOTERMS 1990)办理。
　　The terms "FOB""CIF""CFR(C&F/CNF)" shall be subject to the "International Rules For the Interpretation of Trade Terms"(INCOTERM 1990) trovided by International Chambers of Commerce (ICC) unless otherwise stipulated herein.

(19) 特殊条款 Special Provisions。
(20) 其他条款 Other Terms.
本合同经双方授权代表签字及买方盖章后即生效，双方各执一份，每份具有同等的效力。
This contract becomes effective shile signed by authorized representatives of both parties and sealed by the Buyers. Each party holds one copy. The copies are equivalently valid.

THE SELLER：   THE BUYER：
卖方：   买方：
CHINA NINGBO COOPERATION HOLDING LTD.   Juct Food Co., Ltd
中国宁波合作股份有限公司   Ben. Kamla(签章)
陈永国(签章)

(二) 补充资料

1. INVOICE NO.：自编
2. PACKING：

Ladies' Coats   1 050PCS   PACKED IN ONE CARTON OF 35 PCS EACH
Ladies' Pants   1 075PCS   PACKED IN ONE CARTON OF 25 PCS EACH
Men's Coats   350PCS   PACKED IN ONE CARTON OF 35 PCS EACH
Men's Pants   275PCS   PACKED IN ONE CARTON OF 25 PCS EACH

GROSS WEIGHT：11KGS/CTN

NET WEIGHT：9KGS/CTN

MEASUREMENT：0.045M^3

3. H.S. CODE：8204.11
4. FREIGHT：USD 1 200.00
5. 保险费费率：0.6%
6. 代理报关公司：宁波怡翔货运代理公司(3122668874)
   地址：宁波金山路108号 电话：65789687
   报关员：王明
7. 企业代码：中国宁波合作股份有限公司(3105226789)
8.   配舱回单

TO：王明

贵司已委托我司出运货物，FROM ___宁波___ TO ___横滨___

提单号：12WEYJR741305T   箱量：拼

船名/航次：JIN RONG V.741 E

预计船期：2014-7-29

入港时间：_____

最迟报关时间：2014-7-28 11:00 前

入货时间： 2014-7-28   9:00

装箱场地： 宁波北仑港 DCT 场地

电话：0 411-87596334

联系人：陈世利

* 备注：请提供准确的品名及件、重、尺，以免报关时因 EDI 错误导致退单。
　　　如有任何问题，请及时与我司联系！
单据请邮寄我司地址如下：
宁波市中山区港湾街5号银河花园503室

时间：2014-7-25　　　　　　　　　　　　　　航线操作：杨洋
传真：0411-82751969　　　　　　　　　　　　电话：0411-82751488

请以"单证员"身份，根据上述销售合同及补充资料缮制下列单据。

中国宁波合作股份有限公司
CHINA NINGBO COOPERATION HOLDING LTD.

商 业 发 票
COMMERCIAL INVOICE

POST CODE：
FAX：　　　　　　　　　　　　　　　　INVOICE NO.：＿＿＿＿＿＿＿＿＿＿
TELEX：　　　　　　　　　　　　　　　DATA：＿＿＿＿＿＿＿＿＿＿＿＿＿
TEL：　　　　　　　　　　　　　　　　 S/C NO.：＿＿＿＿＿＿＿＿＿＿＿＿
　　　　　　　　　　　　　　　　　　　 L/C NO：＿＿＿＿＿＿＿＿＿＿＿＿
To Messrs,　　　　　　　　　　　　　　 DATA：＿＿＿＿＿＿＿＿＿＿＿＿＿

FROM ＿＿＿＿＿＿＿＿＿＿＿＿　　　　TO ＿＿＿＿＿＿＿＿＿＿＿＿＿＿

唛头号码 MARKS & NO.	数量与货品名 QUANTITES AND DESCRIPTIONS	单　价 UNIT PRICE	总　值 AMOUT

TOTAL AMOUT：

WE HEREBY CERTIFY THAT THE ABOVE MENTIONED GOODS ARE OF CHINESE ORIGIN

中国宁波合作股份有限公司
CHINA NINGBO COOPERATION HOLDING LTD.

中国宁波合作股份有限公司
CHINA NINGBO COOPERATION HOLDING LTD

PACKING LIST

POST CODE:

FAX: INVOICE NO. : _____

TELEX: DATA: _____

TEL: S/C NO. : _____

L/C NO. : _____

To Messrs, DATA: _____

FROM _____ TO _____

C\NOS.	NOS. &. KINDS OF PKGS ( )	QTY ( )	G. W. ( )	N. W. ( )	MEAS ( )
TOTAL:					

PACKED IN _____ CARTONS

TOTAL GROSS WEIGHT _____

TOTAL NET WEIGHT _____

中国宁波合作股份有限公司
CHINA NINGBO COOPERATION HOLDING LTD.

THE PEOPLE'S INSURANCE COMPANY OF CHINA SHANGHAI BRANCH
出 口 运 输 险 投 保 单

编号 _____

兹将我处出口物资依照信用证规定拟向你处投保国外运输险计开：

被保险人 （中文）			
（英文）	过户		
标记及发票号码	件数	物资名称	保险货物金额
运输工具 （及转载工具）	约 于　年　月　日启运		赔款偿 付地点
运输路程	自　经　到	转载地点	
投保险别：	投保单位签章 　　　年　月　日		

中国人民保险公司
THE PEOPLE'S INSURANCE COMPANY OF CHINA
总公司设于北京　一九四九年创立
Head Office：BEIJING　　Established in 1949

保险单保　　　　　险单次号次
INSURANCE POLICY　　POLICY NO.

中国人民保险公司(以下简称本公司)
THIS POLICY OF INSURANCE WITNESSES THAT PEOPLE'S INSURANCE COMPANY OF CHINA (HEREINAFTER CALLED "THE COMPAY")
根据

AT THE REQUEST OF _____

(以下简称被保险人)的要求,由被保险人向公司缴付约

(HEREINAFTER CALLED "THE INSURED") AND IN CPMSIDERATION OF "THE AGREED PREMIUM PAD" TO THE COMPANY BY THE

定的保险费,按照本保险单承保险别和背面所载条款与下列

INSURED UNDERTAKES TO INSURE THE UNDERMENTIONED GOODS IN TRANSPORTATION SURIECT TO THE CONDITIONS OF THIS POLICY

特款承保下述货物运输保险,特立本保险单。

AS PER THE CLAUSES PRINTED OVERLEAF AND OTHER SPECIAL CLAUSES ATTCHED HEREON.

标记 MARKS & NOS	包装及数量 QUANTITY	保险货物项目 DESCRIPTION OF GOODS	保险金额 AMOUNT INSURED

总保险金额:
TOTAL AMOUNT INSURED _____

保费   费率   装载运输工具
PREMIUM AS ARRAGED   RATE AS ARRAGED   PER CONVEYANCE SS _____

开航日期   自   至
SLG. IN OR ABT _____   FROM _____   TO _____

承保险别
CONDITIONS _____

所保货物,如遇出险,本公司凭本保险单及其他有关证件给付赔偿。

CLAIMS IF ANY PAYABLE ON SURRENDER OF THIS POLICY TOGETHER WITH OTHER RELEVANT DOCUMENTS.

所保货物,如果发生本保险单项下负责赔偿的损失或事故,应立即通知本公司下述代理人查勘。

IN THE EVENT OF ACCIDENT WHEREBY LOSS OR DAMAGE MAY RESULT IN A CLAIM UNDER THIS POLICY IMMEDIATE NOTICE, APPLYING FOR SURVEY MUST BE GIVEN TO THE COMPANY'S AGENT AS MENTIONED HSREUNDER.

中国人民保险公司上海分公司
THE PEOPLE'S INSURANCE CO. OF CHINA SHANGHAI BRANCH

赔款偿付地点
CLAIM PAYABLE AT /IN _____

日期
DATE _____

金发船务有限公司
货运委托书

经营单位 (托运人)		委托书编号	
提单 B/L 项目要求	发货人： Shipper：		
	收货人： Consignee：		
	通知人： Notify Party：		

海洋运费(√) Sea freight	预付（　）或 （　）到付 Prepaid or Collect	提单份数		提单寄送 地　　址	
起运港		目的港		可否转船		可否分批	
集装箱预配数		20′× 　　40′×		装运期限		有效期限	

标记唛码	件数及 包装式样	中英文货号 Description of goods	毛重 (千克)	尺码 (立方米)	成交条件 (总价)

内装箱(CFS) 地址		特种货物 □ 冷藏货 □ 危险品	重件：每件重量
			大件 (长×宽×高)
		特种集装箱：(　　　　　)	
门对门装箱地址		货物备妥日期	
外币结算账号		货物进栈(√)　自送(　)或(　)金发派送	
声明事项		人民币结算单位账号	
		托运人签章	
		电　话	
		传　真	
		联系人	
		地　址	
		制单日期	

Shipper		B/L No.
		中国外运上海公司
		SINOTRANS SHANGHAI COMPANY
Consignee or order		**OCEAN BILL OF LADING**
		SHIPPED on board in apparent good order and condition (unless otherwise indicated) the goods or packages specified herein and to be discharged at the mentioned port of discharge or as near there to as the vessel may safely get and be always afloat.
Notify address		The weight, measure, marks and numbers, quality, contents and value, being particulars furnished by the Shipper, are not checked by the Carrier on loading.
Pre-carriage by	Port of loading	The Shipper Consignee and the Holder of this Bill of Lading hereby expressly accept and agree to all printed, written or stamped provisions, exceptions and conditions of this Bill of Lading, including those on the back hereof.
Vessel	Port of transshipment	IN WITNESS where of the number of original Bills of Lading stated below have been signed, one of which being accomplished, the other(s) to be void.
Port of discharge	Final destination	

Container seal No. or marks and Nos.	Number and kind of packages Description of goods	Gross weight (kgs)	Measurement (M³)

Freight and charges	Regarding Transhipment Information Please Contact		
Ex. rate	Prepaid at	Freight payable at	Place and date of issue
	Total Prepaid	Number of original Bs/L	Signed for or on behalf of the Master As Agent

报 关 委 托 书

(出口)报托　第　　号

××××公司:

我单位现委托贵公司代理货物（出口）报关

合同号:　　　　　货名:　　　　　件数:

毛重:　　　　　　净重:　　　　　价值:

我单位保证遵守《中华人民共和国海关法》及国家有关法规,保证所提供的单位与所报的货物相符,如申报货物有任何问题,责任由我单位承担。本委托书有效期至本委托书项下货物报关、缴税及退税完毕止。

委托单位:(盖章)　　　　　　　代理单位:(盖章)

海关注册登记编码:　　　　　　　海关注册登记编码:

法定代表人姓名:　　　　　　　　法定代表人姓名:

联系电话:　　　　　　　　　　　联系电话:

经办人:　　　　　　　　　　　　经办人:

年　　月　　日

中华人民共和国海关出口货物报关单

预录入编号：　　　　　　　　　　　　　　　　　　海关编号：

出口口岸		备案号	出口日期	申报日期
经营单位		运输方式	运输工具名称	提运单号
发货单位		贸易方式	征免性质	结汇方式
许可证号	运抵国(地区)		指运港	境内货源地
批准文号	成交方式	运费	保费	杂费
合同协议号	件数	包装种类	毛重(千克)	净重(千克)
集装箱号	随附单据		生产厂家	
标记码及备注				

项号	商品编号	商品名称、规格型号	数量及单位	最终目的国(地区)	单价	总价	币制	征免

税费征收情况

录入员　　　录入单位	兹声明以上申报无讹并承担法律责任	海关审单批注及放行日期(签章)	
报关员		审单	审价
单位地址	申报单位(签章)	征税	统计
邮编　　　电话　　　填制日期		查验	放行

SHIPPING ADVICE JP

DATE: _____

SHIPPING DATE _____   LOADING PORT _____
VESSEL NAME _____   UNLOADING PORT _____
CARRIET _____   CONSIGNEE _____

GOODS NAME	QUANTITY	CTN QTY	PRICE (USD)	B/L NO.	CTNR NO.
TOTAL					

COMPANY NAME:

CONTRACT PERSON: MS. XINPING ZHANG
TEL: 00-411-83780896
Fax: 00-411-83780892

项目六　缮制托收项下 CFR 术语出口单据

根据以下制单资料缮制相关单证:
(1) 客户名称地址:AL. BALOUSHI TRADING EST JEDDAH
　　付款方式:20%T/T BEFORE SHIPMENT AND 80% D/P AT SIGHT
　　装运信息:指定 APL 承运,装期:2014.04.29;起运港:NINGBO,目的港:JEDDAH
　　价格条款:CFR JEDDAH
　　　　　　ROYAL
　　　　　　05AR225031
　　　　　　JEDDAH
　　　　　　C/N:1—460
(2) 货物描述:
P. P INJECTIONCASES　14"/22"/27"31"　230SET@USD 42.00/SET
USD 9 660.00
P. P INJECTIONCASES　14"/19"/27"31"　230SET@USD 41.00/SET
USD 9 430.00
(中文品名:注塑箱四件套)

(3) 装箱资料：

箱号	货号	包装	件数	毛重(KGS)	净重(KGS)	体积
1—230	ZL0322＋BC05	CTNS	230	18.5/4 255	16.5/37 95	34M³
1—230	ZL0319＋BC01	CTNS	230	18.5/4 255	16.5/379 5	34M³

(4) 合同号：05AR225031　签订日期：2014年3月30日

(5) 商业发票号：AC05AR031

要求：根据以上资料制作相关单据

中华人民共和国出口货物许可证
EXPORT LICENCE THE PEOPLE'S REPUBLIC OF CHINA

A 类

申领许可证单位　编码 Export	出口许可证编号 Licence No.
发货单位 Consigne	许可证有效期 Validity
贸易方式 Terms of trade	输往国家(地区) Country of destination
合同号 Contract No.	收款方式 Terms of payment
出运口岸 Port of shipment	运输方式 Means of transport
唛头—包装件数 Marks & numbers-number of packages	
商品名称 Description of commodity	商品编码 Commodity No.

商品规格型号 Specification	单位 Unit	数量 Quantity	单价( ) U/price	总值( ) Amount	总值折美元 Amount in USD
总计 Total					

备注 Supplementary details	发证机关盖章 Issuing authority's stamp & signature 发证日期 Date

对外经济贸易部监制　　　　　　　　　　　　　　　　本证不得涂改，不得转让

COMMERCIAL INVOICE

TO		INVOICE NO.	
		INVOICE DATE	
		S/C NO.	
		S/C DATE	
FROM		TO	
Letter of Credit No.		Issued By	
Marks and Numbers	Number and kind of package Description of goods	Quantity	Unit Price	Amount
SAY TOTAL				

SINGED BY _____

PACKING LIST

TO		INVOICE NO.			
		INVOICE DATE			
		S/C NO.			
		S/C DATE			
FROM		TO			
Letter of Credit No.		Date of Shipment			
Marks and Numbers	Number and kind of package Description of goods	Quantity	PACKAGE	G. W.	N. W.	MEAS.
	Total					
SAY TOTAL						

SINGED BY _____

普惠制产地证明书申请书

申请单位(盖章):   证书号:

申请人郑重声明:

    本人被正式授权代表本企业办理和签署本申请书。

    本申请书及普惠制产地证明书格式A所列内容正确无误,如发现弄虚作假,冒充证书所列货物,擅改证书,自愿接受签发机构的处罚并承担法律责任,现将有关情况申报如下:

生产单位		生产单位联系人电话			
商品名称(中英文)		H.S.编码(六位数)			
商品FOB总值(以美元计)		发票号			
最终销售国		证书种类(画"√")		加急证书	普通证书
货物拟出运日期					

贸易方式和企业性质(请在适用处画"√")						
正常贸易 C	来(进)料加工 L	补偿贸易 B	中外合资 H	中外合作 Z	外商独资 D	零售 Y	展卖 M

包装数量或毛重或其他数量

原产地标准:

本项商品系在中国生产,完全符合该给惠国给惠方案规定,其原产地情况符合以下第__条:

(1) "P"(完全国产,未使用任何进口原材料)。

(2) "W"其H.S.税目号为_____(含进口成分)。

(3) "F"(对加拿大出口产品,其进口成分不超过产品出厂价值的40%)。

本批产品系:1. 直接运输从_____到_____。

            2. 转口运输从_____中转国(地区)_____到_____。

申请人说明	领证人(签名): 电 话: 日 期: 年 月 日

现提交中国出口商业发票副本一份,普惠制产地证明书格式A(FORM A)一正二副,以及其他附件____份,请予以审核签证。

注:凡有进口成分的商品,必须要求提交《含进口成分受惠商品成本明细单》。

   商 检 局 联 系 记 录

普惠制产地证书

1. Goods consigned from (Exporter's business name, address, country)	Reference No.
	GENERALIZED SYSTEM OF PREFERENCES CERTIFICA OF ORIGN (Combined Declaration and certificate)
2. Goods consigned to (Consignee's name, address, consigned)	FORM A LSSUED IN THE PEOPLES REPUBLIC OF CHINA (country) See Notes Overleaf
3. Means of transport and route (as for as know)	4. For official use

5. Item number	6. Marks and numbers of packages	7. Number and kind of packages; description of goods	8. Origin criterion (see notes overleaf)	9. Gross weight or other quantity	10. Number and date of invoices

11. certification It is hereby certified, on the basis of control carried out, that the declaration by the exporter is correct	12. declaration by the exporter The undersigned hereby declares that the above details and statements are correct, that all the goods were Produced in CHINA (country) and that they comply with the origin requirements specified for those goods, in the generalized system of preference for goods exported to (importing country)
Place and date, signature and stamp of certifying authority	Place and date, signature of and stamp of authorized signatory

中华人民共和国出入境检验检疫

出境货物报检单

报检单位(加盖公章)　　　　　　　　　　＊编号＿＿＿＿＿＿

报检单位登记号：　　　联系人　　　电话　　　报检日期　年　月　日

发货人	(中文)				
	(外文)				
收货人	(中文)				
	(外文)				
货物名称(中/外文)	H.S.编码	产地	数/重量	货物总值	包装种类及数量
运输工具名称号码		贸易方式		货物存放地点	
合同号		信用证号		用途	
发货日期		输往国家(地区)		许可证/审批号	
启运地		到达口岸		生产单位注册号	
集装箱规格、数量及号码					

合同、信用证订立的检验检疫条款或特殊要求	标记及号码	随附单据(划"√"或补填)	
		□ 合同	□ 包装性能结果单
		□ 信用证	□ 许可/审批文件
		□ 发票	□
		□ 换证凭单	□
		□ 装箱单	□
		□ 厂检单	□

需要证书名称(划"√"或补填)		＊检验检疫费	
□ 品质证书　__正__副	□ 植物检疫证书　__正__副	总金额(人民币元)	
□ 重量证书　__正__副	□ 熏蒸/消毒证书　__正__副		
□ 数量证书　__正__副	□ 出境货物换证凭条__正__副		
□ 兽医卫生证书　__正__副	□	计费人	
□ 健康证书　__正__副	□		
□ 卫生证书　__正__副		收费人	
□ 动物卫生证书　__正__副	□		

报检人郑重声明： 1. 本人被授权报检。 2. 上列填写内容正确属实，货物无伪造或冒用他人的厂名、标志、认证标志，并承担货物质量责任。 　　　　　　　　　签名：	领取证书	
	日期	
	签名	

注：有"＊"号栏由出入境检验检疫机关填写。　　　　　　　　◆国家出入境检验检疫局制

金发船务有限公司
货运委托书

经营单位 (托运人)		委托书 编号	
提单 B/L 项目 要求	发货人： Shipper： 收货人： Consignee： 通知人： Notify Party：		
海洋运费(√) Sea freight	预付（ ）或 （ ）到付 Prepaid or Collect	提单份数		提单寄送 地 址	
起运港		目的港		可否转船		可否分批	
集装箱预配数		20′× 40′×		装运期限		有效期限	
标记唛码	件 数 及 包装式样	中英文货号 Description of goods	毛重 (千克)	尺码 (立方米)	成交条件 (总价)
内装箱(CFS) 地址			特种货物 □ 冷藏货 □ 危险品	重件：每件重量	
				大件 (长×宽×高)	
			特种集装箱（　　　　）		
门对门装箱地址			物资备妥日期		
外币结算账号			物资进栈(√) 自送( )或( )金发派送		
声明事项			人民币结算单位账号		
			托运人签章		
			电 话		
			传 真		
			联系人		
			地 址		
			制单日期：		

Shipper		B/L No.
		中国外运上海公司 **SINOTRANS SHANGHAI COMPANY**
Consignee or order		**OCEAN BILL OF LADING** SHIPPED on board in apparent good order and condition (unless otherwise indicated) the goods or packages specified herein and to be discharged at the mentioned port of discharge or as near there to as the vessel may safely get and be always afloat. The weight, measure, marks and numbers, quality, contents and value, being particulars furnished by the Shipper, are not checked by the Carrier on loading. The Shipper Consignee and the Holder of this Bill of Lading hereby expressly accept and agree to all printed, written or stamped provisions, exceptions and conditions of this Bill of Lading, including those on the back hereof. IN WITNESS where of the number of original Bills of Lading stated below have been signed, one of which being accomplished, the other(s) to be void.
Notify address		
Pre-carriage by	Port of loading	
Vessel	Port of transshipment	
Port of discharge	Final destination	
Container seal No. or marks and Nos.	Number and kind of packages Description of goods	Gross weight (kgs)	Measurement (M^3)
---	---	---	---

Freight and charges	Regarding Transhipment Information Please Contact		
Ex. rate	Prepaid at	Freight payable at	Place and date of issue
	Total Prepaid	Number of original Bs/L	Signed for or on behalf of the Master As Agent

中华人民共和国海关出口货物报关单

预录入编号： 　　　　　　　　　　　　　　　　　　海关编号：

出口口岸		备案号		出口日期		申报日期	
经营单位		运输方式		运输工具名称		提运单号	
发货单位		贸易方式		征免性质		结汇方式	
许可证号		运抵国(地区)		指运港		境内货源地	
批准文号		成交方式		运费		保费	杂费
合同协议号		件数		包装种类		毛重(千克)	净重(千克)
集装箱号		随附单据				生产厂家	
标记唛码及备注							
项号 商品编号 商品名称、规格型号 数量及单位 最终目的国(地区)单价 总价 币制 征免							
税费征收情况							
录入员	录入单位	兹声明以上申报无讹并承担法律责任			海关审单批注及放行日期(签章)		
报关员					审单	审价	
单位地址		申报单位(签章)			征税	统计	
邮编	电话	填制日期			查验	放行	

SHIPPING ADVICE

TEL: INV NO.:

FAX: S/C NO.:

                          L/C NO.:

TO MESSRS:

DEAR SIRS:

WE HEREBY INFORM YOU THAT THE GOODS UNDER THE ABOVE MNTIONED CREDIT HAVE BEEN SHIPPED. THE DETAILS OF THE SHIPMENT ARE STAETD BELOW.

COMMODITY: _____   SHIPPING MARKS

MUMBER OF CTNS: _____

TOTAL G. W.: _____

OCEAN VESSEL: _____

DATE OF DEPARTURE: _____

B/L NO.: _____

PORT OF LOADING: _____

DESTINATION: _____

BILL OF EXCHANGE

凭   信用证

Drawn under _____   L/C NO. _____

日期

Dated _____   支取 Payable with interest @ ____ % 按 ____ 息 ____ 付款

号码   汇票金额   宁波

NO. _____   Exchange for   Ningbo _____ 20

见票 _____ 日后(本汇票之副本未付)付交

AT _____ sight of this FIRST of Exchange(Second of Exchange being unpaid)

Pay to the order of _____ The sum of

款已收讫

Value received

_____

此致

TO: _____

_____

简答

1. 请问当这批货物出口后,应向银行提交哪些单据?

2. 请问这批货物出口时,向海关报关应提交哪些单据?

项目七 缮制开证申请书

根据合同资料缮制开证申请书。

合同资料:

买方:TIANJIN LANSHENG TRADE CORP.
   348 JIEFANG ROAD TIANJIN CHINA
   TEL:022-56043222

卖方:TAKAMRA IMP. & EXP. TRADE CORP.
   324, OTOLIMACH TOKYO, JAPAN TEL:028-54872458

品名:WHISKY ROYAL SALUTE 500CL

单价:USD 1 200.00/PC CIF TIANJIN

数量:200PCS

包装:4PC/CTN

总价:24 000 美元

装运时间:2014 年 8 月 31 日前,不准分批装运和转运

装运港:TOKYO

目的港:TIANJIN

开证方式:电开

支付:不可撤销即期跟单信用证

保险:按发票金额加一成投保一切险和战争险

单据条款:商业发票一式五份,注明信用证号和合同号
     装箱单一式四份
     全套清洁已装船正本提单,做成空白抬头,空白背书,注明运费预付
     检验检疫机构出具的品质检验证书一份
     保险单正本一份,作空白背书

合同号:GWM050831

开户行及账号:中国银行 1357924680

IRREVOCABLE DOCUMENTARY CREDIT APPLICATION
TO: BANK OF CHINA

Beneficiary (full name and address)	L/C No. Ex-Card No. Contract No.
	Date and place of expiry of the credit
Partial shipments ☐ allowed ☐ not allowed	Transshipment ☐ allowed ☐ not allowed	☐ Issue by airmail ☐ With brief advice by teletransmission ☐ Issue by express delivery ☐ Issue by teletransmission (which shall be the operative instrument)
Loading on board/dispatch/taking in change at/from Not later than For transportation to	Amount (both in figures and words)
Description of goods Packing	Credit available with ☐ by sight payment ☐ by acceptance ☐ by negotiation ☐ by deferred payment at ☐ Against the documents detailed herein ☐ and beneficiary's draft for % of the invoice value at on
	☐ FOB ☐ C&F ☐ CIF ☐ or other terms

Document required: (marks with ×)
1. (　) Signed Commercial Invoice in copies indication L/C No. and Contract No.
2. (　) Full set of clean on board bills of Lading made out to order and blank endorsed, marked "freight 〔　〕 to collect/〔　〕 prepaid 〔　〕 showing freight amount" notifying.
3. (　) Air Way bills showing "freight 〔　〕 to collect/〔　〕 prepaid 〔　〕 including freight amount" and consigned to
4. (　) Memorandum issued by　　　consigned to
5. (　) Insurance Policy/Certificate in copies for 　% of the invoice value showing claims payable in China in currency of the draft, blank endorsed, covering (〔　〕 Ocean Marine Transportatio/ 〔　〕 Air Transportation/〔　〕 Over Land Transportation) All Risks, War Risk.
6. (　) Packing List/Weight Memo in copies issued by the quantity/gross and the weights of each packing and packing conditions as called for by the L/C.
7. (　) Certificate of Quantity/Weight in copies issued by an independent surveyor at the loading port, indicating the actual surveyed quantity/weight of shipped goods as well as the packing condition.
8. (　) Certificate of Quantity in copies issued by 〔　〕 manufacturer/〔　〕 public recognized survey or/〔　〕.

（续表）

9. (　　) Beneficiary's certified copy of cable dispatched to the accountees within hours after shipment advising 〔　　〕 name of vessel / 〔　　〕 flight No. / 〔　　〕 wagon No., date, tuantity, weight and value of shipment.
10. (　　) Beneficiary's Certifying that extra copies of the documents have been dispatched according to the contract terms.
11. (　　) Shipping Co's certificate attesting that the carrying vessel is chartered or booked by accountee or their shipping agents.
12. (　　) Other documents, if any.

Additional Instructions：
1. (　　) All banking charges outside the opening bank are for beneficiary's account.
2. (　　) Documents must be presented within days after the date of issuance of the transport documents but with the validity of this credit.
3. (　　) Third party as shipper is not acceptable. Short Form/Blank Back B/L is not acceptable.
4. (　　) Both quantity and amount ％ more or less are allowed.
5. (　　) Prepaid freight drawn in excess of L/C amount is acceptable against presentation of original charges voucher issued by shipping Co. /Air Line / or it's agent.
6. (　　) All documents to be forwarded in one cover, unless otherwise started above.
7. (　　) Other terms, if any.

Account No.：　　　　　　　　　　　　　with _____ (name bank)
Transacted by：　　　　　　　　(Applicant：name signature of authorized person)
Telephone No.：　　　　　　　　　　　　　　　　　　(with seal)

"国家中等职业教育改革发展示范学校建设计划"项目教材
中等职业教育"十三五"规划教材·国际贸易系列

常用国际商务单证制作

主编／徐菊红　章忻雯
副主编／谢富敏
参编／林　炜　李小成
主审／傅　蕾

图书在版编目(CIP)数据

常用国际商务单证制作 / 徐菊红,章忻雯主编. —上海：立信会计出版社,2015.9
ISBN 978-7-5429-4623-2

Ⅰ.①常… Ⅱ.①徐… ②章… Ⅲ.①国际贸易—票据—中等专业学校—教材 Ⅳ.①F740.44

中国版本图书馆 CIP 数据核字(2015)第 229398 号

策划编辑　　陈　瑶
责任编辑　　陈　昕
封面设计　　周崇文

常用国际商务单证制作

出版发行	立信会计出版社			
地　　址	上海市中山西路 2230 号	邮政编码	200235	
电　　话	(021)64411389	传　真	(021)64411325	
网　　址	www.lixinaph.com	电子邮箱	lxaph@sh163.net	
网上书店	www.shlx.net	电　话	(021)64411071	
经　　销	各地新华书店			
印　　刷	常熟市梅李印刷有限公司			
开　　本	787 毫米×1092 毫米	1/16		
印　　张	9.25			
字　　数	192 千字			
版　　次	2015 年 9 月第 1 版			
印　　次	2015 年 9 月第 1 次			
印　　数	1—3 100			
书　　号	ISBN 978-7-5429-4623-2/F			
定　　价	30.00 元(含习题集)			

如有印订差错,请与本社联系调换

编者的话

本教材结合职业教育改革新理念,以岗位职业能力为核心,以工作任务为主线,强调学生在学习过程中认知的心理顺序;与专业所对应的典型职业工作顺序,针对国际商务中履行合同的每一个工作环节来传授相关课程内容,实现实践技能与理论知识的整合,对学生掌握知识与技能有事半功倍的效果。

我们与上海良友(集团)有限公司、上海元初国际物流公司、中国二重货运代理公司等公司合作,搜集了企业各类相关资料,以真实、完整的食品出口业务为主线编写本教材,既突出了食品出口贸易,又兼顾了其他一般商品的出口贸易。学生通过完成本教材工作任务过程中涉及的单证缮制及流转,掌握进出口贸易的合同签订、履行,单据的作用、缮制知识及技能。同时,本教材每个任务之后都附有专项训练,方便老师及时检测学生学习掌握程度;另外,还配套了学生训练手册,供学生课后实战模拟之用,以加深对教材内容的理解与掌握,提高学生单据缮制能力。

本教材包含以下几个板块:①学习天地:掌握国际商务英语基本单词;②工作流程:明确工作任务的完成步骤;③知识窗口:掌握必要的知识和技能,引导学生完成单据的具体缮制方法;④实战演练:进一步巩固所学知识,提高学生的理解力和缮制单据技能。

参编教师依据多年专业教学经验,以及丰富的带队比赛经验和国际商务单证考证培训经验,结合企业实践,在企业一线专家的指导下完成了本教材的编写。本教材可供国际商务专业、物流专业、外贸会计专业等商贸类专业学生使用。本教材由徐菊红、章忻雯主编,谢富敏为副主编,第一篇项目一由李小成编写,项目二、项目八、项目九、项目十由徐菊红编写,项目三、项目四、项目七由章忻雯编写,项目五和项目六由林炜编写;第二篇第一部分由徐菊红编写,第二部分由章忻雯编写。感谢校外企业专家上海良友(集团)有限公司业务部经理傅蕾对该书的审核。

本教材经多届国际商务、现代物流等专业学生使用,反响良好,并每年加以修订,此版为最新版。本教材在多次考证和竞赛辅导中被使用,使学生取得了优异成绩。本教材中难免有疏漏之处,恳请广大读者指正。

徐菊红
2015 年 9 月

目录 CONTENTS

项目一　认识国际商务单证工作 ·········· 1
　任务一　制单工作的意义 ·········· 1
　任务二　制单工作的要求 ·········· 2

项目二　审核信用证 ·········· 4
　任务一　解读出口销售合同 ·········· 4
　任务二　解读信用证 ·········· 13
　任务三　审核并修改信用证 ·········· 16

项目三　缮制商业发票和装箱单 ·········· 24
　任务一　缮制商业发票 ·········· 24
　任务二　缮制装箱单 ·········· 29

项目四　办理出口货物产地证书和运输 ·········· 35
　任务一　缮制出口货物的原产地申请及证明书 ·········· 35
　任务二　缮制出口货物的货运委托书 ·········· 46

项目五　办理出口货物的保险和报检 ·········· 52
　任务一　缮制出口货物的投保单 ·········· 52
　任务二　保险公司签发保险单 ·········· 56
　任务三　缮制出口货物的报检单 ·········· 63

项目六　办理出口货物的报关和出运 ·········· 68
　任务一　缮制出口货物报关单 ·········· 68
　任务二　缮制装运通知 ·········· 73
　任务三　确认船公司签发的海运提单 ·········· 75

项目七　办理出口货物的结汇 ································· 82
  任务一　缮制商业汇票 ··· 82
  任务二　交单议付 ··· 86

项目八　认识其他单据 ··· 87
  任务一　认识商检证书和出口许可证 ··························· 87
  任务二　认识非木质包装证明和受益人证明 ····················· 93
  任务三　认识出口收汇核销单 ··································· 94

项目九　审核单据 ··· 96
  任务一　缮制开证申请书 ······································ 96
  任务二　审核结汇单据 ·· 110

项目十　不同结汇方式下单据的缮制 ··························· 112
  任务一　在信用证方式下根据信用证缮制相关单据 ·············· 112
  任务二　在电汇方式下根据销售合同缮制相关单据 ·············· 120
  任务三　在托收方式下根据销售合同缮制相关单据 ·············· 130

附件 ·· 135
  附件1　常用国际贸易术语 ···································· 135
  附件2　常用支付方式 ·· 137

参考文献 ·· 139

项目一

认识国际商务单证工作

学习目的

◆ 理解制单工作的意义
◆ 明确制单员的工作要求

任务一 制单工作的意义

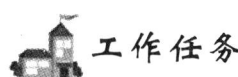 工作任务

小明是今年刚毕业的大学生,通过层层面试,终于进入上海良友(集团)有限公司从事外贸单证员工作。作为一名职场新人,小明在兴奋之余,开始慢慢进入角色。几个月过去了,小明发现外贸单证员的工作也不是那么简单,有时候一笔业务可以起到牵一发而动全身的作用……

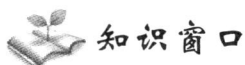 知识窗口

所谓单证是指进出口业务中应用的各种单据和证书,如信用证、商业发票、提单、保险单、原产地证书等,买卖双方凭借这些单证来处理货物的交付、运输、保险、商检和结汇等。单证也是记录整笔国际贸易业务的见证。

单证工作主要有审证、制单、审单、交单和归档五个方面,它贯穿于进出口合同履行的过程,具有工作量大、涉及面广、时间性强和要求高等特点,在进出口业务中具有重要的作用。

一、单证是履行合同的必要手段

各种单证在国际贸易业务的各个环节都有其特定的功能,它们的填制、签发、流转、组合、交换等具体的应用,反映了外贸合同履行的进展情况及相关方的责任、权利和义务的发生、转移及终止。现行的各种单证都有其特定作用,其签发、组合交换都反映了合同履行中不同阶段的作用,也反映了买卖双方责权利的发生、转移和终止。因此,单证是合同履行的不可缺少的手段。

二、单证是货款结算的基本工具

进出口贸易是国与国之间的买卖,是货物与货币的交换。随着国际贸易结算方式的变化,跟单托收和跟单信用证成为国际贸易主要支付方式。在这种支付条件下,随付的单据成为支付的主要凭据。由此,国际货物买卖便转化为单据的买卖,货物与货币的对流演变为单据与货款的交换,卖方以单据代替对货物的交付,买方则以付款赎单表示对货物的收取。

因此,在国际贸易中,全套正确、完整的单据是国际贸易结算的基础工具,只有正确、及时缮制单据,才能保证收汇的安全。

三、单证工作直接影响企业的经济效益

单证工作服务于国际贸易业务的整个过程,它不仅要保证单证的缮制和转递,而且必须要妥善地处理各种问题,保证结汇的安全。例如,单证工作能及时反映货、船、证等业务的管理现状,工作责任心强可及时解决、杜绝差错事故的发生,避免带来不必要的经济损失。同时,单证工作能做到准确、完整、快速,不仅能保证收汇安全,而且又能加快收汇,加速资金周转,为国家多创汇,进而树立企业自身信誉。

四、单证工作是外贸业务管理水平的重要标志

单证工作是国际贸易业务的重要组成部分,单证工作的质量直接反映了外贸业务管理水平的高低。单证工作不能简单地被看作是单证的缮制、复核和流转,它是能否围绕单证及时、妥善处理好国际贸易业务中的各项工作,能否协调和解决业务中的各种矛盾,能否确保顺利结汇及企业的信誉,能否不断提高国际贸易业务管理水平的重要标志。

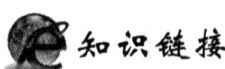

国际商务单证员,是指在国际贸易结算业务中,买卖双方凭借进出口业务中应用的单据、证书来处理货物的交付、运输、保险、商检和结汇等工作的人员。

任务二 制单工作的要求

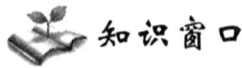

按照我国外经贸部颁布的《外贸企业单证岗位规范(试行)》,结合当前外贸单证工作的特点,对单证员的要求如下:

(一)政治思想与职业道德素质方面

(1)坚持四项基本原则,自觉维护国家利益。

(2)热爱本职工作,具有良好团队精神和解决问题能力,保证及时安全收汇。

(3) 遵守外贸工作纪律,责任心强,努力工作,积极进取。

(二) 专业素质方面

(1) 明确有关我国外贸政策、法规和国际贸易惯例。

(2) 熟悉买卖合同和信用证条款的主要内容以及国际结算、汇兑等专业知识。

(3) 掌握本企业外贸业务的内容、特点和银行对单证的要求,以及运输、保险、报关等工作程序。

(4) 了解进出口贸易业务的一般程序和世界主要港口、航线以及主要贸易国海关对单证的特殊要求。

(三) 技能素质方面

(1) 能阅读英文商务函电和信用证,准确理解有关内容。

(2) 具有独立缮制、操作和管理单证的能力,做到各种单据的准确、完整、及时、简明和整洁,保证证同一致、单证一致、单单一致、单货一致,并能进行单据分类归档。

(3) 正确掌握价格、运价、保险费和汇率等运算。

(4) 熟练掌握计算机英文打字、制单技能以及电子报验、电子报关等电子数据交换(Electrortic Data Interchange,简称 EDI)操作方法。

项目二

审核信用证

学习目的

- ◆ 读懂销售合同主要条款
- ◆ 理解信用证条款
- ◆ 能根据合同条款审核信用证条款
- ◆ 能提出信用证的修改建议

任务一 解读出口销售合同

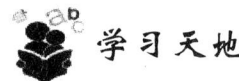 学习天地

销售合同	SALES CONFIRMATION
装运期限	TIME OF SHIPMENT
唛头	SHIPPING MARKS
货物名称及规格	NAME OF COMMODITY AND SPECIFICATION
数量	QUANTITY
单价	UNIT PRICE
总额	AMOUNT
支付方式	TERMS OF PAYMENT

 工作任务

小明接受一项任务,给上海良友(集团)有限公司草拟一份小麦细粉出口的销售合同。

工作流程如图 2-1 所示。

工作流程

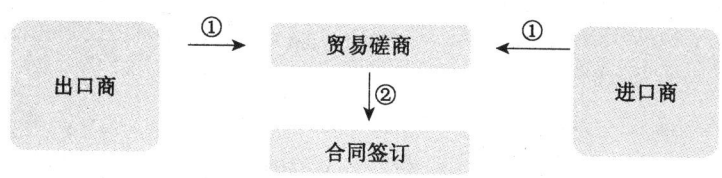

图 2-1 出口销售的工作流程

知识窗口

一、贸易合同的定义

贸易的一方明确表示接受另一方的交易条件，在法律上构成了有效的合同。

二、构成贸易合同的必备条件

构成一项有效的买卖合同的必备条件如下：

(1) 买卖双方当事人应该是具有法律行为能力的人。

(2) 双方当事人在自愿基础上的意思表示一致。

(3) 必须有对价。

(4) 合同的标的和内容必须合法。国际货物买卖合同必须符合法律规定的形式和审批手续。

三、贸易合同的主要内容

书面贸易合同的内容一般包括三个部分：约首、本文和约尾。

(一) 合同的约首部分

约首是合同的首部，它包括合同的名称、编号、订约日期与地点、订约双方当事人名称与地址等。

(二) 合同的本文

合同的本文是合同的主体，它包括各项交易条件，如商品的品名、品质、数量、包装、装运、价格和保险等。

1. 商品的品名、品质条款

该条款是合同中的重要条款，品名应明确、具体并适合商品的特点。而品质条款应列明商品的等级、规格等内容，并可注明商标。如果该商品是凭样品买卖，则要列明样品的编号或寄送日期。

例：悠哈奶糖　UHA Milk Candy。

2. 商品的数量条款

在出口合同中应明确买卖的具体数量、计量单位和数量机动幅度，按重量计量的商品还应包括重量的规定方法,如无明确规定,按国际惯例以净重计算交货数量。对于无法明确具体数量的散装和裸装货,可用溢短装条款加以约定。

例:出口大豆 1 000 公吨,允许有 5% 的多装或少装(Soybeans 1 000 metric tons, with 5% more or less allowed at the buyers' option for chartering purpose)。

3. 商品的包装条款

在进出口合同中,包装条款主要是对包装材料、包装方式、包装费用和包装标志作出相应规定,如,麻袋(Gunny Bags)、纸箱(Carton Case)等。通常包装条款要说明包装的数量以及如何包装。

例:纸箱装,每箱净重 50 公斤(In cartons of 50 kg net each)。

4. 商品的价格条款

货物的价格条款主要包括单价(Unit Price)和总值(Total Amount)两项内容,单价由计价货币、单位价格金额、计量单位和贸易术语构成。

例:CIF 价每打 15 美元 纽约(USD 15.00 Per Dozen CIF NEWYORK)。

5. 商品的装运条款

有关货物的装运条款应包括装运港(地)、目的(地)、装运时间和分批装运或转运等内容。

例:2011 年 9 月份由上海运往伦敦,允许分批和转运(Shipment from Shanghai to London In Sept. 2011, with partial shipments and transshipment allowed)。

6. 商品的支付条款

出口合同中的支付条款要明确规定结算方式,不同的结算方式内容各异,分别说明如下:

(1) 汇付方式(Remittance)。汇付方式通常有预付货款(俗称前 T/T)和赊账交易(俗称后 T/T)等形式。采用汇付方式时,交易双方应在买卖合同中明确规定汇付的时间、具体的汇付方法和金额等。

例:买方应在 2011 年 3 月 10 日前将 100% 的货款以电汇方式预付给卖方(The buyer should pay 100% of the sales proceeds in advance by advance by T/T to reach the seller not later than MAR. 10, 2011)

(2) 托收方式(Collection)。托收方式是指债权人委托当地银行通过它在进口地的分行或代理行向债务人收取货款的支付方式。实际业务中多采用跟单托收。采用托收方式时,必须明确规定交单条件和付款、承兑责任以及付款期限等内容。

例:买方对卖方开具的见票后 30 天付款的跟单汇票,于提示时应即承兑,并应于汇票到期日付款,付款后交单(The buyers shall duly accept the documentary draft drawn by the sellers at 30 days sight upon first presentation and make payment on its maturity. The shipping documents are to be delivered against payment only)。

(3) 信用证(Letter of Credit)。信用证是指开证银行应申请人的要求并按其指示,向第三者开具的载有一定金额,在一定期限内凭符合规定的单据付款的书面保证文件。

信用证从不同的角度可分为跟单信用证、光票信用证、可撤销信用证和不可撤消信用证、即期信用证和远期信用证、可转让信用证和不可转让信用证等。在实际业务中通常使用的是即期不可撤销跟单信用证。

例：买方应通过卖方所接受的银行于装运月份前 30 天开出不可撤销的即期信用证，于装运日后 20 天在中国银行议付(The buyer shall open through a bank acceptable to the sellers an irrevocable Sight Letter of Credit to the sellers 30 days before the month of shipment. Valid for negotiation in bank of china until the 20 days after the date of shipment)。

(4) 托收与信用证相结合方式。这种方式是指部分货款用托收方式支付，部分货款用信用证支付。一般做法是来证规定，出口商出立两张汇票，信用证部分凭光票付款，整套货运单据附在托收部分汇票项下收取。但信用证内必须注明"在发票金额全部付清后方可交单"的条款。

例：货款 50% 应开立不可撤销信用证，余款 50% 见票后即期付款交单。全套货运单据应随托收项下，于申请人付清发票全部金额后交单。如果进口人不付清全部金额，则货运单据由开证银行掌握，听凭卖方处理(50% of the invoice value is available against payment by irrevocable L/C, while the remaining 50% of documents be held against payment at sight on collection basis. The full set of the shipping documents of 100% invoice value shall accompany the collection item and shall only be released after full payment of the invoice value. If the importer fails to pay full invoice value, the shipping documents shall be held by the issuing Bank at the exporter's disposal)。

7. 货运保险条款

出口合同中保险条款视贸易术语而定。①FOB, CFR, FCA, CPT 术语项下的保险条款，保险由买方办理(Insurance to be covered by the buyers)；②CIF, CIP 术语项下的保险条款，应明确规定由谁办理保险，确定投保险别和保险金额以及以何种保险条款为依据，并注明该条款的生效日期。

例：保险由卖方按发票金额的 110% 投保一切险和战争险，按中国人民保险公司 1981 年 1 月 1 日的有关海洋运输货物保险条款为准(To be covered by the Seller for 110% of total invoice value against covering All Risks and War Risks as per and subject to the relevant ocean marine cargo clauses of the People's Insurance Company of China, dated 1/1/1981)。

8. 商品检验检疫条款

商品检验检疫条款一般包括检验权的规定、检验或复验的时间和地点、检验机构、检验项目和检验证书等内容。

例：买卖双方同意以装运港（地）中国出入境检验检疫局签发的质量和重量检验证书作为信用证项下议付所提交的单据的一部分，买方有权对货物的质量和重量进行复验，复验费由买方负担。但若发现质量和(或)重量与合同规定不符时，买方有权向卖方索赔，并提供经卖方同意的公证机构出具的检验报告。索赔期限为货物到达目的港（地）后 180 天内(It's mutually agreed that the Certificate of Quality and Weight issued by the China Exit and Entry Inspection and Quarantine Bureau at the port/place of shipment shall be part of the documents to be presented for negotiation under the relevant L/C. The buyers shall have the right to reinspect the quality and weight of the cargo. The reinspection fee shall be borne by the Buyers. Should the quality and/or weightbe found not in conformity with of the contract, the buyers are entitled to lodge with the sellers a claim which should be supported by survey reports issued by a recognized surveyor approved by the sellers. The claim, if any, shall be lodged within 180 days after arrival of the goods at the port/place of destination)。

9. 不可抗力条款

不可抗力条款主要规定不可抗力的范围及其处理的原则和方法,以及不可抗力发生后通知对方的期限、方法和出具证明机构等内容。

例:由于人力不可抗拒事故,使卖方不能在合同规定期限内交货或不能交货,卖方不负责任,但卖方必须立即以电报通知买方。如买方提出要求,卖方应以挂号函向买方提供由中国国际贸易促进委员会或有关机构出具的发生事故的证明文件(In case of Force Majeure, the seller shall not be held responsible for late delivery or non-delivery of the goods but shall notify the buyer by cable. The seller shall deliver to the buyer by registered mail, if so requested by the buyer, a certificate issued by the China Council for the Promotion of International Trade or competent authorities)。

10. 索赔条款

贸易合同中的索赔条款是由于在履行合约的过程中,有一方违约致使另一方利益受损,受损方提出的赔偿要求,一般规定提出索赔的时效和责任的界定。

例:倘如买方提出索赔,凡属品质异议须于货到目的地口岸之日起 30 天内提出。凡属数量异议须于货到目的地口岸之日起 15 天内提出。对所装货物所提出的任何异议,属于保险公司、轮船公司、其他有关运输机构或邮递机构所负责者,售方不负任何责任(In case of quality discrepancy, claim should be filed by the buyer within 30 days after the arrival of the goods at port of destination, while for quantity discrepancy, claim should be filed by the buyer within 15 days after the arrival of the goods at port of destination. It is understood that the seller shall not be liable for any discrepancy of the goods shipped due to the causes for which the Insurance Company, Shipping Company, other transportation organization/or Post Office are liable)。

11. 仲裁条款

仲裁条款的内容一般包括仲裁地点、仲裁机构、仲裁规则和裁决的效力。在规定仲裁地点时,我方一般首先争取规定在我国仲裁。

例:凡因本合同引起的或与本合同有关的任何争议,均应提交中国国际经济贸易仲裁委员会,按照申请仲裁时现行有效的仲裁规则进行仲裁。仲裁裁决是终局的,对双方均有约束力(Any dispute arising from or connection with this Contract shall be submitted to China International Economic and Trade Arbitration Commission for arbitration which shall be conducted in accordance with the Commission's arbitration rules in effect at the time of applying for arbitration. The arbitral award is final and binding upon both parties)。

(三) 合同的约尾部分

合同的约尾通常载明双方当事人的全称及其代表人的签章和签约的时间。

 缮制说明

上海良友(集团)有限公司
中国上海张杨路88号
SHANGHAI LIANGYOU GROUP CO., LTD.
NO. 88 ZHANGJIANG ROAD SHANGHAI, CHINA 200122

售 货 确 认 书
SALES CONFIRMATION

Tel: 0086-021-85083376　　　　　　　　　编号:
Fax: 0086-021-85083378　　　　　　　　　No.　LY11SC-003-S

　　　　　　　　　　　　　　　　　　　　日期:
　　　　　　　　　　　　　　　　　　　　Date　MAY 24, 2014

TO Messrs:
　FUMING FEED CO., LTD.
　　THAILAND 653, MOO 4, SOI E 6 PATANA 1 RD., SAMUT PRAKAN 10280
　　TEL: 66-2-324-0770　FAX: 66-2-324-0350-1

谨启者:兹确认授予你方下列货品,其成交条款如下:
DEAR SIRS: WE HEREBY CONFIRM HAVING SOLD TO YOU THE FOLLOWING GOODS ON THE TERMS AND CONDITIONS AS SPECIFIED BELOW:

(1) 货物名称及规格 NAME OF COMMODITY AND SPECIFICATION	(2) 数量 QUANTITY	(3) 单价 UNIT PRICE	(4) 总价 AMOUNT
WHEAT FLOUR (FEED GRADE) PACKING: 25KG PER BAG NET N.W.: 210 MT	210 MT	CIF BANGKOK USD 500.00	USD 105 000.00
TOTAL			USD 105 000.00
TOTAL AMOUNT IN WORDS: SAY US DOLLARS ONE HUNDRED AND FIVE THOUSAND ONLY			

(5) 装运期限
TIME OF SHIPMENT: NOT LATER THAN JUL. 30, 2014
SHIPPING MARKS: FUMING, THAILAND
(6) 装运港
PORT OF LOADING: SHANGHAI CHINA
(7) 目的港
PORT OF DESTINATION: BANGKOK THAILAND
(8) 分批装运
PARTIAL SHIPMENTS: ALLOWED
(9) 转船
TRANSSHIPMENT: ALLOWED
(10) 付款条件
TERMS OF PAYMENT: BY AN IRREVOCABLE LETTER OF CREDIT AT 30 DAYS AFTER B/L DATE AVAILBLE WITH ANY BANK IN CHINA REMAIN VAILD FOR NEGOTIATLON TILL AUG. 20, 2014

(11) 保险
THE SELLER SHALL COVER INSURANCE AGAINST WPA AND INSURANCE BREAKAGE & WAR RISKS FOR 110% OF THE TOTAL INVOICE VALUE AS PER
THE RELEVANT OCEAN MARINE CARGO OF P. I. C. C. DATED1/1/1981.

(12) 品质规格
ASH≤1%, MOISTURE≤13.5%, WET GLUTE≥35%, PROTEIN≥12.5%
DETAILED SPECIFICATION

(13) 其他事项

a. ORIGINAL DOCUMENTS SEND TO L/C ISSUING BANK WITHIN TEN WORKING DAYS OTHER AFFAIRS OF B/L DATE.

b. ADVISING BANK IN CHINA:
CHINA MINSHENG BANKING CORP. LTD. ,SHANGHAI BRANCH
SWIFT CODE:MSBCCNBJ005

CONFIRMED BY:

买方 Robert·Meade	卖方 谢红炜
THE BUYER	THE SELLER
FUMING FEED CO., LTD.	上海良友(集团)有限公司 合同专用章

 实战演练

根据买卖双方的磋商文件,请拟定上海凌烽进出口有限公司出口木制玩具的销售合同。

(一)制作依据

(1) 出口商:上海凌烽进出口有限公司,代码:3101082356879。

(2) 进口商:百达贸易公司(BAIDA TRADE CO., LTD), 13 PARK STREET TIVERSTONE 61-02-97573548。

(3) 贸易方式:一般贸易。

(4) 进口国(地区):澳洲悉尼。

(5) 合同号:2011080108。

(6) 付款方式:100%发票金额的不可撤销即期信用证。

(7) 合同签订日期:2014年8月1日。

(8) 装运期限:2014年10月份。

(9) 运输方式:江海运输。

(10) 装运港:上海 SHANGHAI,目的港:悉尼 SYDNEY。

　　　不允许分批装运和转运。

(11) 商品名称:如表2-1所示。

表2-1　　　　　　　　　销售商品信息

木质玩具	(WOODEN TOYS)			共468打		CIF SYDNEY		
规格型号	数量(打)	单价(美元)	包装(箱)	毛重(KG)	净重(KG)	长(CM)	宽(CM)	高(CM)
YW 4002	128	45.00	2打每箱	20	18	40	30	20
YW 4004	340	25.00	4打每箱	22	20	50	30	20

(12) 保险:按发票价的110%投保一切险和战争险。

(二) 要求

制作销售合同。

上海凌烽进出口有限公司
SHANGHAI LINGFENG IMPORT & EXPORT CO., LTD.
NO. 43 CHIFENG ROAD, SHANGHAI CHINA

售　货　确　认　书

SALES CONFIRMATION

Tel: 0086-021-65978916

Fax: 0086-021-65978917

编号:

No. ＿＿＿＿＿＿

日期:

Date ＿＿＿＿＿＿

TO Messrs:

谨启者:兹确认授予你方下列货品,其成交条款如下:

DEAR SIRS: WE HEREBY CONFIRM HAVING SOLD TO YOU THE FOLLOWING GOODS ON THE TERMS AND CONDITIONS AS SPECIFIED BELOW:

(1) 货物名称及规格 NAME OF COMMODITY AND SPECIFICATION	(2) 数量 QUANTITY ( )	(3) 单价 UNIT PRICE ( )	(4) 总价 AMOUNT ( )
		TOTAL	
TOTAL AMOUNT IN WORDS:			

(5) 装运期限

TIME OF SHIPMENT:

(6) 装运港

PORT OF LOADING:

(7) 目的港

PORT OF DESTINATION:

(8) 分批装运

PARTIAL SHIPMENTS:

(9) 转船

TRANSSHIPMENT:

(10) 付款条件

TERMS OF PAYMENT:

(11) 保险

INSURANCE:

(12) REMARKS

CONFIRMED BY:

买方　　　　　　　　　　　　　　　　　　卖方

THE BUYER　　　　　　　　　　　　　　THE SELLER

补充资料

(1) 上海良友(集团)有限公司出口210吨小麦粉的制单补充资料。

货物毛重:211680KGS,体积:200CBM。

商业发票的开票日期:2014.6.20,发票编号:LY11SI-003-5。

装箱单的制单日期:2014.6.20。

实际装船日期:2014.7.15,提单号:SISHLKGA97297。

船名:HALCYON V.1106S。

保险单号:23546890。

出口运费:11 060美元。

保险费:3 465美元。

集装箱号:10×20英尺。

单位编码:62122133-6。

出境货物通关单编号:310900211001591。

出口收汇核销单编号:780594951。

箱号/铅封号:SITU2900605/ITS1019256　　GESU3561102/ITS1019125
　　　　　　GLOU3919424/ITS1019176　　SITU2962567/ITS1019141
　　　　　　TEMU2119838/1019132　　　TEHU2858212/1019297
　　　　　　DFSU2009715/ITS1019251　　BMOU2626150/ITS1019103
　　　　　　SITU2895598/1019117　　　BMOU2744153/1019190

H.S.编码:1101000001。

(2) 上海凌烽进出口有限公司出口木制玩具合同的制单补充资料。

商业发票的开票日期:2014.8.30,发票编号:LLE31VI-007。

装箱单的制单日期:2014.8.30。

实际装船日期:2014.10.23,提单号:SELGAKTA173879。

船名:GETON STAR V.1296W。

保险单号:2345600。

出口运费:690美元。

保险费:130美元。

集装箱号:1×20英尺拼箱货。

单位编码:622342-6。

出口收汇核销单编号:234556947,出境货物通关单编号:310240211001345。

任务二　解读信用证

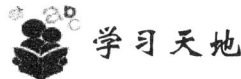
学习天地

IRREVOCABLE CREDIT　　　　不可撤销信用证
REVOCABLE CREDIT　　　　　可撤销信用证
CONFIRMED CREDIT　　　　　保兑信用证
UNCONFIRMED CREDIT　　　　不保兑信用证
DOCUMENTARY CREDIT　　　　跟单信用证
TRANSFERABLE CREDIT　　　　可转让信用证
NEGOTIATIONG CREDIT　　　　议付信用证
SIGHT CREDIT　　　　　　　即期信用证

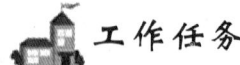
工作任务

小明拿到了通知行转来的福民公司的信用证,仔细阅读信用证所列条款,以便更好地缮制信用证中所规定的单据。

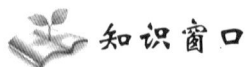
知识窗口

一、信用证的含义

信用证是银行(开证行)应客户(进口商)的要求,对第三人(出口商)所签发的一种有条件的书面付款保证,同意受益人得按所载条件签发以该行或其指定的另一银行为付款人的汇票,并交付全部符合信用证规定的单据,开证行履行付款的责任。

二、信用证的功能

(一) 对出口商的功能

1. 信用证可给出口商获得信用担保

出口商收到信用证后,因有银行信用取代商业信用,所以不必多顾虑进口商的信用,出口商只要按照信用证上所规定的条件装运货物,缮制单据,即可取得货款。

2. 信用证可给出口商获得外汇担保

在外汇管制的国家,信用证的签发通常表示出口商获得外汇批准,因此,出口商无需顾虑货物出口后无法收到外汇货款。

3. 信用证可给出口商获得低利率资金融通便利

出口商只要确实按照信用证所规定的条件装运货物,向议付行交单后即可取得货款,不必等到进口商收到货物后才能取得货款。

(二) 对进口商的功能

1. 信用证可给进口商获得低利率资金融通的便利

凭信用证交易,进口商申请签发信用证,通常仅需缴纳信用证一定金额的保证金,其余由开证银行给予低利率融资。如凭非信用证交易,出口商可能要求进口商预付全部货款后,才能发货。

2. 信用证可确定履行合约的日期

因出口商必须按照信用证所列条款,在规定期限内完成装运,所以进口商可大致确定对方履行合约的日期。

3. 信用证可给进口商获得信用担保

出口商必须按照信用证规定条件办理押汇(或付款),押汇(或付款)银行必须对各种单据严格审查,符合条件才给予办理付款(或押汇)。所以只要信用证条件规定适当,对进口商就有相当的保障。

三、SWIFT 信用证的常见格式

信用证的开立方式主要有信开和电开,随着电信事业的发展,信开方式已被电开方式所取代。电开方式包括电传、电报和 SWIFT 格式。由于 SWIFT 格式的信用证具有高性能、低成本、安全、迅速的特点,已被世界各国广泛使用。通过 SWIFT 开立信用证的电文格式有 MT700 和 MT701,以下主要介绍跟单信用证 SWIFT MT 700 的格式与内容,见表 2-2。

表 2-2 跟单信用证 SWIFT MT700 的格式与内容

项目顺序号		应填内容	要点提示
20	DOCUMENTARY CREDIT HUMBER	信用证号码	
27	SEQUENCE OF TOTAL	电文页次	
31C	DATE OF ISSUE	开证日期	
31D	DATE AND PLACE OF EXPIRY	信用证有效期和有效地点	最迟交单日不能晚于该日期
51A	APPLICANT BANK	信用证开证的银行	
50	APPLICANT	信用证开证申请人,一般为进口商	
59	BENEFICIARY	信用证的受益人,一般为出口商	
32B	CURRENCY CODE, AMOUNT	信用证结算的货币和金额	
39A	PERCENTAGE CREDIT AMOUNT TOLERANCE	信用证金额上下浮动允许的最大范围	数值表示百分比,5/5 为上下浮动,最大 5%
39B	MAXIMUN CREDIT AMOUNT	信用证最大限制金额	
40A	FORM OF DOCUMENTARY CREDIT	跟单信用证形式	通常为不可撤销跟单信用证
41A	AVAILABLE WITH… BY…	指定的有关银行及信用证总付的方式	如果是自由议付信用证,该项目代号为:41D,内容为:ANY BANK IN…
42A	DRAWEE	汇票付款人	
42C	DRAFTS AT…	汇票付款日期	
43P	PARTIAL SHIPPMENTS	分装条款	表示该信用证的货物是否可以分批装运
43T	TRANSSHIPMENT	转运条款	表示该信用证的货物是否可以转运

(续表)

项目顺序号	应填内容	要点提示
44A LOADING ON BOARD/DISPATCH/TAKEING IN CHARGE AT/FORM	装船、发运和接收监管的地点	
44B FOR TRANSPORTATION TO…	货物发运的最终地	
44C LATEST DATE OF SHIPMENT	装船的最迟的日期	
44D SHIPMENT PERIOD	船期	44C 与 44D 不能同时出现
45A DESCRIPTION OF GOODS AND/OR SERVICE	货物描述	有关货物的情况、价格条款
46A DOCUMENTS REQUIRED	单据要求	对各种提交单据的要求
47A ADDITIONAL CONDITIONS	特别条款	
48 PERIOD FOR PRESENTATION	交单期限	如未规定,视为运输单据后21天内交单
49 CONFIRMATION INSTRUCTIONS	保兑指示	CONFIRM:要求保兑行保兑该信用证
71B CHARGES	费用情况	表明费用是否有受益人(出口商)承担

任务三 审核并修改信用证

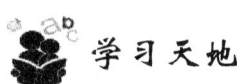学习天地

SEQUENCE OF TOTAL　　　　　　　信用证页数
FORM OF DOCUMENTARY CREDIT　　信用证性质
DOCUMENTARY CREDIT NUMBER　　信用证号码
DATE OF ISSUE　　　　　　　　　开证日期
DATE AND PLACE OF EXPIRY　　　到期日期和地点
APPLICANT　　　　　　　　　　　开证申请人
AMOUNT　　　　　　　　　　　　总额
TERMS OF PAYMENT　　　　　　　支付方式

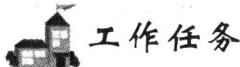
工作任务

福民食品有限公司按时开来信用证,通知行收到信用证,审核无误后在信用证正本上加盖"证实书"的戳印,并随信用证通知书交上海良友(集团)有限公司审核。公司交给小明审核并制作信用证修改通知书。

工作流程

工作流程如图 2-2 所示。

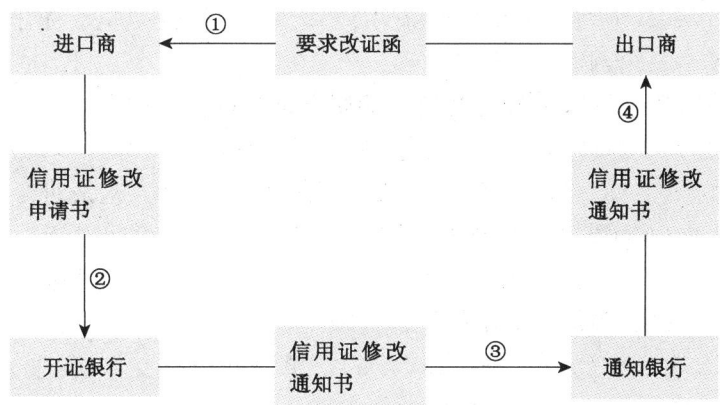

图 2-2 制作信用证修改通知书的工作流程

知识窗口

信用证付款对单据的要求非常严格,如出现单证不符点,一种处理是拒付,另一种处理是对不符点罚款,这两种处理结果都会给出口商带来经济损失。所以审核信用证对出口商是件非常重要的工作,如发现信用证条款和合同条款不一致且不能执行时,应及时通知开证申请人更改。

一、审核信用证的要点

(一)审核信用证的付款保证,如有一项付款得不到保证,就应及时向开证人提出

(1) 应该保兑的信用证是否按要求由有关银行进行保兑。
(2) 附有条件的信用证,如"待获得进口许可证后才能生效"。
(3) 由开证人直接寄送的信用证。
(4) 由开证人提供的开立信用证申请书。

(二)审核信用证的付款时间是否与有关合同规定相一致

(1) 对于信用证中有关货款条款须在向银行交单后若干天内或见票后若干天内付款等情况,应仔细审核其是否与合同相应条款一致。

(2) 信用证在国外到期，由于单据的邮寄风险无法控制，所以一般要求在国内到期。

(3) 如装船期和有效期是同一天的"双到期"信用证，在实际业务操作中，一般在有效期前 10 天装运，以便有合理的时间来制单结汇。

(三) 审核信用证受益人和开证人的名称和地址是否完整和准确

(四) 审核信用证的价格条款是否符合合同规定

(1) 信用证金额是否正确。

(2) 信用证中的单价与总值是否准确，大小写金额是否一致，币制是否正确。

(3) 信用证采用的价格术语是否和合同一致。

(4) 如数量条款中规定了溢短装条款，那么，在信用证中也应作出相应规定，支付金额是否允许有一定幅度的增减。

(五) 审核信用证条款中装运期的有关规定是否符合要求

(1) 信用证规定的装运期太近，无法按期装运，应及时与开证申请人联系改证。

(2) 如实际装运期与信用证规定的交单期时间相距太短，应及时要求改证。

(3) 信用证中如规定了分批出运的时间和数量，应注意能否办到，否则任何一批未按期装运，以后各期均告失效。

(六) 审核信用证规定的交单期是否合理

(1) 信用证有规定的，应严格按规定的交单期向银行交单，但要避免交单期过短，一般按规定装运期后 15 天左右交单。

(2) 信用证没有规定的，向银行交单的日期不得迟于提单日期后 21 天。

实例展示

————————INSTANCE TYPE AND RANSMISSION————————
COPY RECEIVED FROM SWIFT
PRIORITY：NORMAL
MESSAGE OUTPUT REFERENCE：1457 110110 MSBCCNB JA0023409369715
CORRESPONDENT INPUT REFERENCE：1357 110110 KASITHBKA×××1828428653
————————MESSAGE HEADER————————
SWIFT OUTPUT：FIN 700 ISSUE OF A DOCUMENTARY CREDIT
SENDER： KASITHBK×××
KASIKORNBANK PUBLIC COMPANY LIMITED
BANGKOK TH
BECEIVER： MSBCCNB J002
CHINA MINSHENG BANKING CORPORATION, LIMITED
(SHANGHAI BRANCH)
SHANGHAI CN
————————MESSAGETEXT————————
27：SEQUENCE OF TOTAL

1/1

40A: FORM OF DOCUMENTARY CREDIT
   IRREVOCABLE
20: DOCUMENTARY CREDIT NUMBER
   ML 11000632
31C: DATE OF ISSUE
   410610
40E: APPLICABLE RULES
   UCP URR LATEST VERSION
31D: DATE AND PLACE OF EXPIRY
   140409 THAILAND
50: APPLICANT
   FUMING FEED CO., LTD.
   THAILAND 653, MOO 4, SOI E 6 PATANA 1 RD.,
   SAMUT PRAKAN 10280
   TEL: 66-2-324-0770 FAX: 66-2-324-0350-1
59: BENEFICIARY—NAME & ADDRESS
   SHANGHAI LIANG YOU GROUP CO., LTD.
   NO. 88 ZHANGYANG ROAD SHANGHAI,
   CHINA 200122   TEL: 58761831
   FAX: 58767244
32E: CURRENCY CODE, AMOUNT
   CURRENCY: USD(US DOLLAR)
   AMOUNT: 105 000.00.
39A: PERCENTAGE CREDIT AMT TOLERANCE
   5/5
41D: AVAILABLE WITH-BY——NAME & ADDR
   ANY BANK IN CHINA BY NEGOTIATION
42C: DRAFTS AT——
   30 DAYS AFTER B/L DATE
42D: DRAWEE—NAME & ADDRESS
   ISSUING BANK
43P: PARTIAL SHIPMENTS
   NOT ALLOWED
43T: TRANSHIPMENTS
   ALLOWED
44E: PORT OF LOADING/AIRPORT OF DEP
   ANY CHINA PORT
44B: PL OF FINAL DEST / OF DELIVERY
   BANGKOK, THAILAND

44C: LATEST DATE OF SHIPMENT
   110730
45: DESCRIPTN OF GOODS &./ OR SERVICES
   +5 PERCENT MORE OR LESS IN AMOUNT AND QUANTITY ACCEPTABLE
   +210 MT. OF WHEAT FLOUR (FEED GRADE)
   UNIT PRICE AT EUR 500.00 /MT CFR BANGKOK
   SHIPPING MARK: FUMING, THAILAND
46A: DOCUMENTS REQUIRED
   + SIGNED COMMERCIAL INVOICE IN 3 COPIES, PRICE CIF LAT KRABANG INDICATING FOB VALUE, FREIGHT CHARGES, THIS L/C NUMBER AND TERM OF PAYMENT SEPARATELY
   +FULL SET OF THREE CLEAN ON BOARD OCEAN BILL OF LADING MADE OUT OR ENDORSED TO THE ORDER OF KASIKORN BANK PUBLIC CO., LTD., BANGKOK MARKED FREIGHT PREPAID NOTIFY APPLICANT PLUS 3 NON-NEGOTIABLE COPIES
   + FULL SET OF NEGOTIABLE INSURANCE POLICY OR CERTIFICATE BLANK ENDORSED AGAINST WPA AND WAR RISKS FOR 120% OF THE TOTAL INVOICE VALUE AS PER THE RELEVANT OCEAN MARINE CARGO OF P.I.C.C. DATED 1/1/1981
   +PACKING LIST IN 3 COPIES
   +CERTIFICATE OF ANALYSIS IN 3 COPIES
   +CERTIFICATE OF ORIGIN IN 2 COPIES ISSUDE BY OFFICIAL AUTHORITY
   + BENEFICIARY'S CERTIFICATE CERTIFYING THAT DETAIL OF SHIPMENT AND COPY OF ALL DOCUMENTS HAVE BEEN SENT TO APPLICANT AFTER SHIPMENT EFFECTED
47A: ADDITIONAL CONDITIONS
   +PLS USE THIS CORRECT APPLICANT'S ADDRESS INSTEAD OF FIELD 50: — 77/12 MOO 2, RAMA II RD., NAKHOK MANG, SAMUTSAKHORN 74000, THAILAND
           +++ THE END +++
   +ALL DOCUMENTS REQUIRED UNDER THIS L/C MUST BE ISSUED IN ENGLISH LANGUAGE
   +ALL DRAFTS IN DUPLICATE MUST INDICATE THE L/C NUMBER, DATE OF ISSUE AND NAME: KASIKORN BANK PUBLIC COMPANY LIMITED
   +THIS CREDITS IS SUBJECT TO THE UNIFORM CUSTONS AND PRACTICE FOR DOCUMENTARY CREDITS, 2007 REVISION, ICC PUBLICATION NO. 600
71B: CHARGES
   ALL BANK CHARGES OUTSIDE THAILAND
   INCLUDING REIMBURSING CHARGES ARE FOR A/C OF BENEFICIARY
48: PERIOD FOR TRESENTATION
   DOCUMENTS TO BE PRESENTED WITHIN 16 DAYS AFTER SHIPMENT DATE BUT WITHIN VALIDITY OF CREDIT
49: CONFIRMATION INSTRUCTIONS

WITHOUT
53A: REIMBURSING BANK—FI BIC
   KASIUS6L
   KASIKORN BANK PCL
   LOS ANGELES, CA US
57D: 'ADCISE THROUGH' BANK-NAME & ADDR
   SHANGHAI BRANCH
72: SENDER TO RECEIVER INFORMATION
   PLEASE ADVISE BENEFICIARY URGENTLY
———————————————MESSAGE TRAILER———————————————
(CHK: C5FB4A96CC69)
PKI SIGNATURE: MAC-EQUIVALENT

上海良友(集团)有限公司审核上述信用证后，发现多处不符点，提出下列改证要求。

KASIKORN BANK PUBLIC COMPANY LIMITED BANGKOK TH
APPLICATION FOR AMENDMENT
AMENDMENT TO CREDIT NO:
AMENDMENT NO:
AMENDMENT DATE:

TO: CHINA MINSHENG BANKING CORPORATION, LIMITED
   (SHANGHAI BRANCH)

APPLICANT
   FUMING FEED CO., LTD.
   THAILAND 653, MOO 4, SOI E 6 PATANA 1 RD., SAMUT PRAKAN 10280
ADVISING BANK   CHINA MINSHENG BANKING CORPORATION, LIMITED
                    (SHANGHAI BRANCH)

BENEFICIARY   SHANGHAI LIANGYOU GROUP CO., LTD.
                    NO. 88 ZHANGJIANG ROAD SHANGHAI, CHINA 200122
AMUOUT   USD 105 000.00

THE ABOVE MENTIONED CREDIT IS AMENDED AS FOLLOWS:
  1. THE L/C EXPIRY PLACE SHOULD BE IN CHINA NOT IN THAILAND
  2. PARTIAL SHIPMENTS SHOULD BE ALLOWED NOT PROHIBITED
  3. UNITE PRICE IS USD 500.00 PER M/T CIF BANGKOK
  4. THE GOODS INSURED FOR 110% INVOICE VALUE NOT 120%

ALL OTHER TERMS AND CONDITIONS REMAIN UNCHANGED
                              AUTHORIZED SINGNATURE:

THIS AMENDMENT IS SUBJECT TO UNIFORM CUSTOMS AND PRACTICE FOR DOCU-

MENTARY CREDITS (2007 REVISION) INTERNATIONAL CHAMBER OF COMMERCE PUBLICATION NO. 600

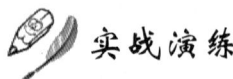 实战演练

根据上海凌烽进出口有限公司出口木制玩具的合同资料审核下列信用证。

(1) 信用证资料如下所示。

COMMONWEALTH BANK OF AUSTRALIA
LEVEL 1, 48 MARTIN PLACE, SYDNEY, NEW SOUTH WALES 2000

FORM OF DOC. CREDIT	*40A: IRREVOVABLE
DOC. CREDIT NUMEBER	*20: SKL1002242
DATA OF ISSUE	31C: 140821
EXPIRY	*31D: DATA 141123 PLACE IN THE COUNTRY OF BENEFICIARY
APPLICANT	*50: BAIDA TRADE CO. ,ILTD 13 PARK STREET TIVERSTONE 61-02-97573548
BENEFICIARY	*59: SHANGHAI LINGFENG IMPORT & EXPORT CO. , LTD. NO. 43 CHIFENG ROAD, SHANGHAI CHINA
AMOUNT	*32B: USD AMOUNT 14 260.00
AVAILABLE WITH/BY	*41D: ANY BANK BY NEGOLATION
DRAFTS AT…	42C: DRAFTS AT SIGHT FOR FULL INVOICE COST
DRAWEE	42A: XCOMMONWEALTH BANK OF AUSTRALIA
PARTIAL SHIPMENTS	43P: ALLOWED
TRANSSHIPMENT	43T: PROHIBITED
LOADING IN CHARGE	44A: SHANGHAI
FOR TRANSPORT TO…	44B: SYDNEY PORT
LATEST DATE OF SHIP.	44C: 141016
DESCRIPT. OF GOODS	45A: WOODEN TOYS CIF SYDENEY

ART	DOZS	U/PRICE (USD)	PACKING (CTN)	G.W. (KG/CTN)	N.W. (KG/CTN)	MEAS (CBM/CTN)
YW 4002	128	45.00	2DOZ/CTN	20	18	0.024
YW 4004	340	25.00	4DOZ/CTN	22	20	0.03

DETAILS OF CHARGES	71B: ALL BANKING CHARGES OUTSIDE JAPAN ARE FOR ACCOUNT OF BENEFICIARY
PRESENTATION PERIOD	48: DOCUMENTS MUST BE PRESENTED WITHIN 15 DAYS AFTER THE DATE OF SHIPMENT BUT WITHIN THE VALIDITY OF THE CREDIT

CONFIRMATION   *49: WITHOUT
DOCUMENTS REQUIRED   46 A:

　　+SIGNED COMMERCIAL INVOICE IN TRIPLICATE

　　+MARINE INSURANCE POLICY OR CERTIFICATE IN DUPLICATE ENDORSED IN BLANK FOR 110 PCT OF INVOICE VALUE WITH CLAIMS TO BE PAYABLE IN JAPAN IN THE CURRENCY OF THE DRAFT COVERING OCEAN MARINE CARGO CLAUSES ALL RISK, OCEAN MARINE WAR CLAUSES, OCEAN MARINE STRIKES RIOTS AND CIVIL COMMOTIONS CLAUSES OF THE PEOPLE'S INSURANCE COMPANY OF CHINA

　　+2/3 SET OF CLEAN ON BOARD OCEAN BILLS OF LADING MADE OUT TO ORDER OF SHIPPER AND BLANK ENDORSED AND MARKED FREIGHT PREPAID AND NOTIFY APPLICANT

　　+OEN COPY OF NON-NEGOTIABLE BILL OF LADING

　　+PACKING LIST IN TRIPLICATE

　　+PHOTOCOPY OF G. S. P. CERTIFICATE OF ORIGIN FORM A IN DUPLICATE

　　+BENEFICIARY'S CERTIFICATE CERTIFYING THAT ONE SET OF ORIGINAL SHIPPING DOCUMEN-TS INCLUDING ONE ORIGINAL G. S. P. CERTIFICATE OF ORIGIN FORM A ORIGINAL 1/3 B/L HAVE BEEN SENT DIRECTLY TO APPLICANT BY SPECIAL COURIER SERVICE B/L SHOULD BEAR VESSEL AGENT'S NAME AND TELEPHONE NUMBER IN JAPAN

（2）合同资料见项目二的任务一，上海凌烽进出口有限公司的销售合同和补充资料。

（3）审核意见如下所述。

THE ABOVE MENTIONED CREDIT IS AMENDED AS FOLLOWS:

项目三

缮制商业发票和装箱单

学习目的

- ◆ 知晓商业发票的作用、主要内容和缮制方法
- ◆ 知晓装箱单的作用、主要内容和缮制方法
- ◆ 会根据合同或者信用证按时出具商业发票
- ◆ 会根据合同和信用证按时出具装箱单

任务一 缮制商业发票

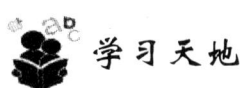 学习天地

JANUARY	1月	JULY	7月
FEBRUARY	2月	AUGUST	8月
MARCH	3月	SEPTEMBER	9月
APRIL	4月	OCTOBER	10月
MAY	5月	NOVEMBER	11月
JUNE	6月	DECEMBER	12月

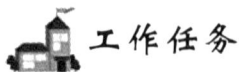 工作任务

上海良友(集团)有限公司的员工小明在规定时间内着手备货,并按销售合同和信用证的规定缮制商业发票。

工作流程

工作流程见图 3-1。

```
出口商备货  →  商业发票  →  交给相关部
                            门履行合同
```

图 3-1 缮制商业发票的工作流程

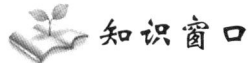

一、发票的种类

根据作用不同,发票可分为商业发票(Commercial Invoice)、海关发票(Customs Invoice)、形式发票(Pro-forma Invoice)、领事发票(Consular Invoice)、厂商发票(Manufacturer's Invoice)、联合发票(Combined Invoice)和证实发票(Certified Invoice)等,其中商业发票是出口业务结汇中最重要的单据之一,是单证工作中的核心单据。

二、商业发票的概述

商业发票简称发票,是卖方向买方签发的载明货物的品质、数量、包装和价格,并凭以索取货款的凭证。其作用主要有:①发票是买卖双方收付货款和记账的依据。②发票是买卖双方办理报关、纳税和计算佣金的依据。③如信用证中不要求提供汇票,发票可代替其作为付款的依据。④发票是全套结汇单据的核心,是缮制其他出口单据的依据。

三、信用证商业发票条款示例

(1) SIGNED COMMERCIAL INVOICE IN THREE COPIES.
签署的商业发票一式三份。

(2) BENEFICIARY'S MANUALLY SIGNED COMMERCIAL INVOICE IN FIVE FOLDS.
受益人手签的商业发票一式五份。

(3) SIGNED COMMERCIAL INVOICE IN THREE COPIES PRICE CIF BANGKOK SHOWING FOB VALUE, FREIGHT, INSURANCE PREMIUM SEPARATELY.
商业发票一式三份的价格 CIF 曼谷分别显示离岸价格价值、运费和保险费。

缮制说明

商业发票由出口企业自行拟制,无统一格式,但基本内容和缮制方法大致相同。

出口商企业名称（中英文）
地址（英文）

商 业 发 票
COMMERCIAL INVOICE

TEL：(1)出口商电话
FAX：(2)出口商传真   INVOICE NO.：(3) 发票号由出口商自编
                              DATE：(4) 发票出票日期
                              S/C NO.：(5)   合同号
                              L/C NO.：(6)   信用证编号

To Messrs(抬头人)(7)
　　　　　进口商名称
　　　　　进口商地址
FROM(8)   装运港   TO(9)   目的港

唛头及号码(10) MARKS & NOS.	数量与货品名(11) QUANTITES AND DESCRIPTIONS	单价(12) UNIT PRICE	总金额(13) AMOUNT
按合同和信用证规定填制	商品品名 具体规格　　　　　对应的成交数量 包装条款 与信用证描述一致或与合同内容相符	贸易术语 单价	数量×单价

TOTAL AMOUT(14)：SAY US DOLLARS ···················ONLY
金额大写

WE HEREBY CERTIFY THAT THE ABOVE MENTIONED GOODS ARE OF CHINESE ORIGIN(声明)

　　　　　　　　　　　　　　　　　　　　（15）开票人签章
　　　　　　　　　　　　　　　　　　　　出口公司名称
　　　　　　　　　　　　　　　　　　　　经办人签名

商业发票的缮制要点如表 3-1 所示。

表 3-1　　　　　　　　　　　商业发票的缮制要点

项目顺序号	应填内容	要点提示
出票人的名称与地址	名称、地址应与合同的卖方或信用证的受益人的名称、地址相同	一般出口企业印刷的空白发票，都事先将该公司的名称、地址、电话和传真印在发票的正上方
(4) 发票日期	发票的出票日期(英文格式)	发票应是整套单据中签发日期最早的单据。可以早于信用证的开证日期，但不可以晚于信用证的议付有效期
(7) 抬头人	进口商名称 进口商地址	信用证项下为开证申请人；托收项下为合同买方。填写时，名称、地址不应在同一行放置，应分行表明
(10) 运输标志(唛头)	货物的唛头(收货人简称、合同号、目的港、件数)	与信用证和合同规定的完全一致，照抄唛头；若信用证和合同显示无唛头时，应填 N/M (NO MARKS)； 若信用证没有规定唛头样式，由出口商自拟唛头
(11) 货物的描述和数量	信用证项下应严格按照信用证要求填写(品名、规格、数量、包装)	规格和数量一一对应，详细填写 凡信用证规定的数量前有"约""大概""大约"或类似的词，交货时允许数量有10%的增减幅度
(12) 单价	由计价货币、单位数量、计量单位和价格术语四部分组成	凡信用证规定的单价前有"约""大概""大约"或类似的词，交货时允许单价有10%的增减幅度
(13) 总金额	若来证要求分别列出运费、保险费和FOB价格，如 CIF TOKYO　USD 30 000 LESS F　　　USD 250 LESS I　　　USD 150 FOB　　　　USD 29 600	不能超过信用证的允许金额，对于佣金和折扣应按信用证规定的处理，如果来证要求分别列出运费、保险费和FOB价格，必须照办
(15) 签署	出票人的公司名称 经办人的签名	如信用证规定手签(MANUALL SIGNED)，则必须按规定照办。对墨西哥、阿根廷的出口，无论信用证是否规定，都必须手签

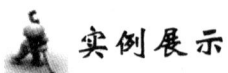 实例展示

上海良友(集团)有限公司
SHANGHAI LIANG YOU GROUP CO., LTD.
NO. 88 ZHANGYANG ROAD SHANGHAI, CHINA 200122
COMMERCIAL INVOICE
商业发票

FAX: 0086-021-85083378　　　　　INVOICE NO.: LY11SI-003-5

　　　　　　　　　　　　　　　　　DATE: JAN. 20, 2015

TEL: 0086-021-85083376　　　　　S/C NO.: LY11SC-003-S

　　　　　　　　　　　　　　　　　L/C NO.: ML11000632

TO MESSRS:
FUMING FEED CO., LTD.
THAILAND 653, MOO 4, SOI E 6 PATANA 1 RD., SAMUT PRAKAN 10280
TEL: 66-2-324-0770　FAX: 66-2-324-0350-1

FROM　SHANGHAI CHINA　　TO　BANGKOK THAILAND

唛头及号码 MARKS & NOS.	货物描述 DESCRIPTION OF GOODS	数量 QTY	单价 UNIT PRICE	总价 AMOUNT
FUMING, THAILAND	WHEAT FLOUR(FEED GRADE) PACKING: 25KG PER BAG NET .... TERM OF PAYMENT: IRREVOCABLE L/C AT 30 DAYS AFTER B/L DATE AVAILABLE WITH ANY BANK IN CHINA BY NEGOTIATION. * * * * * * * * * * * *	8 400BAGS 210MT 8 400BAGS 210MT	CIF BANGKOK USD 500.00/MT	USD 105 000.00 ....

TOTAL: SAY US DOLLARS ONE HUNDRED AND FIVE THOUSAND ONLY

WE HEREBY CERTIFY THAT THE ABOVE MENTIONED GOODS ARE OF CHINESE ORIGIN
SHANGHAI LIANGYOU GROUP CO., LTD.
董勋　AUTHORIZED SIGNATURE

实战演练

请根据上海凌烽进出口有限公司出口木制玩具的信用证、合同和相应资料缮制商业发票。

<table>
<tr><td colspan="2">ISSUER</td><td colspan="3" rowspan="2">商 业 发 票
COMMERCIAL INVOICE</td></tr>
<tr><td colspan="2">TO</td></tr>
<tr><td colspan="2" rowspan="3">TRANSPORT DETAILS</td><td colspan="2">INVOICE NO.</td><td>DATE</td></tr>
<tr><td colspan="2">S/C NO.</td><td>.L/C NO.</td></tr>
<tr><td colspan="2"></td><td></td></tr>
<tr><td>MARKS AND NUMBERS</td><td>NUMBER AND KIND OF PACKAGES; DESCRIPTION OF GOODS</td><td>QUANTITY</td><td>UNIT PRICE</td><td>AMOUNT</td></tr>
<tr><td></td><td></td><td></td><td></td><td></td></tr>
</table>

AMOUNT

SIGNED ____________________

任务二 缮制装箱单

学习天地

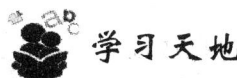

PACKING LIST	装箱单	WEIGHT LIST	重量单
WEIGHT NOTES	磅码单	DETAILED WEIGHT LIST	明细重量单
PACKING	包装	WEIGHT AND MEASUREMENT LIST 重量和尺码单	

WEIGHT	重量	GROSS WEIGHT	毛重
NET WEIGHT	净重	QUANTITY	数量

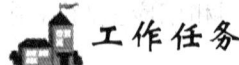 **工作任务**

上海良友(集团)有限公司业务员小明在规定时间内着手备货,并按合同和信用证的规定缮制装箱单。

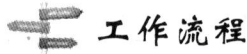 **工作流程**

工作流程见图3-2。

图3-2 缮制装箱单的工作流程

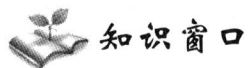 **知识窗口**

一、装箱单的概述

装箱单(Packing List or Packing Specification)又称包装单、码单,是用来说明货物包装细节的清单。装箱单的作用主要是补充发票内容,详细记载包装方式、包装材料、包装件数、货物规格、数量、重量等内容,便于进口商和海关对货物的核准。

装箱单所列各项数据和内容必须与提单等单据的内容相同,还要与货物实际情况相符。

二、信用证装箱单条款示例

(1) PACKING LIST IN 3 COPIES MANUAL SIGNED BY THE BENEFICIARIES.

受益人签署的装箱单一式三份。

(2) PACKING LIST SHOWING GROWS AND NET WEIGHTS EXPRESSED IN KILOS OF EACH TYPE OF GOODS REQUIRED.

装箱单以千克计量,标明货物的毛重和净重。

(3) SEPARATE PACKING LIST IN FULL DETAILS REQUIRED.

独立包装清单中要求显示全部细节。

缮制说明

装箱单由出口企业自行拟制,无统一格式,但基本内容和缮制方法大致相同。

出口商企业名称(中英文)
地址(英文)
装箱单
PACKING LIST

TEL：(1)出口商电话

FAX：(2)出口商传真

INVOICE NO.：(3)　装箱单由出口商自编

DATE：(4)　装箱单出票日期

S/C NO.：(5)　合同号

L/C NO.：(6)　信用证编号

To Messrs(抬头人)(7)
　　　　进口商名称
　　　　进口商地址

FROM(8)　装运港　　　　TO(9)　目的港

唛头及号码 MARKS & NOS. (10)	品名 NOS. & KINDS OF PKGS(11)	箱数 CTNS (12)	数量 QTY (13)	毛重 G.W. (14)	净重 N.W. (15)	尺码 MEAS (16)
按合同和信用证规定填制同发票	品名 具体规格 包装条款 品名和规格必须与信用证的描述相符。规格包括商品规格和包装规格	不同规格货品对应的箱数	不同规格货品对应的数量	不同规格货品对应的毛重	不同规格货品对应的净重	不同规格货品对应的体积
TOTAL (17)		总箱数	总数量	总毛重	总净重	总体积

TOTAL (18)SAY……………………………………ONLY

开票人签章(19)

出口公司名称

经办人签名

装箱单缮制要求如表 3-2 所示。

表 3-2　　　　　　　　　　　装箱单缮制的要点

项目顺序号	应填内容	要点提示
出票人的名称与地址	名称、地址应与合同的卖方或信用证的受益人的名称、地址相同	一般出口企业印刷的空白发票,都事先将该公司的名称、地址、电话和传真印在发票的正上方
(4) 装箱单日期	装箱单的出票日期(英文格式)	
(7) 抬头人	进口商名称 进口商地址	信用证项下为开证申请人;托收项下为合同买方。填写时,名称、地址不应同行放置,应分行表明
(10) 运输标志(唛头)	同发票唛头 货物的唛头(收货人简称、合同号、目的港、件数)	与信用证和合同规定的完全一致,照抄唛头;若信用证和合同显示无唛头时,应填 N/M (NO MARKS);若信用证没有规定唛头样式,由企业自拟唛头
(11) 品名和规格	品名和规格必须与信用证的描述相符,规格包括商品规格和包装规格。	
(12) 箱数	最大外包装件数	若为散装货写明 IN BULK 若为裸装货写明 IN NUDE
(19) 签署	出票人的公司名称 经办人的签名	与发票签章相符,如果信用证规定中性包装,此栏可以不填

实例展示

上海良友(集团)有限公司
SHANGHAI LIANG YOU GROUP CO., LTD.
NO. 88 ZHANGYANG ROAD SHANGHAI, CHINA 200122
PACKING LIST
装箱单

FAX: 0086-021-85083378　　　　　　INVOICE NO.: LY11SI-003-5
　　　　　　　　　　　　　　　　　　DATE: JAN. 20, 2015
TEL: 0086-021-85083376　　　　　　S/C NO.: LY11SC-003-S
　　　　　　　　　　　　　　　　　　L/C NO.: ML11000632

TO MESSRS:

FUMING FEED CO., LTD.

THAILAND 653, MOO 4, SOI E 6 PATANA 1 RD., SAMUT PRAKAN 10280

TEL: 66-2-324-0770　FAX: 66-2-324-0350-1

FROM　SHANGHAI CHINA　　　**TO**　BANGKOK THAILAND

唛头及号码 MARKS & NOS.	品名 NOS. & KINDS OF PKGS	数量 QTY	毛重 G.W.	净重 N.W.	尺码 MEAS
FUMING, THAILAND	HEAT FLOUR(FEED GRADE) PACKING: 25KG PER BAG NET	8 400 BAGS	211 680 KGS	210 000 KGS	200CBM (20CBM ×10)
	PACKED IN 8 400BAGS OF 25KGS EACH	8 400 BAGS	211 680 KGS	210 000 KGS (210MT)	200 CBM
TOTAL: SAY EIGHT THOUSAND FOUR HUNDRED BAGS ONLY					

PACKED IN ___8 400___ BAGS
TOTAL GROSS WEIGHT ___211 680KGS___
TOTAL NET WEIGHT ___210 000KGS___

　　　　　　　　　　　SHANGHAI LIANGYOU GROUP CO., LTD.
　　　　　　　　董勋　AUTHORIZED SIGNATURE

实战演练

请根据上海凌烽进出口有限公司出口木制玩具的信用证、合同和相应资料缮制装箱单。

ISSUER				装箱单 PACKING LIST		
TO				INVOICE NO.		DATE
TRANSPORT DETAILS				S/C NO.		L/C NO.
MARKS AND NUMBERS	NUMBER AND KIND OF PACKAGES; DESCRIPTION OF GOODS	CTNS	QTY	G. W. (KGS)	N. W. (KGS)	MEAS. (CBM)
	TOTAL					

TOTAL (IN WORDS)

SIGNED _____

项目四

办理出口货物产地证书和运输

学习目的

- ◆ 知晓申请签发原产地证书的一般程序及其要求
- ◆ 会根据合同或者信用证填制一般原产地证书
- ◆ 知晓租船订舱业务的一般程序和要求
- ◆ 知晓货运委托书的作用
- ◆ 会根据合同或者信用证按时填制货运委托书

任务一 缮制出口货物的原产地申请及证明书

 **学习天地**

数字

FOURTEEN	十四	HUNDRED	百
FORTY	四十	THOUSAND	千
NINETEEN	十九	MILLION	百万
NINETY	九十	BILLION	十亿

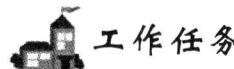 **工作任务**

上海良友(集团)有限公司业务员小明根据信用证的规定,在货物装运前3天向上海贸促会申请签发一般原产地证书。申请签发时,必须提交已缮制的商业发票一份、《中华人民共和国出口货物原产地证明书申请书》一套和《中华人民共和国原产地证明书》一套。

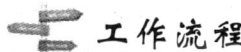 **工作流程**

工作流程见图4-1。

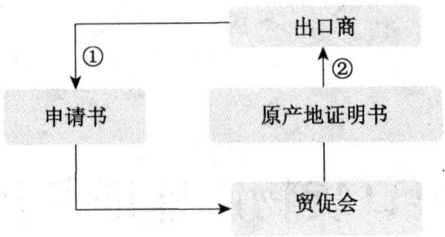

图 4-1　缮制原产地证明书的工作流程

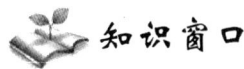

一、产地证明书概述

产地证明书是由出口国政府有关机构签发的一种证明货物原产地或制造地的证明文件。它主要用于进口国海关实行差别关税,实施进口税率和进口配额等不同国别政策的依据。产地证明书是出口商应进口商的要求提供的,有着多种形式。其中应用最多的是原产地证书和普惠制产地证,通常多用于不需要提供海关发票或领事发票的国家或地区。

二、中华人民共和国原产地证明书

中华人民共和国原产地证明书(Certificate of origin of The People's Republic of China)简称原产地证明书,又称一般原产地证明书,是证明本批出口商品的生产地,并符合《中华人民共和国出口货物原产地规则》的一种文件。它是商务部统一规定和印制,由中国出入境检验检疫局或中国国际贸易促进委员会签发。如果信用证或合同对签证机构未作具体规定,一般由中国出入境检验检疫局出具。

三、原产地证书的申请

根据我国有关规定,出口企业最迟于货物出运前 3 天向签证机构申请办理原产地证书,并按签证机构要求提供已缮制的《中华人民共和国出口货物原产地证明书申请书》(又称《一般原产地证明书申请书》)和《中华人民共和国原产地证明书》各一套、出口货物商业发票一份和签证机构所需的其他证明文件。

四、信用证有关原产地证书条款示例

(1) CERTIFICATE OF ORIGINAL IN TRIPLICATE AND CERTIFICATE FROM THE MANUFACTURES IN TRIPLICATE.

生产厂家签发的原产地证明一式三份。

(2) PHOTOCOPY OF ORIGINAL CERTIFICATE OF CHINESE ORIGIN OR GSP FORM A REQUIRED AND SUCH CERTIFICATE COMPINED WITH OR REFERRING TO OTHER DOCUMENTS NOT ACCEPTABLE.

要求提供中国原产地证书复印件或普惠制原产地证书的,其他单据不接受。
(3) CERTIFICATE OF ORIGIN IN THREE COPIES ISSUED BY SELLER.
由卖方签发的产地证一式三份。

 缮制说明

一般原产地证明书申请书

申请单位注册号:出口单位名称　　　　　证书号:

申请人郑重声明:

　　本人被正式授权代表本企业办理和签署本申请书。

　　本申请书及一般原产地证明书所列内容正确无误,如发现弄虚作假,冒充证书所列货物,擅改证书,自愿接受签发机构的处罚并承担法律责任,现将有关情况申报如下:

企业名称	出口单位名称	发票号	
商品名称	货物品名中英文同发票	H.S.编码(六位数)	海关《商品名称及编码协调制度》中商品的八位数字,一般填写前六位
商品FOB总值(以美元计)	FOB价值,若是CIF成交的要扣除国外运费和保费;若是CFR成交的要扣除国外运费	最终目的地国家/地区	填写目的国
拟出运日期	装船日期	转口国(地区)	
贸易方式和企业性质(请在适用处画"√")			
一般贸易		三来一补	其他贸易方式
国有企业	三资企业	国有企业　　三资企业	国有企业　　三资企业
包装数量或毛重或其他数量	一般填最大外包装数量或者总毛重等		
证书种类(画"√")	一般原产地证明书		加工装配证明书
现提交中国出口货物商业发票副本一份,一般原产地证明书/加工装配证明书一正三副,以及其他附件　　份,请予审核签证。			
申请单位盖章	申请人(签名)出口商名称 电话: 日期:　　年　月　日		
商检局联系记录			

ORIGINAL

1. Exporter (full name and address)信用证发货人(受益人)名称/托收是卖方地址、国别	Certificate No. 按检验检疫局指定的编号填制 **CERTIFICATE OF ORIGIN** **OF** **THE PEOPLE'S REPUBLIC OF CHINA**
2. Consignee (full name, address, country)最终收货人的名称(开证申请人)、地址和国别,若信用证有具体规定,应按信用证规定填写	
3. Means of transport and route FROM 装运港　TO 卸货港　BY 运输方式	5. For certifying authority use only 本栏供检验检疫局根据需要加注说明
4. Destination port 按信用证或合同规定的目的港的名称填制,也可同时列出国家或地区名称	

6. Marks and numbers of packages 按信用证或合同中规定的内容进行缮制,且与发票和提单的同项一致,不得留空	7. Description of goods; number and kind of packages 品名 包装件数和种类(填外包装数量及其包装方式) ＊＊＊＊＊＊＊＊＊＊＊＊＊＊＊＊ (以 ＊ 结尾,防止添加)	8. H. S. Code 商品名称和编码	9. Quantity or weight 成交数量如货物计重需注明毛重或净重	10. Number and date of invoice 发票号码和开具发票日期,月份应用英文缩写表示

11. Declaration by the exporter The undersigned hereby declares that the above details and statements are correct; that all the goods were produced in China and that they comply with the Rules of Origin of the People's Republic of China 加盖申请单位章 申报地点和日期,并由经办人签字 Place and date, signature and stamp of authorized signatory	12. Certification It is hereby certified that the declaration by the exporter is correct 在此加盖签证机构印章 发证地点和日期,并由授权人签名 Place and date, signature and stamp of certifying authority

缮制一般原产地证明书申请书的要点如表 4-1 所示。

表 4-1　　　　　　　　　缮制一般原产地证明书申请书的要点

项目顺序号	应 填 内 容	要 点 提 示
(2) 收货人	填最终收货人的名称、地址和国别	信用证项下一般为开证申请人,如果其不是实际收货人,又不知最终收货人,可填提单被通知人或发票抬头人
(3) 运输方式和路线	应按信用证规定填运输路线和运输方式	By steamer（海运）、By train（陆运）、By air（空运）,如中途转运应注明转运地,例：Via Hong Kong。不知转运地则用 W/T 表示
(7) 包装件数、方式和品名	填出口货物最大包装件数和商品名称	如信用证规定单据要加注信用证编号或合同号码等内容,可在此显示
(9) 数量或重量	依据发票和提单有关内容填写	表示重量应注明毛重和净重
(11) 出口商申请日期、地点及签章	申请单位盖章,由授权人手签并注明日期和地点,签字和盖章不得重叠	申报日期不得早于发票日期晚于提单日期
(12) 签证机构证明	签证单位授权人手签并加盖签证当局印章,签字和盖章不得重叠	签证日期不得早于发票日期,也不得早于申请日期

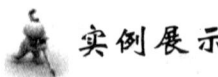
实例展示

一般原产地证明书申请书

申请单位注册号:上海良友(集团)有限公司 　　　证书号:

申请人郑重声明:

本人被正式授权代表本企业办理和签署本申请书。

本申请书及一般原产地证明书所列内容正确无误,如发现弄虚作假,冒充证书所列货物,擅改证书,自愿接受签发机构的处罚并承担法律责任,现将有关情况申报如下:

企 业 名 称	上海良友(集团)有限公司	发 票 号		LY11SI-003-5
商 品 名 称	小麦或混合麦的细粉	H. S. 编码(六位数)		1101000001
商品FOB总值(以美元计)	90 475 美元	最终目的地国家/地区		泰国
拟出运日期	2014.7.15	转口国(地区)		
贸易方式和企业性质(请在适用处画"√")				
一般贸易		三来一补		其他贸易方式
国有企业	三资企业	国有企业	三资企业	国有企业	三资企业
√					
包装数量或毛重或其他数量				8 400 包	
证书种类(画"√")		一般原产地证书√			加工装配证明书
现提交中国出口货物商业发票副本一份,一般原产地证明书/加工装配证明书一正三副,以及其他附件　　份,请予审核签证。				
申请单位盖章		申请人(签名)上海良友(集团)有限公司 电话: 日期:　　年　　月　　日			
商 检 局 联 系 记 录				

ORIGINAL

1. Exporter (full name and address) SHANGHAI LIANGYOU GROUP CO., LTD. NO.88 ZHANGYANG ROAD, SHANGHAI CHINA 200122	Certificate No. C113100220980012
2. Consignee (full name, address, country) FUMING FEED CO., LTD. THAILAND 653, MOO 4, SOIE6 PATANA 1RD., SAMUT PRAKAN 10280 TEL: 66-2-324-0770 FAX: 66-2-324-0350-1	CERTIFICATE OF ORIGIN OF THE PEOPLE'S REPUBLIC OF CHINA
3. Means of transport and route FROM SHANGHAI, CHINA TO BANGKOL, THAILAND BY SEA	5. For certifying authority use only
4. Destination port THAILAND	

6. Marks and numbers of packages FUMING, THAILAND	7. Description of goods; number and kind of packages EIGHT THOUSAND FOUR HUNDRED (8 400) BAGS OF WHEAT FLOUR(FEED GRADE) ＊＊＊＊＊＊＊＊＊＊	8. H. S. Code 1.01	9. Quantity or weight G. W. 211 680KGS	10. Number and date of invoice LY11SI-003-5 JUNE. 20, 2014

11. Declaration by the exporter The undersigned hereby declares that the above details and statements are correct; that all the goods were produced in China and that they comply with the Rules of Origin of the People's Republic of China … 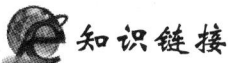 …SHANGHAI, CHINA, JAN 23, 2015… Place and date, signature and stamp of authorized signatory	12. Certification It is hereby certified that the declaration by the exporter is correct …SHANGHAI, CHINA, JAN 26 2015…××× Place and date, signature and stamp of certifying authority

知识链接

1. 普惠制原产地证书(Generalized System of Preferences Certificate of Origin)

普惠制原产地证书简称普惠制产地证(G.S.P.),是指受惠国有关机构就本国出口商向给惠国出口受惠商品而签发的用来证明原产地证明的文件,是给惠国(进口国)给予优惠关税待遇或免税的凭证。普惠制产地证明书主要有普惠制产地证明书A、普惠制产地证明书格式 59A 和普惠制产地证书格式 APR 三种。其中 FORM A (格式 A)使用范围较广,它由我国出入境检验检疫局统一签发。

2. 普惠制产地证的申请

出口企业在货物装运前 5 天,填制《普惠制产地证明书申请书》一份、普惠制产地证明书 FORM A 一套和商业发票一份以及签证机构要求提供的其他文件,递交给签证机构审核签发。如果出口商品含有进口成分,还应交纳《含进口成分受惠商品成本明细单》一式两份。本证书一律不得涂改,一般使用英文填制,也可以使用法文。

普惠制产地证明书申请书

申请单位(盖章):   证书号:

申请人郑重申明:

  本人被正式授权代表本企业办理和签署本申请书。

  本申请书及普惠制产地证明书格式A所列内容正确无误,如发现弄虚作假,冒充证书所列货物,擅自证书,自愿接受签发机构的处罚并承担法律责任,现将有关情况申报如下:

生产单位	生产企业名称	生产单位联系人电话	
商品名称 (中英文)	货物品名统称	H.S.编码(六位数)	海关《商品名称及编码协调制度》中商品的八位数字,一般填写前六位
商品FOB总值 (以美元计)	FOB价值,若是CIF成交的要扣除国外运费和保费;若是CFR成交的要扣除国外运费	发票号	商业发票号
最终销售国	最终目的国国名	证书种类(画"√")	加急证书 普通证书
货物拟出运日期		装运日期	
贸易方式和企业性质(请在适用处画"√")			
正常贸易 C	来(进)料加工 L	补偿贸易 B	中外合资 H	中外合作 Z	外商独资 D	零售 Y	展卖 M
包装数量或毛重或其他数量		外包装数量或总毛重	
原产地标准: 本项商品系在中国生产,完全符合该给惠国给惠方案规定,其原产地情况符合以下第___条: (1)"P"(完全国产,未使用任何进口原材料)。 (2)"W"其H.S.税目号为_____(含进口成分)。 (3)"F"(对加拿大出口产品,其进口成分不超过产品出厂价值的40%)。 本批产品系:1.直接运输从_____到_____。 2.转口运输从_____中转国(地区)_____到_____。			
申请人说明		领证人(签名) 电话 日 期: 年 月 日	
现提交中国出口商业发票副本一份,普惠制产地证明书格式A(FORM A)一正两副,以及其他附件___份,请予以审核签证。 注:凡有进口成分的商品,必须要求提交《含进口成分受惠商品成本明细单》。			
商 检 局 联 系 记 录			

普惠制产地证书

1. Goods consigned from (Exporter's business name, address, country) 出口商名称地址	Reference No. **GENERALIZED SYSTEM OF PREFERENCES CERTIFICA OF ORIGN** **(COMBINED DECLARATION AND CERTIFICATE)** **FORM A** **LSSUED IN THE** **PEOPLES REPUBLIC OF CHINA** (COUNTRY)
2. Goods consigned to (Consignee's name, address, consigned) 进口商名称地址	
3. Means of transport and route (as for as know) FROM 装运港 TO 目的港 BY 运输方式	4. For official use 官方机构使用,不填

5. Item number 商品项目号,同批商品不同品种分列"1""2""3",单项商品填"1"	6. Marks and numbers of packages 唛头	7. Description of goods; number and kind of packages 品名(可不写具体规格) 包装件数和种类 (填外包装数量及其包装方式) ＊＊＊＊＊＊＊ (以＊结尾,防止添加)	8. Origin criterion (see notes overleaf) 原产地标准,无进口成分填"P"	9. Gross weight or other quantity 成交数量 如货物计重需注明毛重或净重	10. Number and date of invoices 发票号码和开具发票日期,月份应用英文缩写表示

11. Certification It is hereby certified, on the basis of control carried out, that the declaration by the exporter is correct 在此加盖签证机构印章 发证地点和日期,并由授权人签名 Place and date, signature and stamp of certifying authority	12. Declaration by the exporter The undersigned hereby declares that the above details and statements are correct, that all the goods were Produced in …CHINA…… (country) and that they comply with the origin requirements specified for those goods, in the generalized system of preference for goods exported to ………………………………… (importing country) 加盖申请单位章 申报地点和日期,并由经办人签字 Place and date, signature of authorized signatory

缮制普惠制产地证明书的要点如表 4-2 所示。

表 4-2　　　　　　　　　　缮制普惠制产地证明书的要点

项目顺序号	应填内容	要点提示
(3) 运输方式和路线	应按信用证规定填运输路线和运输方式	By steamer (海运)、By train (陆运)、By air (空运),如中途转运应注明转运地,例:Via Hong Kong。不知转运地则用 W/T 表示
(7) 包装件数、方式和品名	填出口货物最大包装件数和商品名称	如信用证规定单据要加注信用证编号或合同号码等内容,可在此显示
(8) 原产地标准	进口国海关审核的重点	完全出口国自产,填"P" 有进口成分,出口至欧盟、挪威、瑞士和日本,填"W+产品 H.S. 编码" 有进口成分,出口至加拿大,填"F" 有进口成分,出口至波兰、俄罗斯等 6 国,填"Y"+进口成分占产品离岸价的比重 出口至澳大利亚、新西兰,此栏留空
(9) 数量或重量	依据发票和提单有关内容填写	表示重量应注明毛重和净重
(11) 签证机构证明	签证单位授权人手签并加盖签证当局印章,签字和盖章不得重叠	签证日期不得早于发票日期,也不得早于申请日期
(12) 出口商申请日期、地点及签章	申请单位盖章,由授权人手签并注明日期和地点,签字和盖章不得重叠	申报日期不得早于发票日期晚于提单日期

实战演练

请根据上海凌烽进出口有限公司出口木制玩具的信用证、合同和相应资料缮制原产地申请及证书。

一般原产地证明书申请书

申请单位注册号：　　　　　　　　　证书号：

申请人郑重声明：

本人被正式授权代表本企业办理和签署本申请书。

本申请书及一般原产地证明书所列内容正确无误，如发现弄虚作假，冒充证书所列货物，擅改证书，自愿接受签发机构的处罚并承担法律责任，现将有关情况申报如下：

企业名称		发票号	
商品名称		H. S. 编码(六位数)	
商品FOB总值(以美元计)		最终目的地国家/地区	
拟出运日期		转口国(地区)	
贸易方式和企业性质(请在适用处画"√")			
一般贸易		三来一补		其他贸易方式	
国有企业	三资企业	国有企业	三资企业	国有企业	三资企业
包装数量或毛重或其他数量					
证书种类(画"√")		一般原产地证书		加工装配证明书	
现提交中国出口货物商业发票副本一份，一般原产地证明书/加工装配证明书一正三副，以及其他附件　　份，请予审核签证。 　　申请单位盖章　　　　　　　　　　　　申请人(签名) 　　　　　　　　　　　　　　　　　　　　电话： 　　　　　　　　　　　　　　　　　　　　日期：　　年　　月　　日					
商检局联系记录					

ORIGINAL

1. Exporter (full name and address)	CERTIFICATE No. **CERTIFICATE OF ORIGIN** **OF** **THE PEOPLE'S REPUBLIC OF CHINA**
2. Consignee (full name, address, country)	
3. Means of transport and route	5. For certifying authority use only
4. Country/Region of destination	

6. Marks and numbers of packages	7. Description of goods; number and kind of packages	8. H. S. Code	9. Quantity or weight	10. Number and date of invoices

11. Declaration by the exporter The undersigned hereby declares that the above details and statements are correct; that all the goods were produced in China and that they comply with the Rules of Origin of the People's Republic of China .... Place and date, signature and stamp of authority signatory	12. Certification It is hereby certified that the declaration by the exporter is correct .... Place and date, signature and stamp of certifying authority

任务二 缮制出口货物的货运委托书

学习天地

CONSIGNOR　　　　　发货人　　　CONSIGNEE　　　　　收货人

SHIPPER	托运人
CARRIER	承运人
NOTIFY PARTY	通知方
SHIPPING AGENT	装运代理人、发货代理人
SHIPPING/SHIPMENT	装船,交运
DATE OF SHIPMENT	装船日期,装运期

工作任务

上海良友(集团)有限公司业务员小明在 CIF 条件下及时办理租船订舱手续,并在货物装运完毕后,及时通知买方。为此,小明及时向××国际货运代理公司办理了出口货物托运手续。

工作流程

工作流程见图 4-2。

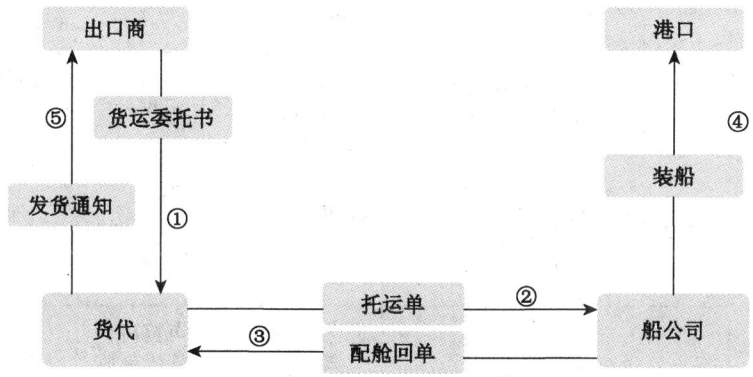

图 4-2　缮制货运委托书的工作流程

知识窗口

海运货物货运委托书是出口企业在办理出口货物托运时,将有关货名、数量、航线等有关内容制成委托书,向承运人或其代理人提出申请,是承运人或其代理人制作提单的依据。

外贸业务人员应根据信用证规定的最迟装运期及货源和船源情况安排委托出运。一般情况应提前 10 天左右或更长时间,以便留出机动时间应付意外情况发生。

缮制说明

货运委托书并无统一格式,各货运代理公司制作的货运委托书/订舱委托书内容大致相同。

货运委托书一般格式如表 4-3 所示。

表 4-3　　　　　　　　　　　　货 运 委 托 书

经营单位(托运人)(1)		出口商名称(中文)		编号(2)		货代公司提供填写		
提单 B/L 项目要求	发货人:(3) Shipper:出口商名称							
	收货人:(4) Consignee:根据信用证规定填写							
	通知人:(5) Notify Party:通常写进口商名称,并注明地址和电话。若信用证有规定,按信用证规定填写							
海洋运费(√)(6) Sea freight	预付(　)或(　)到付 Prepaid or Collect		提单份数(7)		按信用证要求填制	提单寄送地址(8)		根据合同和信用证要求,一般为卖方地址
起运港(9)	装运港		目的港(10)	目的港	可否转船(11)	按信用证	可否分批(12)	按信用证
集装箱预配数(13)	20×集装箱数 40×集装箱数				装运期限(14)	装船日期	有效期限(15)	最迟装运日
标记唛码(16)	件数及包装式样(17)		中英文货号(18) Description of goods		毛重(千克)(19)		尺码(立方米)(20)	成交条件(总价)(21)
同发票 按信用证或合同规定填写	最大外包装数		货物品名中英文		同装箱单总毛重		同装箱单总体积数	填发票总价
					特种货物 □冷藏货 □危险品		重件:每件重量	
内装箱(CFS)地址							大件(长×宽×高)	
门对门装箱地址(22)			根据合同要求填写		特种集装箱:(　　　)			
					资物备妥日期			
声明事项					托运人签章(25)	一般为卖方公章		
					电　话	卖方联系方式		
					传　真			
					联系人			
					地　址			
					制 单 日 期:(26) 早于装运日期,晚于发票装箱单日期			

缮制货运委托书的要点如表 4-4 所示。

表 4-4　　　　　　　　　　　　缮制货运委托书的要点

项目顺序号	应填内容	要点提示
发货人(3)	信用证项下通常是信用证受益人 托收项下为合同卖方	如信用证无具体规定,可以第三方为托运人。本栏应包括托运人的全称和地址,如信用证无规定,地址可省略
收货人(4)	信用证方式下应按信用证规定填写 托收项下填"TO ORDER"或"TO ORDER OF SHIPPER"	如信用证规定: (1) "FULL SET OF B/L CONSIGNED TO A. B. C. Co.",此栏填"CONSIGNED TO A. B. C. Co." (2) "FULL SET OF B/L MADE OUT TO ORDER",此栏填"TO ORDER" (3) "FULL SET OF B/L MADE OUT TO OUR ORDER",此栏填"TO ORDER OF …BANK" (4) "FULL SET OF B/L MADE OUT TO ORDER OF SHIPPER",此栏填"TO ORDER OF SHIPPER" (5) "B/L ISSUED TO ORDER OF APPLICANT",此栏填"TO ORDER OF A. B. C. Co.",(注:A. B. C. Co. 为开证人名称)
通知人(5)	信用证方式下,应按信用证要求填制,通常为开证申请人名称和地址 托收项下的提单可填合同的买方	如信用证规定: (1) NOTIFY PARTY…,将……打在通知栏即可 (2) NOTIFY PARTY APPLICANT,此栏开证人全称和地址 (3) NOTIFY PARTY APPLICANT AND US,需打开证人和开证行全称
海洋运费(6)	根据信用证,预付还是到付打勾	CIF 或 CFR 是运费预付 FOB 是运费到付
集装箱预配数(13)	根据合同和信用证资料填写	若一个 40 英尺集装箱 填 20′×　　40′×1 若两个 20 英尺集装箱 填 20′×2　　40′×

实例展示

货运委托书

经营单位(托运人)		上海良友(集团)有限公司		编号				
提单 B/L 项目要求	发货人: Shipper:上海良友(集团)有限公司							
	收货人: Consignee:TO THE ORDER OF KASIKORN BANK PUBLIC CO., LTD.							
	通知人:FUMING FEED CO., LTD. Notify Party:THAILAND 653, MOO 4, SOI E 6 PATANA 1 RD., SAMUT PRAKAN 10280 TEL: 66-2-324-0770 FAX: 66-2-324-0350-1							
海洋运费(√) Sea freight	预付(√)或( ) 到付 Prepaid or Collect		提单份数	3	提单寄送地址		上海市张杨路88号	
起运港	SHANGHAI	目的港	BANGKOK	可否转船	允许	可否分批		允许
集装箱预配数		20×10 40×		装运期限	2014.07.15	有效期限		2014.07.30
标记唛码	件数及包装式样	中英文货号 Description of goods	毛重 (千克)		尺码 (立方米)		成交条件 (总价)	
FUMING, THAILAND	8 400 包	小麦或混合麦的细粉 WHEAT FLOUR (FEED GRADE)	211 680		200		USD 105 000.00	
			特种货物 ☐ 冷藏货 ☐ 危险品		重件:每件重量			
					大件 (长×宽×高)			
内装箱(CFS)地址	上海市张杨路88号		特种集装箱:( )					
门对门装箱地址			物资备妥日期					
声明事项			托运人签章		上海良友(集团)有限公司(印章)			
			电 话					
			传 真					
			联系人		×××			
			地 址		上海市张杨路88号			
			制单日期:2015.6.30					

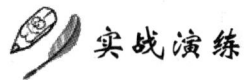实战演练

请根据上海凌烽进出口有限公司出口木制玩具的信用证、合同和相应资料缮制货运委托书。

货 运 委 托 书

经营单位(托运人)			编号		
提单B/L项目要求	发货人：Shipper：				
	收货人：Consignee：				
	通知人：Notify Party：				
海洋运费(√)Sea freight	预付(√)或( )到付Prepaid or Collect		提单份数	提单寄送地址	
起运港		目的港		可否转船	可否分批
集装箱预配数		20′× 40′×		装运期限	有效期限
标记唛码	件数及包装式样	中英文货号Description of goods	毛重(千克)	尺码(立方米)	成交条件(总价)
内装箱(CFS)地址			特种货物□冷藏货□危险品	重件:每件重量	
				大件(长×宽×高)	
门对门装箱地址			特种集装箱:( )		
			物资备妥日期		
外币结算账号			物资进栈(√) 自送( )或( )派送		
			人民币结算单位账号		
声明事项			托运人签章		
			电 话		
			传 真		
			联系人		
			地 址		
			制单日期：		

项目五

办理出口货物的保险和报检

学习目的

- ◆ 知晓投保单的作用和主要内容
- ◆ 知晓保险单的作用和主要内容
- ◆ 知晓报检单的作用和主要内容
- ◆ 会根据合同和信用证缮制投保单
- ◆ 会根据合同和信用证确认保险单
- ◆ 会根据合同和信用证缮制报检单

任务一 缮制出口货物的投保单

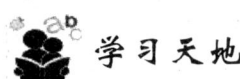 学习天地

INSURANCE	保险	AMOUNT INSURED	保险金额
ICC	协会海运货物险条款	CIC	中国保险条款
FPA	平安险	WA/WPA	水渍险
ALL RISKS	一切险	WAR RISK	战争险
STRIKES	罢工险	TAINT OF ODOUR	串味险

工作任务

上海良友(集团)有限公司需根据合同与信用证保险条款的规定办理出口货物运输保险。对此公司业务员小明缮制了投保单,并向中保财产保险有限公司上海市分公司办理了保险手续。

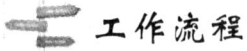 工作流程

工作流程见图 5-1。

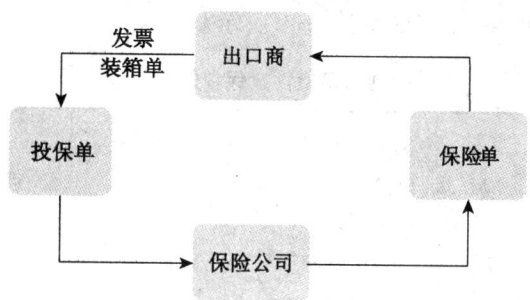

图 5-1 缮制出口货物投保单的工作流程

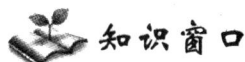

我国出口货物运输保险业务中,投保人向保险公司办理保险时,先填制投保单(Application for Insurance),并随附发票、提单、信用证和合同向保险公司申请投保,保险公司在审核无误后出具保险单或其他保险单据。

投保单是保险公司接受投保、出具保单的依据。经保险公司签署后的保险单即成为向银行进行议付的重要单据。

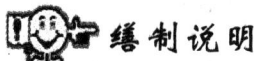

THE PEOPLE'S INSURANCE COMPANY OF CHINA,LTD. SHANGHAI BRANCH APPLICATION FORM FOR I/E MARINE CARGO INSURANCE
进出口货物运输保险投保单

(1) 被保险人　信用证项下:发货人(受益人)名称 　　　　　　　托收项下:卖方				
(2) 发票号码(出口用)或合同号码(进口用)	(3) 件数		(4) 保险货物项目	(5) 保险货物金额
发票编号	最大包装件数		货物名称(统称)	CIF 发票总额再加10%计算的金额,去尾数进位取整数
(6) 运输工具及转载工具	一般填写船名、航次	(7) 约于　　年　月　日启运装船日期	(8) 赔款偿付地点	目的港
(9) 运输路程	自　　装运港经的港	中转地　　到目	转载地点	
(10) 投保险别:合同或信用证要求填写的承保险别		(11) 投保单位签章 　　　　　　出口商名称 　　　　　　　年　月　日		

缮制出口货物投保单的要点如表 5-1 所示。

表 5-1　　　　　　　　　缮制出口货物投保单的要点

项目顺序号	应填内容	要点提示
(5) 保险金额	CIF 发票总额再加 10% 计算的金额	如发票为 FOB 或 CFR 金额,则先换为 CIF 价后,再加一成(按惯例投保加一成) 保险金额＝CIF 价(或 CIP 价)×(1＋投保加成率) 此栏金额去尾数进位取整,如 USD 11 200.01 元,此栏填 USD 11 201.00 元整
(6) 运输工具	海运填船名、航次	中途转船应在一程船名后加填二程船名,如"BY S.S DONG FEN/CHANG JIANG V.112" 铁路和空运填班次与航班名称,联运应注明联运方式,如陆空联运
(7) 开航日期	按实际出运日期填写	海运方式下可填 AS PER B/L
(8) 赔付地及币制	目的港(地)	如有特殊要求可事先说明,币制应与信用证的货币相同
(9) 承保险别	合同保险条款规定	常见的海运主险有中国人民保险公司的平安险、水渍险、一切险
(10) 投保单位签章	出口企业全称	由经办人签名,注明签发日期(早于提单等运输单据签发日)

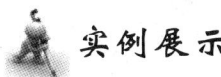
实例展示

THE PEOPLE'S INSURANCE COMPANY OF CHINA, LTD. SHANGHAI BRANCH APPLICATION FORM FOR I/E MARINE CARGO INSURANCE
进出口货物运输保险投保单

(1) 被保险人 SHANGHAI LIANGYOU GROUP CO., LTD.			
(2) 发票号码(出口用)或合同号码(进口用)	(3) 件数	(4) 保险货物项目	(5) 保险货物金额
LY11SI-003-5	8 400BAGS	WHEAT FLOUR (FEED GRADE)	USD 115 500.00
(6) 运输工具及转载工具	HALCYON V.1106S	(7) 约于 2014 年 7 月 15 日启运	(8) 赔款偿付地点 BANGKOK
(9) 运输路程	自 SHANGHAI 经 到 BANGKOK	转载地点	
(10) 投保险别 FOR 110% OF THE TOTAL INVOICE VALUE AS PER THE RELEVANT OCEAN MARINE CARGO OF P. I. C. C. DATED1/1/1981		(11) 投保单位签章 SHANGHAI LIANGYOU GROUP CO., LTD. 2014年7月13日	

实战演练

请根据上海凌烽进出口有限公司出口木制玩具的信用证、合同和相应资料缮制投保单。

THE PEOPLE'S INSURANCE COMPANY OF CHINA, LTD. SHANGHAI BRANCH APPLICATION FORM FOR I/E MARINE CARGO INSURANCE

进出口货物运输保险投保单

被保险人				
发票号码(出口用)或合同号码(进口用)	件数	保险货物项目		保险货物金额
运输工具及转载工具		约于　年　月　日启运	赔款偿付地点	
运输路程	自　　经　　到	转载地点		
投保险别：			(投保单位签章)　年　月　日	

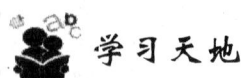

任务二　保险公司签发保险单

学习天地

INSURANCE POLICY　　　　　　　　　　保险单
INSURANCE CERTIFICATE　　　　　　　　保险凭证
COMBINED INSURANCE CERTIFICATE　　　联合保险凭证
OPEN POLICY　　　　　　　　　　　　　预约保险单

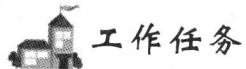 **工作任务**

上海良友(集团)有限公司需根据合同与信用证保险条款的规定办理出口货物运输保险,并向中保财产保险有限公司上海市分公司办理了保险手续。随后,保险公司签发了货物运输保险单。保险单一般由保险公司审单员根据投保人提供的投保单等材料进行缮制。

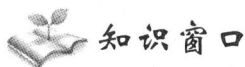 **知识窗口**

保险单是保险人与被保险人之间订立保险合同的一种书面文件,又是保险人出具的承保证明。其主要作用是:当被保险货物遭受损害时,保险单是被保险人向保险人进行索赔的依据,也是保险公司理赔的必要条件。保险单是一种权利的凭证,经背书后可以随货物所有权的转移而进行转让。

1. 保险单的种类

(1) 保险单,俗称"大保单",是正式的保险单据。除正面项目外,背面印就保险双方当事人的权利义务条款,是保险人与被保险人之间的保险合同。

(2) 保险凭证,俗称"小保单",是保险单的简化形式,省略了背面的保险条款,但保险条款仍以保险单为准,与保险单具有同等的法律效力。

(3) 预约保险单,又称预约保险合同,是保险公司与投保人事先订立在一定时期内承保多批货物的保险合同。合同中规定了承保范围、险制、费用、责任等条款,凡在合同约定时期内,货物一旦起运就自动承保,由出口商向保险公司发出"装运通知"或"保险声明"作为正式保单生效的标志。

2. 信用证保险单条款示例

(1) MARINE INSURANCE POLICY/CERTIFICATE COVERING ALL RISKS AND WAR RISK FOR 110 PERCENT OF THE CIF INVOICE VALUE.

(提供)海运保险单,承保险别有一切险、战争险,依据发票金额的110%投保加成。

(2) COVER INSURANCE AGAINST WPA AND INSURANCE BREAKAGE & WAR RISKS FOR 110% OF THE TOTAL INVOICE VALUE AS PER.

THE RELEVANT OCEAN MARINE CARGO OF P. I. C. C. DATED 1/1/1981.

承保险别有中国人民保险条款的水渍险、碰损破碎险、战争险,依据发票金额的110%投保加成。

(3) INSURANCE POLICY OR CERTIFICATES INDUPLICATE, ENDORSED IN BANKFOR 110% OF INVOICE VALUE COVERING INSTITUTE CARGO CLAUSES (A).

(提供)不可转让的海运保险单,承保险别有英国伦敦保险协会条款的A险,依据发票金额的110%投保加成。

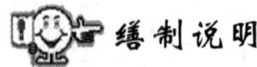 缮制说明

中国人民保险公司
THE PEOPLE'S INSURANCE COMPANY OF CHINA

总公司设于北京　一九四九年创立
HEAD OFFICE: BEIJING　ESTABLISHED IN 1949

货物运输　保险单
CARGO TRANSPORTATION INSURANCE POLICY

发票号码：　　　　　　　　　　　　　　保险单次号次
NO. (1)发票编号　　　　　　　　　　　NO. (2)保险单编号

中国人民保险公司(以下简称本公司)
THIS POLICY OF INSURANCE WITNESSES THAT PEOPLE'S INSURANCE COMPANY OF CHINA (HEREINAFTER CALLED "THE COMPAY") AT THE REQUEST OF.

根据(3)投保人的名称，一般为出口商名称(以下简称被保险人)的要求，由被保险人向公司缴付约定的保险费，按照本保险单承保险别和背面所载条款与下列特款承保下述货物运输保险，特立本保险单。
(HERE INAFTER CALLED "THE INSURED") AND IN CPMSIDERATION OF THE AGREED PREMIUM PAID TO THE COMPANY BY THE INSURED UNDERTAKES TO INSURE THE UNDERMENTIONED GOODS IN TRANSPORTATION SURIECT TO THE CONDITIONS OF THIS POLICY.

AS PER THE CLAUSES PRINTED OVERLEAF AND OTHER SPECIAL CLAUSES ATTCHED HEREON.

(4) 标记 MARKS & NOS	(5) 包装及数量 QUANTITY	(6) 保险货物项目 DESCRIPTION OF GOODS	(7) 保险金额 AMOUNT INSURED
唛头	最大包装件数	货物名称(统称)	CIF发票总额再加10%计算的金额，去尾数进位取整数

总保险金额
TOTAL AMOUNT INSURED

(8) 保险金额大写_____

保费　　　　　　　装载运输工具
PREMIUM AS ARRANGED PER CONVEYANCE SS　(9)船名、航次

开航日期　　　自　　　至
SLG. ON OR ABT (10)运输单据签发日期　　FROM (11)装运港　　TO 目的港

承保险别 CONDITIONS　(12) 合同保险条款_____

所保货物,如遇出险,本公司凭本保险单及其他有关证件给付赔偿所保货物,如果发生本保险单项下负责赔偿的损失或事故应立即通知本公司下述代理人查勘。

CLAIMS IF ANY PAYBLE ON SURRENDER OF THIS POLICY TOGTEHER WITH OTHER RELEVANT DOCUMENTS IN THE EVENT OF ACCIDENT WHEREBY LOSS OR DAMAGE MAY RESULT IN A CLAIM UNDER THIS POLICY IMMEDIATE NOTICE APPLYING FOR SURVEY MUST BE GIVEN TO THE COMPANY'S AGENT AS MENTIONED HSREUNDER.

中国人民保险公司
THE PEOPLES INSURANCE COMPANG OF CHINA

赔款偿付地点 CLAIM PAYABLE AT/IN　(13)目的地及赔付的货币名称＿＿＿＿＿

日期　DATE　(14)保险单签发日期＿＿＿＿＿

地址:中国上海中山东路23号 TEL 323405 3217466-44　TELEX:33128 PICCS CN
ADDRESS 23 ZHONGSHAN DONG YI LU SHANGHAI, CHINA CABLE 42001 SHANGHAI

GENERAL MANAGER 保险公司签章

缮制出口货物保险单的要点如表5-2所示。

表5-2　　　　　　　缮制出口货物保险单的要点

项目顺序号	应 填 内 容	要 点 提 示
(3) 被保险人(Insured)	出口商名称	托收项下的保险单应填出口商名称 CIF条件下的信用证支付应按信用证要求填制,如信用证规定"TO ORDER",此栏转录,且受益人要在保险单背面作空白背书;信用证要求"TO ORDER OF…或 IN FAVOUR OF…",此栏应写成 TO ORDER OF 加上被保险人名称,并作记名背书;信用证对此无具体规定,受益人应视为被保险人,并作空白背书
(4) 标记(Marks & Nos.)	发票上的唛头	也可填"AS PER INVOICE NO …"
(5) 包装及数量(Quantity)	最大包装件数	散装货填"IN BULK"。如果货物价格以重量计价,除表示件数外,还应注明毛重或净重
(7) 保险金额(Amount Insured)	发票总值110%	信用证项下应按信用证规定计算填入,如发票金额须扣除佣金时,应按原金额加成投保;发票金额须扣除折扣时,应按扣除的金额加成投保。保险金额小数点后的尾数应进位取整,如 USD2 304.1 应进位取整为 USD2 305

(续表)

项目顺序号	应填内容	要点提示
(9) 装载运输工具 (Per Conveyance S.S.)	海运填写船名和航次	中途转船应在一程船名后加填二程船名,如"By S.S. DONG FANG/TOKYO V.108";其他运输方式为:BY RAILWAY(陆运),BY AIRPLANE(空运)
(10) 开航日期 (Slg. on or Abt.)	货物运输单据的签发日期	海运可填"AS PER B/L"
(11) 起讫地点 (From … To …)	在 From 后填装运港(地)名称,To 后填目的港(地)名称	须转运时应在目的港(地)后加注 W/T AT…(转运港/地名称),并与提单或其他运输单据相一致。如海运至目的港,保险承保到内陆城市,应在目的港后注明。如"FROM … TO LIVERPOOL AND THENCE TO BIRMINGHAM"

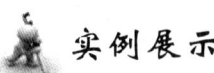

实例展示

中国人民保险公司
THE PEOPLE'S INSURANCE COMPANY OF CHINA

总公司设于北京　　一九四九年创立
HEAD OFFICE：BEIJING　　ESTABLISHED IN1949
货物运输　保险单
CARGO TRANSPORTATION INSURANCE POLICY

发票号码：　　　　　　　　　　　　　　　　保险单次号次
NO. LY11SI-003-5　　　　　　　　　　　　NO. 23546890

中国人民保险公司 (以下简称本公司)
THIS POLICY OF INSURANCE WITNESSES THAT PEOPLE'S INSURANCE COMPANY OF CHI-NA (HEREINAFTER CALLED. "THAT THE REOUEST OF PAY") AT THE REOUEST OF.
根据___SHANGHAI LIANGYOU GROUP CO., LTD.(以下简称被保险人)的要求,由被保险人向公司缴付约定的保险费,按照本保险单承保险别和背面所载条款与下列特款承保下述货物运输保险,特立本保险单。(HEREINAFTER CALLED "THE INSURED") AND IN CPMSIDERATION OF THE AGREED PREMIUM PAID TO THE COMPANY BY THE INSURED UNDERTAKES TO INSURE

THE UNDERMENTIONED GOODS IN TRANSPORTATION SURIECT TO THE CONDITIONS OF THIS POLICYPER THE CLAUSES PRINTED OVERLEAF AND OTHER SPECIAL CLAUSES ATTCHED HEREON.

标记 MARKS & NOS	包装及数量 QUANTITY	保险货物项目 DESCRIPTION OF GOODS	保险金额 AMOUNT INSURED
FUMING, THAILAND	8 400BAGS	WHEAT FLOUR (FEED GRADE)	USD 115 500.00

总保险金额
TOTAL AMOUNT INSURED SAY US DOLLARS ONE HUNDRED AND FIFTEEN THOUSAND FIVE HUNDRED ONLY

保费　　　　　　　　装载运输工具
PREMIUM AS ARRANGED PER CONVEYANCE SS HALCYON V. 1106S

开航日期　　　　　　　　自　　　　至
SLG. ON OR ABT AS PER B/L　　FROM SHANGHAI TO BANGKOK

承保险别　CONDITIONS
COVER INSURANCE AGAINST WPA AND INSURANCE BREAKAGE & WAR RISKS
FOR 110% OF THE TOTAL INVOICE VALUE AS PER.
THE RELEVANT OCEAN MARINE CARGO OF P. I. C. C. DATED1/1/1981.

所保货物,如遇出险,本公司凭本保险单及其他有关证件给付赔偿所保货物,如果发生本保险单项下负责赔偿的损失或事故应立即通知本公司下述代理人查勘。
CLAIMS IF ANY PAYBLE ON SURRENDER OF THIS POLICY TOGTEHER WITH OTHER RELEVANT DOCUMENTS IN THE EVENT OF ACCIDENT WHEREBY LOSS OR DAMAGE MAY RESULT IN A CLAIM UNDER THIS POLICY IMMEDIATE NOTICE APPLYING FOR SURVEY MUST BE GIVEN TO THE COMPANY'S AGENT AS MENTIONED HSREUNDER.

中国人民保险公司
THE PEOPLES INSURANCE COMPANG OF CHINA

赔款偿付地点：CLAIM PAYABLE AT/IN LAT KRABANG IN USD
日期：DATE JUL. 14, 2015
地址：中国上海中山东路23号 TEL 323405 3217466-44　TELEX：33128 PICCS CN
ADDRESS 23 ZHONGSHAN DONG YI LU SHANGHAI, CHINA CABLE 42001 SHANGHAI

GENERAL MANAGER 保险公司签章

实战演练

请根据上海凌烽进出口有限公司出口木制玩具的信用证、合同和相应资料缮制保险单。

中国人民保险公司
THE PEOPLE'S INSURANCE COMPANY OF CHINA

总公司设于北京　一九四九年创立
HEAD OFFICE: BEIJING　ESTABLISHED IN1949

货物运输　保险单
CARGO TRANSPORTATION INSURANCE POLICY

发票号码：　　　　　　　　　　　　　　　　保险单次号次
NO. _____　　　　　　　　　　　NO. _____

中国人民保险公司（以下简称本公司）
THIS POLICY OF INSURANCE WITNESSES THAT PEOPLE'S INSURANCE COMPANY OF CHINA (HEREINAFTER CALLED "THE COMPAY") AT THE REOUEST OF

根据_____（以下简称被保险人）的要求，由被保险人向公司缴付约定的保险费，按照本保险单承保险别和背面所载条款与下列特款承保下述货物运输保险，特立本保险单。
(HEREINAFTER CALLED "THE INSURED") AND IN CPMSIDERATION OF THE AGREED PREMIUM PAID TO THE COMPANY BY THE INSURED UNDERTAKES TO INSURE THE UNDERMENTIONED GOODS IN TRANSPORTATION SURIECT TO THE CONDITIONS OF THIS POLICY PER THE CLAUSES PRINTED OVERLEAF AND OTHER SPECIAL CLAUSES ATTCHED HEREON.

标记 MARKS & NOS	包装及数量 QUANTITY	保险货物项目 DESCRIPTION OF GOODS	保险金额 AMOUNT INSURED

总保险金额：TOTAL AMOUNT INSURED _____

保费　　　　　　　　装载运输工具
PREMIUM　AS ARRANGED　　PER CONVEYANCE SS _____

开航日期　　　自_____　VIA_____　至_____
SLG. ON OR ABT _____　FROM_____　VIA_____　TO_____

承保险别　CONDTIONS：_____

所保货物，如遇出险，本公司凭本保险单及其他有关证件给付赔偿所保货物，如果发生本保险单项下负责赔偿的损失或事故应立即通知本公司下述代理人查勘。
CLAIMS IF ANY PAYBLE ON SURRENDER OF THIS POLICY TOGTEHER WITH OTHER RELEVANT DOCUMENTS IN THE EVENT OF ACCIDENT WHEREBY LOSS OR DAMAGE MAY RESULT IN A CLAIM UNDER THIS POLICY IMMEDIATE NOTICE APPLYING FOR SURVEY MUST BE GIVEN TO THE COMPANY'S AGENT AS MENTIONED HSREUNDER.

中国人民保险公司
THE PEOPLES INSURANCE COMPANG OF CHINA

赔款偿付地点：CLAIM PAYABLE AT/IN _____
日期：DATE _____
地址：中国上海中山东路23号 TEL 323405 3217466-44 TELEX:33128 PICCS CN
ADDRESS 23 ZHONGSHAN DONG LU SHANGHAI, CHINA CABLE 42001 SHANGHAI

GENERAL MANAGER 保险公司签章

任务三 缮制出口货物的报检单

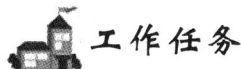

上海良友(集团)有限公司需根据我国有关检验检疫法规,向上海出入境检验检疫局办理了出口货物报检手续,申请签发出境货物通关单。为此,小明根据信用证与合同条款的有关规定填写了出境货物报检单。

工作流程见图5-2。

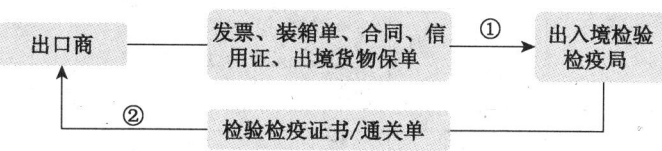

图5-2 缮制出口货物报检单的工作流程

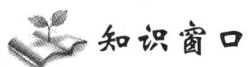

出境检验检疫的报检范围

1. 法律与行政法规所规定的实施检验检疫的出境对象
(1) 列入《出入境检验检疫机构实施检验检疫的进出境商品目录》内的货物。
(2) 对出口危险货物的包装容器的性能检验和使用鉴定。
(3) 出境集装箱。
(4) 出境动植物、动植物产品和其他检疫物。
(5) 装载动植物、动植物产品和其他检疫物的装载容器、包装物、铺垫材料。
(6) 装载出境动植物、动植物产品和其他检疫物的运输工具。
(7) 出境人员、交通工具、运输设备以及可能船舶检疫传染病的行李、货物和邮包物品。
(8) 其他法律、行政法规规定需经检验检疫机构实施检验检疫的其他出境对象。
2. 输入国家或地区所规定须凭检验检疫机构出具的证书方准入境的对象
3. 凡我国作为成员的国际条约、公约和协定所规定的实施检验检疫出境货物
4. 凡贸易合同约定的须凭检验检疫机构签发的证书进行交接、结算入境货物

缮制说明

中华人民共和国出入境检验检疫
出境货物报检单

报检单位（加盖公章）:(1) 报检单位全称　　编号(2) 电子报检自动生成

报检单位登记号:(3) 在商检局登记号　联系人:(4) 报检员姓名　电话:(5) 联系号码　报检日期:(6)

(7) 发货人	（中文）	出口商名称			
	（外文）				
(8) 收货人	（中文）	进口商名称(一般输入＊＊＊＊＊＊)			
	（外文）				
(9) 货物名称(中/外文)	(10) H.S.编码	(11) 产地	(12) 数/重量	(13) 货物总值	(14) 包装种类及数量
合同中货物名称	税则编码	生产（加工）地	成交总数、总重量毛重或净重	发票金额	包装种类及数量
(15) 运输工具名称号码	船名、航次	(16) 贸易方式	一般填一般贸易	(17) 货物存放地点	工厂仓库
(18) 合同号	合同编号	(19) 信用证号	信用证编号	(20) 用途	依据实际情况填写
(21) 发货日期	出口装运日	(22) 输往国家(地区)	进口国（地区）	(23) 许可证/审批号	相关号码
(24) 启运地	出口口岸	(25) 到达口岸	最终目的地	(26) 生产单位注册号	商检局注册登记编号
(27) 集装箱规格、数量及号码		若以集装箱运输，填写集装箱规格、数量及号码			
(28) 合同、信用证订立的检验检疫条款或特殊要求		(29) 标记及号码		(30) 随附单据(划"✓"或补填)	
合同订立的质量、卫生等特别条款		唛头		☑合同　☐包装性能结果单 ☑信用证　☐许可/审批文件 ☑发票　☐ ☐换证凭单　☐ ☑装箱单　☐ ☐厂检单	
(31) 需要证单名称(划"✓"或补填)				(32) 检验检疫费	
☑品质证书　　__正__副 ☑重量证书　　__正__副 ☐数量证书　　__正__副 ☐兽医卫生证书 __正__副 ☐健康证书　　__正__副 ☐卫生证书　　__正__副 ☐动物卫生证书 __正__副		☐植物检疫证书　　__正__副 ☐熏蒸/消毒证书　__正__副 ☑出境货物换证凭单 __正__副		总金额 （人民币元） 计费人 收费人	
(33) 报检人郑重声明： 1. 本人被授权报检。 2. 上列填写内容正确属实，货物无伪造或冒用他人的厂名、标志、认证标志，并承担货物质量责任。 　　　　　　　　签名：　报检员姓名手签				(34) 领 取 证 单	
				日期	领单日
				签名	报检员

缮制出口货物报检单的要点如表 5-3 所示。

表 5-3　　　　　　　　　缮制出口货物报检单的要点

项目顺序号	应填内容	要点提示
(2) 编号	商检机构报检受理人员填写	前 6 位检验检疫机构代码、前 7 位报检类代码、前 8、前 9 位为年代码、第 10 至 15 位为流水号
(16) 贸易方式	依实际情况填写	选填一般贸易、来料加工、进料加工、易货贸易和补偿贸易
(20) 用途	依实际情况填写	选填食用、奶用、观赏或演艺、伴侣动物、试验、药用、其他等
(29) 标记及号码	本批货物标记、号码	没有则填："N/M"
(30) 随附单据	向商检机构提供的实际单据	没有的单据可以后补
(31) 需要证单名称	商检机构要求出具的单据	正副本数量

实例展示

中华人民共和国出入境检验检疫
出境货物报检单

报检单位(加盖公章):(1) 上海良友(集团)有限公司　编　号 (2)

报检单位登记号:(3)　　联系人:(4) 徐红　电话:(5)　报检日期:(6) 2014年7月10日

(7) 发货人	(中文)	上海良友(集团)有限公司					
	(外文)	SHANGHAI LIANGYOU GROUP CO., LTD.					
(8) 收货人	(中文)	＊＊＊＊＊＊＊＊＊＊					
	(外文)	FUMING FEED CO., LTD.					
(9) 货物名称(中/外文)		(10) H.S.编码	(11) 产地	(12) 数/重量	(13) 货物总值	(14) 包装种类及数量	
小麦粉(无品牌) WHEAT FLOUR (FEED GRADE)		1101000001	上海	毛重 211 680千克	105 000美元	8 400包	
(15) 运输工具名称号码		HALCYON V.1106S	(16) 贸易方式	一般贸易	(17) 货物存放地点		上海浦东
(18) 合同号		LY11SC-003-S	(19) 信用证号	ML 11000632	(20) 用途		
(21) 发货日期		2014.7.15	(22) 输往国家(地区)	泰国	(23) 许可证/审批号		
(24) 启运地		上海	(25) 到达口岸	曼谷	(26) 生产单位注册号		
(27) 集装箱规格、数量及号码		20′×10					
(28) 合同、信用证订立的检验检疫条款或特殊要求			(29) 标记及号码		(30) 随附单据(划"✓"或补填)		
			FUMING, THAILAND		☑合同 ☑信用证 ☑发票 ☐换证凭单 ☑装箱单 ☐厂检单	☐包装性能结果单 ☐许可/审批文件	
(31) 需要证单名称(划"✓"或补填)					(32) 检验检疫费		
☑品质证书　1正__副 ☑重量证书　__正__副 ☐数量证书　__正__副 ☐兽医卫生证书　__正__副 ☐健康证书　__正__副 ☐卫生证书　__正__副 ☐动物卫生证书　__正__副			☐植物检疫证书　__正__副 ☐熏蒸/消毒证书　__正__副 ☑出境货物换证凭单 　　　　　　　__正__副		总金额 (人民币元) 计费人 收费人		
(33) 报检人郑重声明: 　1. 本人被授权报检。 　2. 上列填写内容正确属实,货物无伪造或冒用他人的厂名、标志、认证标志,并承担货质量责任。 　　　　　　　签名:_____					(34) 领取证单 日期 签名		

实战演练

请根据上海凌烽进出口有限公司出口木制玩具的信用证、合同和相应资料缮制报检单。

中华人民共和国出入境检验检疫
出境货物报检单

报检单位（加盖公章）：　　　　　编　号　(1)

报检单位登记号：　　联系人：　　电话：　　报检日期：　　年　月　日

发货人	（中文）	
	（外文）	
收货人	（中文）	
	（外文）	

货物名称(中/外文)	H.S.编码	产地	数/重量	货物总值	包装种类及数量

运输工具名称号码		贸易方式		货物存放地点	
合同号		信用证号		用途	
发货日期		输往国家(地区)		许可证/审批号	
启运地		到达口岸		生产单位注册号	

集装箱规格、数量及号码

合同、信用证订立的检验检疫条款或特殊要求	标记及号码	随附单据(划"✓"或补填)
		☑ 合同 ☑ 信用证 ☑ 发票　　□ 包装性能结果单 □ 换证凭单　□ 许可/审批文件 ☑ 装箱单 □ 厂检单

需要证单名称(划"✓"或补填)　　　　　　检验检疫费

☑ 品质证书 __正__副	□ 植物检疫证书 __正__副	总金额（人民币元）	
☑ 重量证书 __正__副	□ 熏蒸/消毒证书 __正__副		
□ 数量证书 __正__副	☑ 出境货物换证凭单 __正__副	计费人	
□ 兽医卫生证书 __正__副	□		
□ 健康证书 __正__副	□	收费人	
□ 卫生证书 __正__副	□		
□ 动物卫生证书 __正__副	□		

报检人郑重声明：
1. 本人被授权报检。
2. 上列填写内容正确属实，货物无伪造或冒用他人的厂名、标志、认证标志，并承担货物质量责任。
　　　　　　签名：_____

领取证单

日期
签名

注：有"*"号栏由出入境检验检疫机关填写。　　　　　　◆国家出入境检验检疫局制
　　　　　　　　　　　　　　　　　　　　　　　　　　[1-2 (2012.1.1)]

项目六

办理出口货物的报关和出运

学习目的

- 知晓申请办理出口报关的一般程序及其要求
- 知晓装运通知的作用
- 会根据信用证和合同缮制出口货物报关单
- 会根据信用证和合同缮制装运通知
- 会根据信用证和合同缮制海运提单
- 知晓商业保险单的作用、主要内容和缮制方法

任务一 缮制出口货物报关单

 学习天地

THE EXPORT DECLARATION	出口报关单
MODE (TERM) OF TRADE	贸易方式
TERMS AND COUNTRY	贸易条件
NAME OF TRADING COUNTRY	贸易国
DATE OF IMPORTATION	进口日期

 工作任务

上海良友(集团)有限公司需根据我国有关检验检疫法规,向上海外港海关办理了出口货物报关手续。为此,小明根据信用证与合同条款的有关规定填写了出口货物报关单。

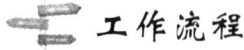 **工作流程**

工作流程见图 6-1。

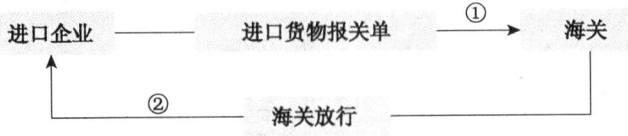

图 6-1 缮制出口货物报关单的工作流程

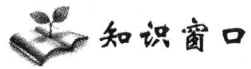

出口报关单的含义与作用:

(1) 出口报关单是由海关总署统一格式印制,由出口企业在装运前填制,经海关审核、签发后生效的法律文书。出口报关单是海关依法监管货物出口、征收关税、编制海关统计以及处理其他海关业务的重要凭证。

(2) 报关单根据业务性质的不同,有一般贸易出口货物报关单、进料加工专用报关单、出口退税专用报关单和来料加工、补偿贸易专用报关单,其主要内容大致相同,填制方法略有差异。

中华人民共和国海关出口货物报关单

预录入编号:(1)　　　　　　　　　　　　　　　　　　　　　海关编号:(2)海关填写

出口口岸(3) 出境口岸的海关名称代码		备案号(4) 加工手册或征免税证明号	出口日期(5) 运输工具出境日期	申报日期(6) 办出口报关手续日期
(7) 经营单位 出口企业及编码(10位)		(8) 运输方式 实际运输方式	(9) 运输工具名称 船名、航次	(10) 提运单号 运输单据编号
(11) 发货单位 在境内的生产或销售单位		(12) 贸易方式 一般贸易等其他贸易方式	(13) 征免性质 一般征税等其他性质	(14) 结汇方式 信用证等结汇方式
(15) 许可证号 出口许可证编号		(16) 运抵国(地区) 出口运抵的国家	(17) 指运港 最终目的港	(18) 境内货源地 货物在国内的产地
(19) 批准文号 出口核销单编号	(20) 成交方式 依具体情况填	(21) 运费 货币代码/ 费用/代码	(22) 保费 货币代码/ 费用/代码	(23) 杂费 货币代码/ 费用/代码
(24) 合同协议号 合同编号	(25) 件数 外包装实际件数	(26) 包装种类 实际种类	(27) 毛重(千克) 实际总毛重	(28) 净重(千克) 实际总净重
(29) 集装箱号 集装箱号/规格/集装箱自重 (此处填写一个,剩余写备注栏内)		(30) 随附单据 官方监管单据(如通关单等)	(31) 生产厂家 境内生产企业	
(32) 标记唛码及备注 唛头,剩余的随附单据号码,剩余的集装箱号码				

项号	商品编号	商品名称规格型号	数量及单位	最终目的国(地区)	单价	总价	币制	征免
序号	商品编码	中文名称 规格型号	实际成交数量 成交数量及 计量单位	最终目的地	单价	总价	货币 代码	照章 征税

税费征收情况				
录入员	录入单位	兹声明以上申报无讹并承担法律责任	海关审单批注及放行日期(签章)	
报关员 单位地址 邮编　　电话　　　　　填制日期		申报单位(签章) 报关专用章	审单　　　审价 征税　　　统计 查验　　　放行	

缮制出口货物报关单的要点如表 6-1 所示。

表 6-1　　　　　　　　　缮制出口货物报关单的要点

项目顺序号	应 填 内 容	要 点 提 示
(4) 备案号	依贸易方式不同填写	如是一般贸易就不填写,如是加工贸易就须填报有关文件的编号
(8) 运输方式	依实际情况填写	水路运输、铁路运输、汽车运输、航空运输等
(12) 贸易方式	依实际情况填写	一般贸易、易货贸易、来料加工、补偿贸易、来料深加工、进料对口等
(13) 征免性质	依实际情况填写	其他情况有:进料加工、中外合资、中外合作、外资企业、边境小额等
(14) 结汇方式	依实际情况填写	其他情况有:电汇、信汇、票汇、付款交单、承兑交单、先出后结、先结后出等
(20) 成交方式	依实际情况填写	情况有:FOB、CFR、CIF、市场价、垫仓等
(21) 运费	依实际情况填写	代码有:3——运费总价,1——运费率,2——运费单价
(22) 保费	依实际情况填写	代码有:3——保险费总价,1——保险费率
(23) 杂费	依实际情况填写	代码有:3——杂费总价,1——杂费率
(25) 件数	实际件数	裸装货物填"1"
(27) 毛重(千克)	实际重量	不足 1 千克应填"1"
(28) 净重(千克)	实际重量	不足 1 千克应填"1"
(30) 随附单据	依实际情况填写	合同、发票、装箱单和许可证等必备随附单证可以不填
(31) 征免	依实际情况填写	其他情况有:1——照章征税;2——折半征税;3——全免等

项目六 办理出口货物的报关和出运

 实例展示

中华人民共和国海关出口货物报关单

预录入编号：　　　　　　　　　　　　　　海关编号：

出口口岸 外港海关 2225	备案号		出口日期 2014-07-15	申报日期 2014-07-13
经营单位 上海良友(集团)有限公司	运输方式 水路运输 2		运输工具名称 HALCYON/1106S	提运单号 SISHLKGA97297
发货单位 上海良友(集团)有限公司	贸易方式 一般贸易　0110		征免性质 一般征税(101)	结汇方式 信用证
许可证号 11-AD-400021	运抵国(地区) 泰国(136)		指运港 曼谷(136)	境内货源地 上海浦东
批准文号 780594951	成交方式 CIF	运费	保费	杂费
合同协议号 LY11SC-003-S	件数 8 400	包装种类 包	毛重(千克) 211 680	净重(千克) 210 000
集装箱号 SITU2900605/20/1280	随附单据 B: 310900211001591		生产厂家	
标记唛码及备注 FUMING, THAILAND GESU3561102/20/1280　　　GLOU3919424/20/1280　　　SITU2962567/20/1280 TEMU2119838/20/1280　　　TEHU2858212/20/1280　　　DFSU2009715/20/1280 BMOU2626150/20/1280　　　SITU2895598/20/1280　　　BMOU2744153/20/1280					

项号	商品编号	商品名称 规格型号	数量及单位	最终目的国(地区)	单价	总价	币制	征免
01	1101000001	小麦细粉 WHEAT FLOUR (FEED GRADE)	210 000.00 千克 8 400 包	泰国	500.00	115 000	USD	照章

税费征收情况			
录入员　　录入单位	兹声明以上申报无讹并承担法律责任	海关审单批注及放行日期(签章)	
报关员	申报单位(签章)	审单	审价
单位地址		征税	统计
邮编　　电话　　填制日期		查验	放行

071

实战演练

请根据上海凌烽进出口有限公司出口木制玩具的信用证、合同和相应资料缮制出口货物报关单。

中华人民共和国海关出口货物报关单

预录入编号：　　　　　　　　　　　　　海关编号：

出口口岸	备案号		出口日期		申报日期	
经营单位	运输方式		运输工具名称		提运单号	
发货单位	贸易方式		征免性质		结汇方式	
许可证号	运抵国(地区)		指运港		境内货源地	
批准文号	成交方式	运费		保费		杂费
合同协议号	件数	包装种类		毛重(千克)		净重(千克)
集装箱号		随附单据		生产厂家		
标记唛码及备注						

项号	商品编号	商品名称规格型号	数量及单位	最终目的国(地区)	单价	总价	币制	征免

税费征收情况				
录入员　　录入单位	兹声明以上申报无讹并承担法律责任	海关审单批注及放行日期(签章)		
报关员	申报单位(签章)	审单		审价
单位地址		征税		统计
邮编　　电话	填制日期	查验		放行

任务二 缮制装运通知

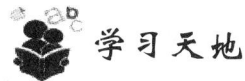

SHIPPING ADVICE	装运通知	SHIPPING NOTICE	装运通知单
ADVISE SHIPPING DATE	装运通知日期	OCEAN BILL OF LADING	提单
FREIGHT	运费	FREIGHT CHARGES	运费

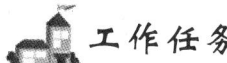

上海良友(集团)有限公司根据信用证和合同的有关条款规定,在货物装船后缮制了装运通知书,并在规定的时间发出。

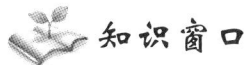

装运通知书的作用
在 CFR 与 CIF 条件下,出口商应在货物装船后,及时发出装运通知书。其作用有:
(1) 装运通知书是出口商向银行议付单据之一。
(2) 进口商获得装运通知后,可以及时办理进口货物保险或做好接收货物的准备。

SHIPPING ADVICE

INVOICE NO.：__发票编号__
S/C NO.：__合同编号__
L/C NO.：__信用证编号__
DATE：__签发日期__

TO MESSRS：
　　　　__进口方(信用证项下开证申请人;托收项下买方)__
COMMODITY：__商品名称__　　　SHIPPING MARKS
NUMBER OF CTNS：__最大包装件数__　　唛头
TOTAL GROSS WEIGHT：__总毛重__
OCEAN VESSEL：__船名 航次__
B/L NO.：__提单编号__
PORT OF LOADING：__装运港__
DATE OF DEPARTURE：__装运日期__
DESTINATION：__目的港__

实例展示

SHIPPING ADVICE

INVOICE NO.: LY11SI-003-5
S/C NO.: LY11SC-003-S
L/C NO.: ML11000632
DATE: JUL. 15, 2014

TO MESSRS:
　　FUMING FEED CO., LTD.
　　THAILAND 653, MOO 4, SOIE 6 PATANA 1 ROAD, SAMUT PRAKAN 10280
COMMODITY: WHEAT FLOUR
NUMBER OF CTNS: 8 400 BAGS
TOTAL GROSS WEIGHT: 211 680 KGS
OCEAN VESSEL: HALCYON V1106S
B/L NO: SISHLKGA97297
PORT OF LOADING: SHANGHAI CHINA
DATE OF DEPARTURE: JUL. 15, 2014
DESTINATION: BANGKOK
　　SHIPPING MARKS
　　FUMING, THAILAND

实战演练

请根据上海凌烽进出口有限公司出口木制玩具的信用证、合同和相应资料缮制装运通知。

SHIPPING ADVICE

INVOICE NO.: ＿＿＿＿＿＿＿
S/C NO.: ＿＿＿＿＿＿＿
L/C NO.: ＿＿＿＿＿＿＿
DATE: ＿＿＿＿＿＿＿

TO MESSRS:

COMMODITY: ＿＿＿＿＿＿＿
NUMBER OF CTNS: ＿＿＿＿＿＿＿
TOTAL GROSS WEIGHT: ＿＿＿＿＿
OCEAN VESSEL: ＿＿＿＿＿＿＿
B/L NO.: ＿＿＿＿＿＿＿
PORT OF LOADING: ＿＿＿＿＿＿＿
DATE OF DEPARTURE: ＿＿＿＿＿
DESTINATION: ＿＿＿＿＿＿＿
SHIPPING MARKS

任务三　确认船公司签发的海运提单

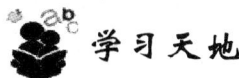

NEW YORK	纽约
LOS ANGELES	洛杉矶
SYDNEY	悉尼
LONDON	伦敦
TOKYO	东京
BUSAN	釜山
LONG BEACH	长滩
MELBOURNE	墨尔本
LIVERPOOL	利物浦
OSAKA	大阪
YOKKAICHI	横滨
LNCHON	仁川

上海良友(集团)有限公司出口的货物经海关放行后,获取盖有放行章的报关单,作为港口装船的依据。装船后,由船长或大副向船运公司签发收货单,船运公司或国际货运代理公司凭收货单缮制海运提单,并向出口商签发。

工作流程

工作流程见图6-2。

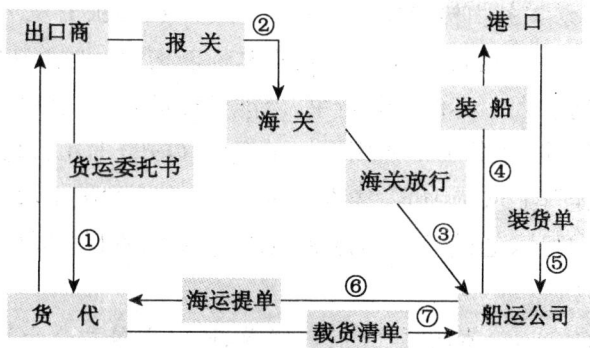

图6-2　缮制海运提单的工作流程

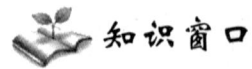知识窗口

一、海运提单的概念

海运提单(Bill of Lading)简称提单,是由船公司或其代理人收到承运货物时或将其装船后,向托运人签发的货物收据。

二、提单的分类

1. 按货物是否已经装船,分已装船提单和备运提单

已装船提单(On Board B/L)是指货物装船后,由承运人签发给托运人的提单,它必须载明装货船名和装船日期。由于这种提单对收货人按时收货有保障,因此,在买卖合同和信用证中一般都规定卖方须提供已装船提单;备运提单(Received for Shipment B/L)又称收讫待运提单,是承运人在收到托运货物等待装船期间,向托运人签发的提单。由于这种提单没有确切的装船日期,且不注明装运船只的名称,因此,实际业务中一般不使用这种提单。

2. 按提单上对货物外表状况有无不良批注,分清洁提单和不清洁提单

清洁提单(Clean B/L)指交运货物的外表状况良好,承运人未加有关货损或包装不良之类批注的提单。不清洁提单(Unclean B/L or Foul B/L)指凡承运人加注了表明货物外表状况不良或存在缺陷之类批注的提单。对于不清洁提单,银行都拒绝接受。

3. 按提单的抬头不同,分记名提单、不记名提单和指示提单

记名提单(Straight B/L)是指发给指定的收货人的提单,在提单中的收货人栏内,具体填明收货人的名称。这种提单只能是指定的收货人提货,不能转让,虽避免了转让带来的风险,但也失去了转让流通的便利,故银行不愿接受这种提单作为议付证件,因而在国际贸易实务中极少使用。不记名提单(Black B/L or Open B/L)是指在提单上收获栏内不填写收货人或指示人的名称而留空,或只填写"来人"(Bearer)字样的提单。提单持有人可不作任何背书,就能凭提单转让货物所有权或提取货物。因其安全性极差,故实际业务中不使用。指示提单(Order B/L)是指在提单上收货人一栏内填写:"凭指定"(To Order)、"凭发货人指定"(To Order of Shipper)等字样的一种提单。指示提单可以通过背书的方法转让给他人,在国际贸易实务中使用较为普遍。

4. 按不同运输方式,分直达提单、转船提单、联运提单和联合运输单据

直达提单(Direct B/L)是指货物从装运港直接运抵目的港的提单。直达提单中只列有装运港和目的港名称,不得有"中途转船""在某港转船"等批注。转船提单

(Transhipment B/L)是指货物须经中途转船才能到达目的港而由承运人在装运港签发的全程提单。转船提单上一般注有"在某港转船"字样,甚至转船船名等。货物在中途港口转船换装,常常会增加货物受损及等候船舶延误到货时间的风险。因此,除另有约定外,进口方一般不允许转船。联运提单(Through B.L)是指货物须经过海运和其他运输方式联合运输时,由第一程承运人所签发的,包括全程运输,并能在目的港或目的地凭以提货的提单。

5. 按提单内容繁简,分全式提单和略式提单

全式提单(Long Form B/L)是指提单上除有正面条款之外,还在背面印有承运人和托运人权利、义务等详细条款的提单。略式提单(Short Form B/L)是指仅有提单正面内容如船名、货号、标志、件数、装运港、目的港,而略去了提单背面全部条款的提单。

三、提单的主要作用

(1) 提单是货物收据。证明承运人或其代理人已按提单所列内容收到货物。

(2) 提单是物权凭证。提单合法持有人有权凭提单在目的港向承运人提取货物,也能将提单转让,或凭以向银行办理抵押贷款,是一份有价证券。

(3) 提单是运输合同的证明。提单条款明确规定了托运人和承运人之间的权利与义务,责任与豁免,是索赔和理赔的法律依据。

四、信用证提单条款示例

(1) FULL SET OF CLEAN ON BOARD OCEAN BILLS OF LADING MADE OUT TO ORDER, BLANK ENDORSED, MARKED "FREIGHT PREPAID" AND NOTIFY APPLICANT.

全套正本已装船的清洁提单,凭托运人的指示、空白抬头、运费预付,通知开证申请人(进口方)。

(2) 3/3 CLEAN ON BOARD OCEAN BILLS OF LADING MADE OUT TO THE ORDER OF ABC BANK, BLANK ENDORSED, MARKED "FREIGHT COLLECT" AND NOTIFY APPLICANT.

全套正本已装船的清洁提单,凭 ABC 银行的指示、空白抬头、运费已付,通知开证申请人(进口方)。

(3) 1/3 CLEAN ON BOARD OCEAN BILLS OF LADING MADE OUT TO ORDER OF ABC COMPANY, BLANK ENDORSED, MARKED "FREIGHT PREPAID" AND NOTIFY APPLICANT.

一本正本结汇,已装船的清洁提单,凭 ABC 公司的指示、空白抬头、运费预付,通知开证申请人(进口方)。

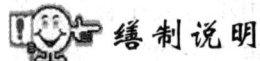 缮制说明

BILL OF LADING

(1) SHIPPER 出口商名称地址	(2) B/L NO. 提单编号
(3) CONSIGNEE 托收项下合同填 TO ORDER 或 TO ORDER OF SHIPPER 信用证项下,应按信用证要求填制	**COSCO SHIPPING**
(4) NOTIFY RARTY 托收项下是合同买方 信用证项下,应按信用证要求填制	

(5) PRE-CARRIAGE BY 需转运,填第一程船名,如无需转运,则不填	(6) VESSEL 船名	(7) VOYAGE NO. 航次	(8) PORT OF LOADING 装运港
(9) PORT OF DISCHARGE 卸货港		(10) PLACE OF DELIVERY 最终目的地	
(11) NO. OF PKGS 件数、包装种类 集装箱编号和唛头	(12) DESCRIPTION OF GOODS 货物名称(统称)	(13) G. W. 总的毛重	(14) MEAS(M^3) 总的尺码(体积)

REGARDING TRANSHIPMENT INFORMATIONPLEASE CONTACT	(15) FREIGHT AND CHARGES CIF 或 CFR 术语下,是运费预付

	PREPAID AT	FREIGHT PAYABLE AT	(16) PLACE AND DATE OF ISSUE 签发日期和地点
EX. Rate	TOTAL PREPAID	(17) NUMBER OF ORIGINAL BS/L 正本份数	(18) SIGNED FOR OR ON BEHALF OF THE MASTER 承运人签字

缮制海运提单的要点如表 6-2 所示。

表 6-2　　　　　　　　　　　缮制海运提单的要点

项目顺序号	应填内容	要点提示
(1) 托运人	发货人	托收项下为合同卖方,信用证项下通常是信用证受益人。如信用证无具体规定,可以第三方为托运人。本栏应包括托运人的全称和地址,如信用证无规定,地址可省略
(2) 提单编号	提单号码由承运人或其代理人提供	提单必须注明承运人或其代理人规定的提单号码,以便核查,否则该提单无效
(3) 收货人	信用证方式下应按信用证规定填写 托收项下填"TO ORDER"或"TO ORDER OF SHIPPER"	如信用证规定: (1) "FULL SET OF B/L CONSIGNED TO A. B. C. Co.",此栏填"CONSIGNED TO A. B. C. Co." (2) "FULL SET OF B/L MADE OUT TO ORDER",此栏填"TO ORDER" (3) "FULL SET OF B/L MADE OUT TO OUR ORDER",此栏填"TO ORDER OF … BANK" (4) "FULL SET OF B/L MADE OUT TO ORDER OF SHIPPER",此栏填"TO ORDER OF SHIPPER" (5) "B/L ISSUED TO ORDER OF APPLICANT",此栏填"TO ORDER OF A. B. C. Co."(注:A. B. C. Co. 为开证人名称)
(4) 被通知人	信用证方式下,应按信用证要求填制。通常为开证申请人名称和地址。 托收项下的提单可填合同的买方	如信用证规定: (1) NOTIFY PARTY…,将……填在通知栏即可; (2) NOTIFY PARTY APPLICANT,此栏填开证人全称和地址; (3) NOTIFY PARTY APPLICANT AND US,需填开证人和开证行全称
(9) 卸货港	目的港	信用证支付方式下,应按来证规定填制:如卸货港有两个以上选择港(例:LONDON/HAMBURG/ROTTERDAM)只能选择其中一个港口名称;如中途转运,应填转船地
(11) 件数、包装种类	包装数量和包装单位	如为散装货,用"IN BUK"表示;如为裸装货,应加件数(例:100 头牛,填 100 HEADS);如为多种包装,应分别注明件数和包装单位,并计算总数
(16) 签发日期和地点	装运日期及装运地	提单签发日则是装运日期,应不晚于信用证或合同规定的最迟装运时间
(18) 承运人签字	承运人或其代理人	提单必须由承运人或其代理人签字方能生效。如信用证要求手签,应按规定执行,签字时必须表明其身份

 实例展示

BILL OF LADING

SHIPPER SHANGHAI LIANGYOU GROUP CO., LTD. NO. 88 ZHANGYANG ROAD, SHANGHAI CHINA 200122	B/L NO.: SISHLKGA97297	
CONSIGNEE TO ORDER OF KASIKORN BANK PUBLIC CO., LTD. BANGKOK	SITC CONTAINER LINE CO., LTD. BILL OF LADING	
NOTIFY RARTY FUMING FEED CO., LTD. 77/12 MOO 2, RAMA II RD NAKHOK MUANG SAMUTSAKHORN 74000, THAILAND		

PRE-CARRIAGE BY	VESSEL HALCYON	VOYAGE NO. V1106S	PORT OF LOADING SHANGHAI, CHINA
PORT OF DISCHARGE BANGKOK, THAILAND		PLACE OF DELIVERY	

NO. OF PKGS	DESCRIPTION OF GOODS	G.W.	MEAS(M³)
FUMING, THAILAND	WHEAT FLOUR (FEED GRADE)	211 680 KGS	200 CBM

TOTAL NO OF CONTAINERS
OR PACKAGES(IN WORDS)   SAY EIGHT THOUSAND FOUR HUNDRED BAGS ONLY

REGARDING TRANSHIPMENT INFORMATIONPLEASE CONTACT		FREIGHT AND CHARGES FREIGHT PREPAID	
EX. RATE	PREPAID AT	FREIGHT PAYABLE AT SHANGHAI	PLACE AND DATE OF ISSUE SHANGHAI JUL. 15, 2014
	TOTAL PREPAID	NUMBER OF ORIGINAL BS/L THREE	SIGNED FOR OR ON BEHALF OF THE MASTER SITC CONTAINER LINE CO., LTD. AS AGENTS

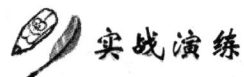 **实战演练**

请根据上海凌烽进出口有限公司出口木制玩具的信用证、合同和相应资料缮制海运提单。

BILL OF LADING

SHIPPER		B/L NO.:	
CONSIGNEE		COSCO SHIPPING	
NOTIFY RARTY			
PRE-CARRIAGE BY	VESSEL	VOYAGE NO.	PORT OF
PORT OF DISCHARGE		PLACE OF DELIVERY	
NO. OF PKGS	DESCRIPTION OF GOODS	G. W.	MEAS(M³)
TOTAL NO OF CONTAINERS OR PACKAGES(IN WORDS)			
REGARDING TRANSHIPMENT INFORMATIONPLEASE CONTACT		FREIGHT AND CHARGES	
EX. RATE	PREPAID AT	FREIGHT PAYABLE AT	PLACE AND DATE OF ISSUE
	TOTAL PREPAID	NUMBER OF ORIGINAL BS/L	SIGNED FOR OR ON BEHALF OF THE MASTER

项目七

办理出口货物的结汇

学习目的

◆ 知道商业汇票的作用
◆ 会缮制信用证项下的商业汇票
◆ 会缮制托收项下的商业汇票

任务一　缮制商业汇票

学习天地

AT SIGHT	见票	AMOUNT	金额
BILL OF EXCHANGE	汇票	BILL OF COLLECTION	托收汇票
BRANCH	分行、分支机构	BANK	银行
BANK OF CHINA	中国银行	D/P	付款交单
DRAFT	汇票	D/A	承兑交单
EXCHANGE	兑换、汇票		

工作任务

上海良友(集团)有限公司已按时将货发运并整理了相关的单据,现要求财务部小江缮制商业汇票,并连同信用证所要求的单据向议付行提交结汇。

工作流程

工作流程见图7-1。

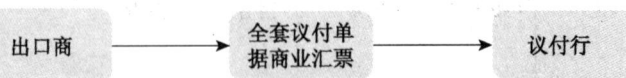

图7-1　缮制商业汇票的工作流程

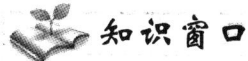 知识窗口

汇票是出票人签发的,委托付款人在见票时或者在指定日期无条件支付确定金额给付款人或持票人的票据。汇票是一种代替现金的支付工具,是有价证券,并能代替货币进行转让或流通。汇票一般有两张正本,其具有同等效力,付款人付一不付二,付二不付一,先到先付,后到无效。根据出票人不同,汇票有银行汇票和商业汇票两种形式,采用信用证和托收结算方式,多使用出口商出具的商业汇票。

 缮制说明

BILL OF EXCHANGE

凭　　　　　　　　　　　　　　　　　信用证　第　　　号
Drawn under(1)　　开证行名称　　　**L/C No.** (2)　　信用证号

日期
Dated(3)　开证日期　　支取 Payable with interest @　% per annum 按年息　　付款

号码　　　汇票金额　　　　　　　　　　　　　　　　　　　年　月　日
No. 一般为发票　**Exchange for**(4)　汇票金额(小 (5) 议付地点,一般 (6) 议付日期,在提
编号　　　　　　　　　　　　写)一般情况同 在出口商营业地 单日期后,交单期内
　　　　　　　　　　　　　　发票金额　　　　　　　　　　　即可

见票　　　日后(本汇票之副本未付)付交
At(7) 付款期限　sight of this **FIRST** of Exchange (Second of exchange being unpaid)

Pay to the order of (8)　受款人,一般填议付行名称
The sum of (9)
金额
信用证金额(大写)和小写金额一致

款已收记
Value received

此致
To(10) 付款人,信用证项下为付款银行名称　(11) 出票人签章(常见是出口商签章)
　　　地址

缮制商业汇票的要点如表7-1所示。

表 7-1　　　　　　　　　　　缮制商业汇票的要点

项目顺序号	应填内容	要点提示
(4) 汇票金额小写	汇票面值	信用证或合同无特别规定,其金额与发票金额一致。如信用证规定部分信用证付款,部分托收,应作两套汇票:信用证下支款的金额按信用证金额支取;托收项下的支款金额按合同规定支取。发票金额是两套汇票相加之和
(7) 付款期限	分为即期和远期付款两类	即期填＊＊＊ 远期看信用证中的汇票条款,根据规定填写
(8) 受款人	汇票的抬头人,收款人	信用证项下一般为议付行,托收项下为托收银行 此栏有三种形式: A. 指示性抬头 PAY TO THE ORDER OF… B. 限制性抬头 PAY TO … ONLY C. 来人抬头 PAY TO BEARDER
(10) 付款人	汇票的受票人,填其名字和地址	信用证项下一般为开证银行或其指定银行,未明确时以开证行为付款人 托收项下填进口商名称地址

实例展示

BILL OF EXCHANGE

凭 **Drawn under**　KASIKORNBANK PUBLIC COMPANY LIMITE　　信用证　第　号 **L/C No.**　ML 11000632

日期 **Dated**　20140110　　支取 Payable with interest @　% per annum 按年息　付款

号码 **No.** LY11SI-003-5　　汇票金额 **Exchange for**　USD 105 000.00　SHANGHAI　　年 月 日　JUL. 20, 2015

见票 **At**　30 DAYS AFTER B/L DATE　　日后(本汇票之副本未付)付交 sight of this **FIRST** of Exchange (Second of exchange being unpaid)

Pay to the order of　CHINA MINSHENG BANKING CORP. LTD., SHANGHAI BRANCH

金额 **The sum**
SAY US DOLLARS ONE HUNDRED AND FIVE THOUSAND ONLY

款已收讫 Value eceived

此致 **To:**
KASIKORNBANK PUBLIC COMPANY LIMITED BANGKOK

(SHANGHAI LIANGYOU GROUP CO., LTD.

项目七 办理出口货物的结汇

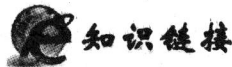
知识链接

托收项下的汇票缮制。

BILL OF EXCHANGE

| 凭 Drawn under | 货物情况和合同号 | 信用证 第 号 L/C No. | 不填 |

日期 Dated 不填　　　　　　支取 Payable with interest @ ‰ per annum 按年息 付款

号码月 日
No. 一般为发票号　　Exchange for　　汇票小写金额　　议付地点,一般在出口商营业地　　议付日期,在提单日期后,交单期内即可

见票　　　　　　　　　　　日后(本汇票之副本未付)付交
At 付款期限 * 标明是 D/P 或 D/A　sight of this **FIRST** of Exchange (Second of exchange being unpaid)
Pay to the order of　　受款人,一般填议付行名称
金额
The sum

汇票金额(大写)和小写金额一致

款已收讫
Value received
此致
To:
付款人,托收项下为进口商名称地址　　　　　出票人签章(常见是出口商签章)

实战演练

请根据上海凌烽进出口有限公司出口木制玩具的信用证、合同和相应资料缮制商业汇票。

BILL OF EXCHANGE

凭 Drawn under　　　　　　　　　　信用证 第 号 L/C No.

日期 Dated　　　　　　　　　支取 Payable with interes ‰ per annum 按年息付款

号码 No.　　汇票金额　　　　　　　　　　　　　　　　年 月 日
　　　　　　　Exchange for
见票　　日后(本汇票之副本未付)付交
At　　sight of this **FIRST** of Exchange (Second of exchange being unpaid)
Pay to the order of
金额
The sum of

款已收讫
Value received
此致
To:

任务二 交单议付

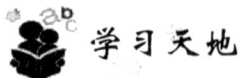 学习天地

BALE	包	BAG	袋
CARTON	纸箱	BOTTLE	瓶
BOX	盒	BARREL	桶
CASE	箱	CONTAINER	集装箱

工作任务

财务部小江缮制好商业汇票,连同商业发票、装箱单、普惠制原产地证明、保险单和海运提单,在信用证规定的有效期和交单期内在民生银行上海分行办理交单议付手续。

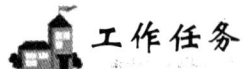 知识窗口

全套相关单据缮制完毕后,要求制单人员自己审核,如有差错应立即更正,以保证迅速有效地向银行交单,确保安全、及时收汇。

一、单据的自审

(一)审单的依据

在信用证方式下,审单依据是信用证条款。在托收方式下,审单依据是该买卖合同。

(二)审单的要求

(1) 单据齐全。包括单据的种类与份数是否符合信用证或合同要求。
(2) 内容完整。各种单据内容和签章是否完整。
(3) 单据名称是否与信用证或合同相符。
(4) 确保单证一致、单同一致、单单一致和单货一致。
(5) 确保该套单据之间的签发日期没有矛盾。

二、单据的提交

出口商在缮制并审核全套单据后,在信用证的有效期和交单期内,及时向议付银行交单,以确保安全及时结汇。

三、归档

国际商务单证在国际贸易中占有极其重要的地位,卖方凭单交货,买方凭单付款,单据具有法律效力,因此保存一套完整的副本单据是十分重要的,也是非常必要的。

项目八

认识其他单据

学习目的

- ◆ 知晓其他单据的种类
- ◆ 会缮制出口许可证和植物检疫证书
- ◆ 会缮制非木质包装证明和受益人证明
- ◆ 会缮制出口收汇核销单

任务一 认识商检证书和出口许可证

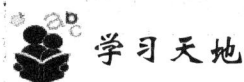 学习天地

PIECE	件、个、只、块、张	PACKAGE	件、包
POUND	磅	FREIGHT TON	运费吨
FEET	英尺	KG	千克

 工作任务

上海良友(集团)有限公司要出口一批小麦,要求业务员小明申领出口许可证和植物检验证书。

 知识窗口

进出口许可证是由国家对外经贸行政管理部门代表国家统一签发的批准某项商品进出口的具有法律效力的证明文件,也是海关查验放行进出口货物的依据。

根据规定,凡是国家宣布实行进出口许可证管理的商品,不管任何单位或个人,也不分任何贸易方式,进出口前均需申领进出口许可证;非外贸经营单位或个人运往国外的货物,不论该商品是否实行进出口许可证管理,价值在人民币1 000元以上的,一律须申领许可证。

我国执行审批并签发进出口许可证的机关有:商务部及其派驻在主要口岸的特

派员办事处；各省、自治区、直辖市以及国务院批准的计划单列市的对外经贸行政管理部门，实行按商品、按地区分级发证办法。

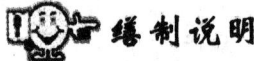 缮制说明

中华人民共和国出口货物许可证
EXPORT LICENCE THE PEOPLE'S REPUBLIC OF CHINA A 类

1. 出口商 Export 出口商名称及其公司编码			3. 出口许可证号 Export Licence No. 由发证机关编排	
2. 发货人 Consignor 通常是出口商名称及其公司编码			4. 出口许可证有效截止日期 Export licence expiry date 由发证机关视商品而定	
5. 贸易方式 Terms of trade 合同中的贸易方式			8. 输往国家(地区) 进口国 Country of destination	
6. 合同号 Contract No. 合同编号			9. 付款方式 Terms of payment 结汇方式	
7. 报关口岸 Port of shipment 装运港			10. 运输方式 Means of transport 江海运输或航空运输等	
11. 商品名称 商品统称 商品编码 H.S.编码 Description of commodity Commodity No.				
12. 规格、等级 Specification	13. 单位 Unit	14. 数量 Quantity	15. 单价( ) U/price	16. 总值( ) Amount	17. 总值折美元 Amount in USD
具体规格	成交计量单位	成交数量	单价	单价×数量	单价×数量
总计 Total		总成交数量		总金额	总金额
备注 Supplementary details			发证机关盖章 Issuing authority's stamp & signature 发证日期 实际发证日期 Date		

中华人民共和国商务部监制（2007） 本证不得涂改，不得转让

 **实例展示**

中华人民共和国出口货物许可证
EXPORT LICENCE THE PEOPLE'S REPUBLIC OF CHINA A 类

1. 出口商　3100631221336 Export　上海良友(集团)有限公司	3. 出口许可证号 Export Licence No.　11-AD-400021
2. 发货人　3100631221336 Consignor　上海良友(集团)有限公司	4. 出口许可证有效截止日期 Export licence expiry date 2014 年 07 月 25 日
5. 贸易方式 Terms of trade　一般贸易	8. 输往国家(地区) Country of destination　泰国
6. 合同号 Contract No.　LY11SC-003-5	9. 付款方式 Terms of payment　信用证
7. 报关口岸 Port of shipment　上海海关	10. 运输方式 Means of transport　海上运输

| 11. 商品名称　小麦或混合麦的细粉　商品编码　1101000001
Description of commodity　　　　　　　　Code of goods |

12. 规格、等级 Specification	13. 单位 Unit	14. 数量 Quantity	15. 单价(USD) U /price	16. 总值(USD) Amount	17. 总值折美元 Amount in USD
小麦细粉	千克	210 000	0.50	105 000.00	$105 000.00
总计 Total	千克	210 000		105 000.00	$105 000.00

| 备注
Supplementary details
限于出口至中国香港、澳门以外地区 | 发证机关盖章
Issuing authority's stamp & signature
发证日期　实际发证日期
Date |

中华人民共和国商务部监制（2007）　　　　　　本证不得涂改，不得转让

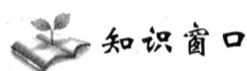工作流程

工作流程见图8-1。

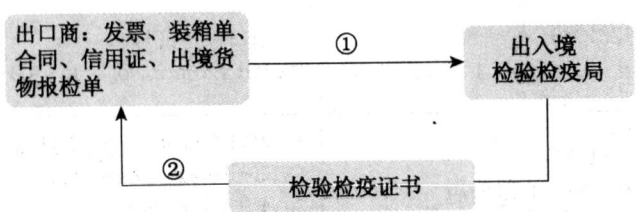

图8-1 缮制出入境检验检疫证书的工作流程

知识窗口

出入境检验检疫证书是出入境检验检疫机构依法对涉及健康、卫生、安全、环保和关系到国计民生的重要出入境货物,运输工具及疫病、疫情进行检验检疫或监督管理后,签发的结果证明文书。

出入境检验检疫机构是《中华人民共和国国境卫生检疫法》《中华人民共和国进出境动植物检疫法》《中华人民共和国进出口检验法》《中华人民共和国食品卫生法》的实施或组织实施部门。出入境检验检疫机构既是公正的检验检疫职能部门,同时又承担着出入境检验检疫的监督管理工作。它所签发的检验检疫证书既是检验检疫的结果证明文书,又是出入境检验、检疫和监督管理的措施。

根据规定,检验检疫证书是出入境检验检疫机构依法对涉及健康、卫生、安全、环保和关系到国计民生的重要出入境货物,运输工具及疫病、疫情进行检验检疫或监督管理后,签发的证明文书;是对外贸易双方证明履约与责任情况的有效证件,是办理索赔的证明文件,也是进行贸易统计、指定非关税壁垒措施的有效凭证。

目前,我国检验检疫机构签发的检验证书主要有:品质检验证书(Inspection Certificate of Quality)、植物检疫证书(Phytosanitary Certificate)、重量或数量检验证书(Inspection Certificate of Weight Quantity)、包装检验证书(Inspection Certificate of Packing)、兽医检验证书(Veterinary Inspection Certificate)、卫生检验证书(Sanitary Inspection Certificate)、消毒检验证书(Inspection Certificate of Disinfection)、熏蒸/消毒证书(Fumigation/Disinfection Certificate)、温度检验证书(Certificate of Temperature)等。

 缮制说明

中华人民共和国出入境检验检疫
ENTRY-EXIT INSPECTION AND QUARRANTINE OF THE PEOPLE'S PRPUBLIC OF CHINA

植物检疫证书
PHYTOSANITARY CERTIFICATE

编号：
No.：

发货人名称及地址：出口商名称
Name and Address of Consignor……………………………………………
收货人名称及地址：进口商名称
Name and Address of Consignee…………………………………………
品名： 货物名统称   植物学名称：该货物的植物学名
Description of Produce………   Botanical Name of Plants…………
报验数量：成交数量   标记及号码：唛头
Quantity Declared……………   Mark & No.
包装种类及数量：外包装数量
Number and Type of Package…………………
产地：制造地
Place of Origin………………………………………
到达口岸：目的港
Port of Destination……………………………
运输工具：船名航次   检验日：送检日期
Means of Conveyance………… Date of Inspection……………

　　此证明上述植物、植物产品或其他检疫物已经按照规定程序进行检查和检验，被认为不带有输入国或地区的规定的检疫性有害物，并且基本上不带有其他的有害物，因而符合输入国或地区现行的植物检疫要求。
　　This to certify the plants, plant products or other regularted described above have been inspected and tested according to appropriate procedures and are considerde to be free from quarantine pests apecified by the importiong country/region, and practically free from other injurious pests; and that they are considered to confor with current phytosanitary requirements of the importing country/region.

杀虫和/灭菌处理 DISINFESTATION AND/OR DISINFE TREATMENT
日期：   药剂及浓度：
Date:……………………   Chemical & Concentration……………
处理方法：   持续时间及温度：
Treatment………………   Duration & Temperature………………
附加声明：
ADDITIONAL DECLARATION   CREDIT NUMBER：
印章：   签证地点：   签证日期：
Stamp   Place of Issue…………   Place of Issue…………
               授权签字人：   签名：
               Authorized Officer……… Signature………………

中华人民共和国出入境检验检疫机关及官员或代表不承担签发本证书的任何财经责任。
No. financial liability with respect to this certificate shall attach to the entry-exit inspection and quarantine authorities of the P. R. of China or any of its officers or represetives.

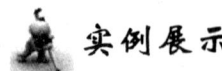

中华人民共和国出入境检验检疫
ENTRY-EXIT INSPECTION AND QUARRANTINE
OF THE PEOPLE'S PRPUBLIC OF CHINA

植物检疫证书
PHYTOSANITARY CERTIFICATE

编号 No.: 310900211001591

发货人名称及地址:
Name and Address of Consignor   SHANGHAI LIANGYOU GROUP CO., LTD.

收货人名称及地址:
Name and Address of Consignee   FUMING FEED CO., LTD.

品名: 植物学名称:
Description of Produce   WHEAT FLOUR   Botanical Name of Plants   ×××
                         (FEED GRADE)

报验数量: 标记及号码:
Quantity Declared   210 000KGS   Mark & No.

包装种类及数量:
Number and Type of Package   8 400BAGS   FUMING, THAILAND

产地:
Place of Origin   SHANGHAI

到达口岸:
Port of Destination   ***

运输工具: 检验日:
Means of Conveyance   BY CONTAINER   Date of Inspection   2015.03.07

　　此证明上述植物、植物产品或其他检疫物已经按照规定程序进行检查和检验,被认为不带有输入国或地区的规定的检疫性有害物,并且基本上不带有其他的有害物,因而符合输入国或地区现行的植物检疫要求。

　　This to certify the plants, plant products or other regularted described above have been inspected and tested according to appropriate procedures and are considerde to be free from quarantine pests apecified by the importiong country/region, and practically free from other injurious pests; and that they are considered to confor with current phytosanitary requirements of the importing country/region.

杀虫和/灭菌处理 DISINFESTATION AND/OR DISINFE TREATMENT

日期: 药剂及浓度:
Date   ***   Chemical & Concentration   ***

处理方法: 持续时间及温度:
Treatment   ***   Duration & Temperature   ***

                                             附加声明:
                                             ADDITIONAL DECLARATION
                                             * * * * * * * * * * * *

印章: 签证地点: 签证日期:
Stamp   Place of Issue   SHANGHAI   Place of Issue   MAR. 07, 2015
                     授权签字人: 签名:
                     Authorized Officer   ZHANGGE   Signature

中华人民共和国出入境检验检疫机关及官员或代表不承担签发本证书的任何财经责任。
No. financial liability with respect to this certificate shall attach to the entry-exit inspection and quarantine authorities of the P. R. of China or any of its officers or representatives.

任务二 认识非木质包装证明和受益人证明

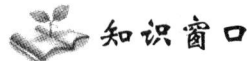

受益人证明是一种信用证受益人自制的,内容多样、格式简单,证明自己履行了信用证规定的条款,根据信用证的有关规定缮制的单据。例如,证明所交货物的品质、证明运输包装的处理、证明按要求寄单等,需严格与信用证规定的名称与内容相符。

1. 非木质包装声明

出口公司英文名称
出口公司英文地址
NON WOODEN PACKING DECLARATION

VESSEL NAME：船名　　　　　　　　　　　　VOYAGE NUMBER：　航次
CONSIGNMENT IDENTIFIER'(S) OR NUMERICAL LINK(S)：箱号
ALL TIMBER PACKAGING USED IN THE CONSIGNMENT CONTAINS NO SOLID WOOD MATERIALS.

SIGNED：___出口公司公章_____　　　　　　DATE OF ISSUE：开具日期
　　COMPANY REPRESENTATIVE

2. 受益人证明

出口商英语名称
出口商英语地址
BENEFICIARY'S CERTIFICATE

TO：进口商名称　　　　　　　　　　　　　　INVOICE NO.：发票号
S/C NO.：销售合同号　　　　　　　　　　　　L/C NO.：信用证编号

DEAR SIRS：
　　根据信用证要求填写

　　　　　　　　　　　　　　　　　　　　　　　　　　　出口商名称(公章)
　　　　　　　　　　　　　　　　　　　　　　　　　　　　　×××

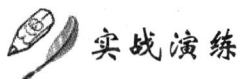

请根据上海凌烽进出口有限公司出口木制玩具的信用证、合同和相应资料缮制非木质包装证明和受益人证明。

1. 非木质包装声明

SHANGHAI LIANGYOU GROUP CO., LTD.
NO. 88 ZHANGYANG ROAD, SHANGHAI, CHINA 200122
NON WOODEN PACKING DECLARATION

VESSEL NAME:HALCYON   VOYAGE NUMBER: V1106S
CONSIGNMENT IDENTIFIER'(S) OR NUMERICAL LINK(S):8 400BAGS
ALL TIMBER PACKAGING USED IN THE CONSIGNMENT CONTAINS NO SOLID WOOD MATERIALS.

SIGNED:＿＿＿董勋＿＿＿＿   DATE OF ISSUE:＿JUL. 01,2014＿
COMPANY REPRESENTATIVE

2. 受益人证明

SHANGHAI LIANGYOU GROUP CO., LTD.
NO. 88 ZHANGYANG ROAD, SHANGHAI, CHINA 200122
BENEFICIARY'S CERTIFICATE

TO: FUMNING FEED CO., LTD.   INVOICE NO.: LY11SI-003-5
S/C NO.: LY11SC-003   L/C NO.: ML11000632

DEAR SIRS:
　　We hereby that one set of non-negotiable shipping documents together with the original from A have been sent to the applicant by airmail within 48 hours after the shipment.

SHANGHAI LIANGYOU GROUP CO., LTD
董勋

任务三　认识出口收汇核销单

CNY	人民币	HKD	港币
GBP	英镑	USD	美元
JPY	日元	AUD	澳元
EUR	欧元	CAD	加拿大元

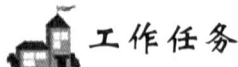

　　上海良友(集团)有限公司已收到银行的结汇水单，派小明去外汇管理局办理出口收汇核销手续。

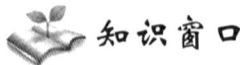

　　外汇管理局通过网上外汇核销管理出口收汇的工作。出口企业必须凭核销单及其他有关单据向海关办理出口货物报关，出口企业待货物装运后，向银行交单结汇，凭银行收款通知单才可以办理核销手续，提高了收汇管理工作的效率。

　　出口收汇核销是由国家外汇管理局统一印制，由出口企业和银行缮制，海关据以受理报关，各级外汇管理部门据以核销外汇的凭证。它由核销单存根、出口收汇核销单及其出口退税专用三联构成。

缮制说明

出口收汇核销单存根	出口收汇核销单	出口收汇核销单出口退税用
(沪)编号:统一印制	(沪)编号:	(沪)编号:

出口收汇核销单存根:
- 出口单位:出口商名并盖章
- 单位编码:税务登记的企业代码
- 出口币种总价:发票金额
- 收汇方式:合同规定收汇方式
- 约计收款日期:
- 报关日期:
- 备注:
- 此单报关有效截止到装运日期

出口收汇核销单:
- 出口单位盖章
- 出口单位:出口商名并盖章
- 单位编码:税务登记的企业代码
- 银行签注栏 | 类别 | 币种金额发票金额 | 盖章
- 海关签注栏:
- 外汇局签注栏: 年 月 日(盖章)

出口收汇核销单出口退税用:
- 出口单位盖章
- 出口单位:出口商名并盖章
- 单位编码:税务登记的企业代码
- 货物名称品名统称 | 数量外包装数量 | 币种总价发票金额
- 海关盖章
- 报关单编号:
- 外汇局签注栏: 年 月 日(盖章)

实例展示

出口收汇核销单存根	出口收汇核销单	出口收汇核销单出口退税用
(沪)编号:325623454	(沪)编号:325623454	(沪)编号:325623454

出口收汇核销单存根:
- 出口单位:上海良友(集团)有限公司
- 单位编码:62122133-6
- 出口币种总价:105 000.00 美元
- 收汇方式:L/C
- 约计手款日期:
- 报关日期:
- 备注:
- 此单报关有效截止到装运日期

出口收汇核销单:
- 出口单位盖章
- 出口单位:上海良友(集团)有限公司
- 单位编码:62122133-6
- 银行签注栏 | 类别 | 币种金额 105 000.00 美元
- 海关签注栏:
- 外汇局签注栏: 年 月 日(盖章)

出口收汇核销单出口退税用:
- 出口单位盖章
- 出口单位:上海良友(集团)有限公司
- 单位编码:62122133-6
- 货物名称 | 数量 | 币种总价 105 000.00 美元
- 海关盖章
- 报关单编号:
- 外汇局签注栏: 年 月 日(盖章)

项目九

审核单据

学习目的

◆ 知晓开证申请书的格式和内容
◆ 能根据合同正确填写信用证开证申请书
◆ 能知晓审核结汇单据的常见差错
◆ 能了解对不符点的灵活处理方法

任务一 缮制开证申请书

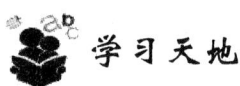

ISSUING BANK	开证银行
ADVISING BANK	通知银行
NEGOTIATION BANK	议付银行
OPENING BANK	开证银行
BILLS OF LADING	海运提单
AIR WAYBILLS	空运单
RAILWAY BILLS	铁路运单
CERTIFICATE OF ORIGIN	原产地证明
CERTIFICATE OF QUALITY	品质证明
BENEFICIARY'S CERTIFICAE	受益人证明

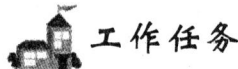

上海良友(集团)有限公司要进口原料,希望小明能够熟悉开证申请书的格式,并能学会缮制开证申请书。

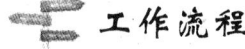

工作流程见图 9-1。

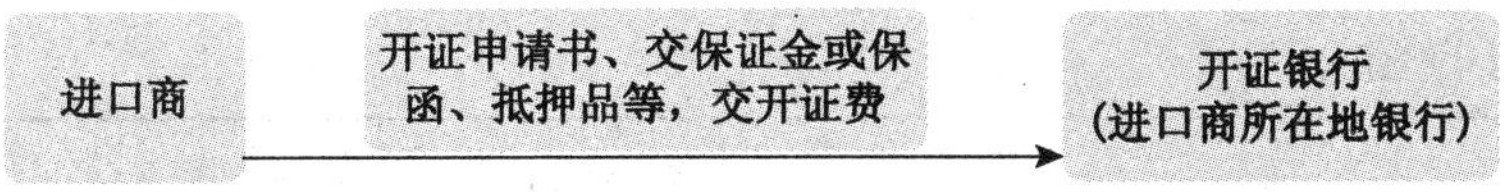

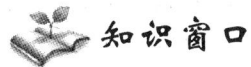

图 9-1 缮制开证申请书的工作流程

知识窗口

一、开证申请书的概念

开证申请书是银行开立信用证的依据,是申请人与开证行之间明确各自权利和义务的证明文件,也是双方的一种契约。采用信用证支付方式,进口商应在合同规定的开证时间内,尽快将信用证开出并由银行传递给出口商。

二、开立信用证应注意的问题

1. 开证申请书的依据

当进出口商在销售合同中约定,采用信用证支付方式时,应在合同中明确信用证的开出时间、开证行、信用证的种类等,以避免日后为信用证的开立引发争议,影响合同的履行。而开证申请书必须以买卖双方签订的销售合同为基础,认真缮制,因为合同条款中的品质条款、数量条款、支付条款、装运条款等,都会反映在信用证条款中。

2. 开立信用证应注意的问题

(1) 申请开立信用证前,对于国家监管商品,务必要落实好进口批准手续,做好购汇准备。

(2) 开证申请书填写完毕后,为节约日后的改证费用等,可先将填写好的开证申请书传真或电邮给出口商审核,双方达成一致后,再开立信用证。

(3) 由于在信用证支付方式下,付款银行是第一付款人,所以开证时必须列明受益人所需提交的单据种类及份数。

(4) 国际贸易也是"单据交易",付款人某些时候付款是以单据符合要求为前提的,并不管货物质量如何,因此在开证时要求受益人提供双方认可的检验检疫机构出具的检验证书。

(5) 开证申请书文字应力求规范。进口商要求开证银行在信用证上载明的事项,必须完整、明确,避免使用"适宜海运""尽快装运"字样。

缮制说明

凡经营国际结算业务的银行都有自己的信用证开证申请书,格式不尽相同,但内容基本一致。

开证申请书（Application for Issuing L/C）

TO(1)：开证行名称

Applicant(full name and address) (2) 进口商名称、地址	L/C NO. (3) ×××××××××× Ex-Card No. Contract No. 合同号		
Beneficiary (full name and address)(4) 出口商名称、地址	Date and place of expiry of the credit(5)到期时间和地点 到期时间：合同最迟装运日＋交单天数 到期地点一般为出口国境内		
Partial shipments（6）分批装运 ○ allowed ○ not allowed	Transshipment（7）转运 ○ allowed ○ not allowed	○ Issue by airmail 以信开方式 ○ With brief advice by teletransmission 以简电方式 ○ Issue by express delivery 快递 ○ Issue by teletransmission (which shall be the operative instrument) 简电后随寄电报证实书 （8）信用证传递方式	
Loading on board / dispatch / taking in（9）charge at / from 装运港 Not later than 最迟装运期 for transportation to 目的港	Amount (both in figures and words)(10) 信用证金额大小写同时填列		
Description of goods(11) 方法一：具体写品名、规格、数量、单价、术语 方法二：写品名统称 AS PER S/C NO. ×××××	Credit available with(12)汇票条款 ○ by sight payment 即期付款 ○ by acceptance 承兑付款 ○ by negotiation 议付 ○ by deferred payment at 延期付款 against the documents detailed herein ○ and beneficiary's draft for 100 ％ of the invoice value 汇票金额 at sight 汇票付款期限 on 开证行名称		
	○ FOB ○ or other terms（13）成交方式	○ CFR	○ CIF
Documents required：(marked with ×)(14)提交单据要求，明确勾选单据种类及份数 (　　) Signed Commercial Invoice in ____ copies indicating invoice no., contract no. 签署的商业发票，一式____份，显示发票号、合同号。 (　　) Full set of clean on board ocean Bills of Lading made out to order ____ and blank endorsed, marked "freight (　　) to collect / (　　) prepaid (　　) and notifying.			

(续表)

全套的海运提单,凭____指示和空白背书,注明运费(____)到付/(____)预付,并通知____。
(   ) Air Waybills showing freight (   ) to collect / (   ) prepaid (   ) and consigned to _____.
收货人为申请人的航空运单,标明"运费到付/预付"并显示运费金额。
(   ) Memorandum issued by _____ consigned to _____.
由_____出具的发货备忘录,以_____为收货人。
(   ) Insurance Policy / Certificate in _____ copies for _____% of the invoice value showing claims payable in China in currency of the draft, bank endorsed, covering (   ) Ocean Marine Transportation / (   ) Air Transportation / (   ) Over Land Transportation) _____.
全套保险单或(预约保险下的)保险凭证(包括正本与副本),投保发票金额____%,标明赔付地点为中国赔付货币与汇票所用货币相同,空白背书,投保"海洋运输/航空运输/陆路运输"的一切险与战争险。
(   ) Packing List / Weight Memo in _____ copies indicating quantity / gross and net weights of each package and packing conditions as called for by the L/C.
装箱单/重量单正本与副本,由××签发,显示每件货物的数量,毛净重及L/C所要求的包装状况。
(   ) Certificate of Quantity / Weight in _____ copies issued an independent surveyor at the loading port, indicating the actual surveyed quantity / weight of shipped goods as well as the packing condition.
数量/重量证明的正本与副本,在装运港由_____签发,显示出运货物的实测数量/重量及包装状况。
(   ) Certificate of Quality in ____ copies issued by (   ) manufacturer / (   ) public recognized surveyor.
品质证明的正本与副本,由制造商/公共机构签发。
(   ) Beneficiary's certifie copy of FAX dispatched to the accountees with ____ days after shipment advising (   ) name of vessel / (   ) date, quantity, weight and value of shipment.
受益人在货物出运后××小时内告知申请人"船名/航班号/车厢号",出货日期,数量,重量及出运货物货值的"电报/电传/传真"证明。
(   ) Beneficiary's Certificate certifying that extra copies of the documents have been dispatched according to the contract terms.
受益人证明,根据合同条款所要求的那些文件的额外副本已被提交。
(   ) Shipping Co's Certificate attesting that the carrying vessel is chartered or booked by accountee or their shipping agents.
船公司证实装运船只由开证申请人或货代租用或预定。
(   ) Other documents, if any:
其他单据要求:
(a) Certificate of Origin in 3 copies issued by authorized institution.
    权威机构签发的原产地证明三份。
(b) Certificate of Health in 3 copies issued by authorized institution.
    权威机构签发的健康/检疫证明三份。
Additional instructions:
(1) (   ) All banking charges outside the opening bank are for beneficiary's account.
    除开证行之外的所有银行费用由受益人承担。
(2) (   ) Documents must be presented with _____ days after the date of issuance of the transport documents but within the validity of this credit.
    运输单据提交后____日内,在信用证的有效期内相关文件必须提交。
(3) (   ) Third party as shipper is not acceptable. Short Form / Blank Back B/L is not acceptable.
    禁止第三方作发货人,简式/背面空白提单不被接受。
(4) (   ) Both quantity and amount _____% more or less are allowed.
    数量与金额允许有____%的溢短装。
(5) (   ) Prepaid freight drawn in excess of L/C amount is acceptable against presentation of origi-

(续表)

> nal charges voucher issued by Shipping Co. / Air line / or it's agent.
> 在提交船公司/航空公司/其代理签发的原始费用凭证后,其超出信用证规定金额的预付费用可以授受。
> (6) (　) All documents to be forwarded in one cover, unless otherwise stated above.
> 除非上述另有规定外,所有单据要求一次全部提交。
> (7) (　) Other terms, if any.
> Advising bank:
> 通知行

Account No.:进口商账号

Transacted by:进口商名称

(Applicant: name, signature of authorized person)

 实例展示

SHANGHAI JINYUN FLOORING TECHNOLOGY CO., LTD.
1000 JUDAI ROAD, EAST IND. DISTRICT, WAI-GANG, JIA-DING SHANGHAI, CHINA

TEL:+86(21) 69475968　　FAX:+86(21) 69476967

购货合同

PURCHASES CONTRACT

卖方:TRICON DRY CHEMICALS, CO., LTD.
Sellers:

Contract No.: JY2012X06

Date: Mar 11st, 2015

Signedat: SHANGHAI

地址:
Address:888 POST OAK BLVD SUITE 670　HOUSTON TEXAS 77056 USA

This Sales Contract is made by and between the sellers and the buyers, whereby the sellers agree to sell and buyers agree to buy the under—mentioned goods according to the terms and conditions stipulated below:

(1) 货号、品名及规格 Name of Commodity and specifications	(2) 数量 Quantity	(3) 单位 Unit	(4) 单价 Unit Price	(5) 金额 Amount
PVC SUSPENSION RESIN PVC 225P PACKING: BIG BAG IN 40FT CONTAINER COUNTRY OF ORIGIN: USA	506	MT	CIFSHANGHAI USD 1 000 /MT	USD 506 000.00
	Total AMOUNT			USD 506 000.00

(6) Packing：CARTON (7) Delivery From ANY PORT IN USA to SHANGHAI, CHINA.

(8) Time of Shipment：APR 15TH, 2015, allowing transshipment and partial shipment.

(9) Terms of Payment：By 100% Irrevocable Letter of Credit in favor of the sellers to be available by after 60 days of B/L date draft to be opened and to reach the seller before APR. 10, 2015 and to remain valid for negotiation in China until the 21th days after the foresaid time of shipment.

(10) Insurance：To be effected by sellers for 110% of full invoice value covering ALL RISKS AND WAR RISK up to USA.

(11) Arbitration：Allstipuations arising from the execution of or in connection with this contract shall be settled amicabley negotiation. The arbitral award is final and binding upon both parties for settling the dispute. The fee for arbitration shal be borne by the losing party unless otherwise awarded.

The Seller：	The Buyer：
TRICON DRYCHEMICALS, CO. LTD	SHANGHAI JINYUN FLOORING TECHNOLOGY CO., LTD
MARTIN	李今云

ABCS(2009)3011a

(See box marked with "×"　　用"×"在方框中标识)

APPLICATION FOR IRREVOCABLE DOCUMENTARY CREDIT
开立不可撤销跟单信用证申请书

Date 日期：Mar 31st, 2015

This Credit is subject to Uniform Customs and Practice for Documentary Credits (2007 Revision) International Chamber of Commerce Publication No. 600.

此信用证遵循国际商会第 600 号出版物《跟单信用证统一惯例》(2007 年版本)

To：AGRICULTURAL BANK OF CHINA BRANCH 致：中国农业银行 嘉定支 行	Credit No. 信用证号码
[ ] Issued by mail 信开 [ ] With brief advice by teletransmission 简电开 [×] Issued by swift 电开	Expiry Date　　May 6th, 2015 Expiry Place　　有效交单地 [ ] _____(开证行所在国家/地区) [ ] _____(指定银行所在国家/地区) [×] in ___USA___(受益人所在国家/地区)
Applicant 申请人 SHANGHAI JINYUN FLOORING TECHNOLOGY CO., LTD. 1000 JUDAI ROAD, EAST IND. DISTRICT, WAI-GANG, JIA-DING, SHANGHAI, CHINA TTEL：+86(21) 69475968 FAX：+86(21) 69476967	Beneficiary(with full name and address)受益人 (全称和详细地址) TRICON DRY CHEMICALS, LLC 888POST OAK BLVD SUITE 670 HOUSTON TEXAS 77056 USA

(续表)

Advising Bank(if blank, at your option)通知行 RABOBANK NEDERLAND SWIFT CODE:RABONL2U	Currency and Amount(in figures & words)币种及金额(大、小写) USD 506 000.00

[ ] Place of taking in charge/Dispatch from…/Place of receipt 接管/从……发送/收货地
[ ] Place of final destination/For transportation to…/place of delivery 目的地/运至……/交付地
[×] Port of loading 装货港   ANY PORT IN USA   [ ] Airport of departure 起飞机场
[×] Port of discharge 卸货港   SHANGHAI, CHINA   [ ] Airport of destination 目的地机场
[×] Latest date of Shipment 最迟装运日   APR 15TH, 2015

Instalment Shipment(Specify, if any)分期装运: (如有,请具体列明)	Credit available with 此证由 __ANY BANK,__ (bank 银行) by [ ] sight payment 即期付款 [ ] deferred payment at _____ days after _____ date ____日后____天延期付款 [ ] acceptance 承兑 [×] negotiation 议付 against the documents required herein 连同下列所需单据, [×] and beneficiary's draft(s) [ ] at _____ day(s) sight/[×] at __60__ days after __B/L__ date drawn on __ISSUING BANK__ for __100__ % of invoice value. 及受益人按发票金额_____%,做成以_____为付款人,期限为_____□见票后____天/□_____日后_____天的汇票。
Partial shipments 部分装运 [×] allowed 允许 [ ] not allowed 不允许	Transhipment 转运 [×] allowed 允许 [ ] not allowed 不允许
Trade term 贸易术语 [ ] FOB [ ] CFR [×] CIF __SHANGHAI__ [ ] FCA [ ] CPT [ ] CIP __ [ ] other(please specify) 其他(请列明)____	

Description of goods 货物描述 PVC SUSPENSION RESIN PVC225P 506.00MTS AT USD 1 000.00/MT CIF SHANGHAI
PACKING:BIG BAG IN 40FT CONTAINER COUNTRY OF ORIGIN:USA
[ ] see attachment(s) 详见附件
Documents required:
[×] Signed Commercial Invoice in __3__ original(s) and in ____ copy(copies) indicating L/C No. and Contract No. __JY2015X06__.
　经签字的商业发票正本__份,副本__份,标明信用证号和合同号_____。
[×] Full /[ ] ____ set of clean on board Ocean Bill of Lading made out[×] to order /[ ] to ____ and blank endorsed, marked "freight [×] prepaid/ [ ] to collect", [ ] showing freight amount and notifying __Applicant__.
[ ] 全套/[ ] ____套清洁已装船海运提单做成[ ]空白抬头/[ ]____为抬头、空白背书,注明"运费[ ]已付/[ ]待付",[ ]标明运费金额,并通知_____。
[ ] Clean Air Waybill consigned to _____ marked "freight [ ] prepaid/ [ ] to collect" notifying

(续表)

清洁空运单收货人为＿＿＿＿＿＿＿＿＿＿＿＿＿＿＿＿＿，注明"运费〔　〕已付/〔　〕待付"，并通知＿＿＿＿＿＿＿＿＿＿＿＿＿＿。

〔×〕 Insurance Policy/Certificate in full set for __110__ % of the 〔×〕 invoice value/〔　〕Value of goods, blank endorsed, indicate that the risks are covered at least between ＿＿＿＿＿ (place of taking in charge or shipment) and ＿＿＿＿＿ (place of discharge or final destination) showing claims payable at __In China__, in the currency of the draft, covering All risks, War risk as per ocean marine transportation.

　　全套保险单/保险凭证，按〔　〕发票金额/〔　〕货物价值的＿＿＿％投保，空白背书，注明至少包括从＿＿＿＿＿(接管或发运地)到(卸货地或最终目的地)的风险，注明赔付＿＿＿＿＿，以汇票同种货币支付，投保一切险，战争险＿＿＿＿＿。

〔×〕 Packing List/Weight Memo in __3 originals indicating total quantity, total gross weight and total net weight__ original(s) and in ＿ copy(copies) indicating quantity, gross and net weight of each package.

　　装运单/重量证明正本＿份，副本＿份，注明每一包装的数量、毛重和净重。

〔　〕 Certificate of Quantity/Weight in original(s) and in ＿ copy(copies) issued by ＿＿＿＿＿.

　　数量/重量证明正本＿＿份，副本＿＿份，由＿＿＿＿＿＿＿＿＿＿出具。

〔×〕 Certificate of Quality in ＿＿ original(s) and in __3__ copy(copies) issued by __Beneficiary__.

　　品质证正本＿份，副本＿份，由＿＿＿＿＿＿＿＿＿＿出具。

〔×〕 Certificate of Origin in __3__ original(s) and in ＿ copy(copies) issued by __Beneficiary__.

　　产地证正本＿份，副本＿份，由＿＿＿＿＿＿＿＿＿＿出具。

〔　〕 Beneficiary's Certified copy of fax/telex dispatched to the applicant within ＿＿＿＿ day(s) after shipment advising L/C No., name of Vessel/flight No., date of shipment, name of goods, quantity, weight and value of goods.

　　受益人传真/电传方式通知申请人装运证明副本。该证明须在装运后＿＿＿＿天内发出，并注明该信用证号、船名/航班号、装运日以及货物的名称、货物的数量、重量和金额。

〔×〕 Other documents or see attachment(s), if any. 其他单据或详见附件。

(1) Beneficiary's certificate certifying that solid wood packing materials has been fumigated(MB) or heat treated (HT) and marked in accordance with regulations or shipment contains no solid wood packing material.

(2) Original beneficiary's certificate certifying that a non-negotiable set of documents has been faxed to the applicant by Fax ＋＋86(21) 69476967 Attn: Stephen Chang after shipment

Additional instructions: 附加条款

〔×〕 All banking charges outside the Issuing Bank andreimbursing charges 〔　〕 and ＿＿＿＿＿ charges are for account of Beneficiary.

　　开证行以外的所有银行费用(包括可能产生的偿付费用及＿＿＿＿＿费用)由受益人承担。

〔×〕 All document(s) must be made within __21__ days after date of shipment but not later than the expiry date of Credit.

　　包含运输单据正本的单据，须在装运日后＿＿＿天内提交，但不得迟于信用证有效期。

〔×〕 Both quantity and Credit amount __5__ % more or less are 〔×〕 allowed 〔　〕 not allowed.

　　数量及信用证金额〔　〕允许 〔　〕不允许 有＿＿＿％的增减。

〔　〕 Confirmation instruction: 〔　〕 Without 〔　〕 May add 〔　〕 Confirm

　　保兑指示:〔　〕不加保 〔　〕可以加保 〔　〕保兑

〔×〕 Other terms and conditions or see attachment(s), if any. 其他条款或详见附件。

(1) All document to be forwarded in one cover. Unless otherwise stated above.

(2) All documents presented under this credit must be expressed in theEnglish language.

(续表)

(3) The number and date of the credit and name of bank must be quoted on all drafts required.
(4) Insurance certificate must be 1 originals plus 1 duplicate.
(5) Third Party documents are acceptable except invoice and draft.

本信用证为履行第_____号进口合同开立,开证前应存开证保证金为开证金额的_____%,即(币种及金额大写)_____,其余信用证金额申请减免保证金。本笔开证业务受编号为_____的 □《进口开证合同》/□《进口开证额度合同》的约束。

申请人声明:贵行已依法向我方提示了本申请书及其背面承诺书相关条款(特别是黑体字条款),应我方要求对相关条款的概念、内容及法律效果做了说明,我方已经知悉并理解上述条款。

申请人(签章)
法定代表人
或授权代理人
年　月　日

ABCS(2009)3011b

开证申请人承诺书

我公司已依法办妥一切必要的进口手续,兹谨请贵行直接或通过贵行上级行为我公司依照本申请书所列条款开立不可撤销跟单信用证,并承诺如下:

一、遵守《开立不可撤销跟单信用证申请书》和《进口开证合同》/《进口开证额度合同》的约定。同意贵行依照国际商会第600号出版物《跟单信用证统一惯例》办理该信用证项下的一切事宜,并同意承担由此产生的一切责任。

二、及时提供贵行要求我公司提供的真实、有效的文件及资料,接受贵行的审查监督。

三、在贵行规定期限内支付该信用证项下的各种款项,包括货款及贵行和有关银行的各项手续费、杂费、利息以及国外受益人拒绝承担的有关银行费用等。

四、当实际存入保证金币种与开证币种不同时,愿意承担汇率变动风险。在信用证付款时,由于汇率变动导致所缴纳保证金不足的,我公司保证补交其中的差额。

五、在贵行《对外付款/承兑通知书》/《境内付款/承兑通知书》规定的期限内,书面通知贵行办理对外付款/承兑/确认延期付款/拒付手续。否则,贵行有权自行确定对外付款/承兑/确认延期付款/拒付,并由我公司承担全部责任。

六、我公司如因单证有不符之处而拟拒绝付款/承兑/确认延期付款时,将在贵行《对外付款/承兑通知书》/《境内付款/承兑通知书》规定期限内向贵行提出书面拒付请求,一次列明所有不符点。对单据存在的不符点,贵行有独立的终结认定权和处理权。经贵行根据国际惯例审核认为不属可据以拒付的不符点的,贵行有权主动对外付款/承兑/确认延期付款,我公司对此放弃抗辩权。

七、该信用证如需修改,由我公司向贵行提出书面申请,贵行可根据具体情况确定能否办理修改。我公司确认所有修改当受益人接受时才能生效。

八、经贵行承兑的远期汇票或确认的延期付款,我公司无权以任何理由要求贵行止付。

九、按上述承诺,贵行在对外付款时,有权主动借记我公司在贵行的账户款项。若发生任何形式的垫付,我公司将无条件承担由此而产生的债务、利息和费用等,并按贵行要求及时清偿。

十、在收到贵行开出信用证、修改书的副本之后,及时核对,如有不符之处,将在收到副本后的两个工作日内书面通知贵行。否则,视为正确无误。

十一、该信用证如因邮寄、电讯传递发生遗失、延误、错漏,贵行概不负责。

十二、本申请书及附件一律用英文填写。如用中文填写而引发的歧义,贵行概不负责。

十三、因信用证申请书及附件字迹不清或词意含混而引起的一切后果均由我公司负责。

十四、如发生争议需要诉讼或仲裁的,约束本笔开证业务的《进口开证合同》/《进口开证额度合同》,合同有约定的从其约定,无约定的由贵行住所地法院管辖。

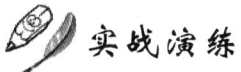 实战演练

上海良友(集团)有限公司
中国上海张杨路88号
SHANGHAI LIANGYOU GROUP CO., LTD.
NO. 88 ZHANGJIANG ROAD SHANGHAI, CHINA 200122

购货合同
PURCHASES CONTRACT

卖方 TARAKA FOOD COMPANY　　　　　ContractNo.:1Y2013T106
Sellers:　　　　　　　　　　　　　　　　Date:AUG.08,2014
地址:　　　　　　　　　　　　　　　　　Signedat:SHANGHAI
Address:1-15 ISUKI-CHONHAKI, TOKYO, JAPAN

This Sales Contract is made by and between the Sellers and the Buyers, whereby the sellers agree to sell and buyers agree to buy the under—mentioned goods according to the terms and conditions stipulated below:

(1) 货号、品名及规格 Name of Commodity and specifications	(2) 数量 Quantity	(3) 单位 Unit	(4) 单价 Unit Price	(5) 金额 Amount
JAPANESE RICE F.A.Q. 2014 BROKEN GRAINE<18% ADMIXTURE<0.2% MOISTURE<8% COUNTRY OF ORIGIN:JAPAN	1 000	KG	CFR SHANGHAI USD 36.00/KG	USD 36 000.00
	Total AMOUNT			USD 36 000.00

(6) Packing:5KGS/BAG.

(7) Delivery From TOKYO JAPAN to SHANGHAI CHINA.

(8) Time of Shipment: DEC 15TH, 2014, transshipment and partial shipment not allowing.

(9) Terms of Payment: The buyer shall open an L/C at sight draft to reach the sellers before SEP. 12, 2014 and to remain valid for negotiation in China until the 21th days after the foresaid Time of Shipment.

(10) Insurance: To be effected by Sellers for 110% of full invoice value covering ALL RISKS as per and subject to Ocean Marine Cargo Clauses of PICC date 1/1/1981.

(11) Arbitration: All stipuations arising from the execution of or in connection with this contract shall be settled amicabley negotiation. The arbitral award is final and binding upon both parties for settling the Dispute. The fee for arbitration shal be borne by the losing party unless otherwise awarded.

The Seller:
TARAKA FOOD COMPANY CO., LTD.
KATE
ABCS(2009)3011a

The Buyer:
SHANGHAI LIANGYOU GROUP
傅雷

(See box marked with "×" 用"×"在方框中标识)

APPLICATION FOR IRREVOCABLE DOCUMENTARY CREDIT
开立不可撤销跟单信用证申请书

Date 日期:_____

This Credit is subject to Uniform Customs and Practice for Documentary Credits (2007 Revision) International Chamber of Commerce Publication No. 600.
此信用证遵循国际商会第 600 号出版物《跟单信用证统一惯例》(2007 年版本)

To: AGRICULTURAL BANK OF CHINA BRANCH 致:中国农业银行嘉定支行	Credit No. 信用证号码
[ ] Issued by mail 信开 [ ] With brief advice by teletransmission 简电开 [ ] Issued by swift 电开	Expiry Date Expiry Place 有效交单地 [ ] _____(开证行所在国家/地区) [ ] _____(指定银行所在国家/地区) [ ] in _____(受益人所在国家/地区)
Applicant 申请人	Beneficiary(with full name and address)受益人 (全称和详细地址)
Advising Bank(if blank, at your option)通知行	Currency and Amount(in figures & words)币种及金额(大、小写)

（续表）

[ ] Place of taking in charge/Dispatch from…/Place of receipt 接管/从……发送/收货地 [ ] Place of final destination/For transportation to…/place of delivery 目的地/运至……/交付地 [ ] Port of loading 装货港 [ ] Airport of departure 起飞机场 [ ] Port of discharge 卸货港 [ ] Airport of destination 目的地机场 [ ] Latest date of Shipment 最迟装运日	

Instalment Shipment(Specify, if any) 分期装运：（如有，请具体列明）		Credit available with 此证由_____（bank 银行）by [ ] sight payment 即期付款 [ ] deferred payment at ____ days after ____ date ____ 日后____天延期付款 [ ] acceptance 承兑 [ ] negotiation 议付 against the documents required herein 连同下列所需单据， [ ] and beneficiary's draft(s)[ ] at _____ day(s) sight/[ ] at _____ days after ___ date drawn on _____ for ____ % of invoice value. 及受益人按发票金额_____ %，做成以_____为付款人，期限为_____[ ]见票后____天/[ ]_____日后____天的汇票。
Partial shipments 部分装运 [ ] allowed 允许 [ ] not allowed 不允许	Transhipment 转运 [ ] allowed 允许 [ ] not allowed 不允许	
Trade term 贸易术语 [ ] FOB [ ] CFR [ ] CIF [ ] FCA [ ] CPT [ ] CIP [ ] other(please specify)其他（请列明）____		

Description of goods 货物描述
 	
[ ] see attachment(s) 详见附件
Documents required：
[ ] Signed Commercial Invoice in ____ original(s) and in __ copy(copies) indicating L/C No. and Contract No. _____.
    经签字的商业发票正本__份，副本__份，标明信用证号和合同号_____。
[ ] Full /[ ] ____ set of clean on board Ocean Bill of Lading made out[×] to order /[ ] to ____ and blank endorsed, marked "freight [ ] prepaid/ [ ] to collect", [ ] showing freight amount and notifying _____.
    []全套/[ ]____套清洁已装船海运提单做成[ ]空白抬头/[ ]_____为抬头、空白背书，注明"运费[ ]已付/[ ]待付"，[ ]标明运费金额，并通知_____。
[ ] Clean Air Waybill consigned to _____ marked "freight [ ] prepaid/ [ ] to collect" notifying _____。
    清洁空运单收货人为_____，注明"运费[ ]已付/[ ]待付"，并通知_____。
[ ] Insurance Policy/Certificate in full set for ____ % of the [×]invoice value/ [ ] Value of goods, blank endorsed, indicate that the risks are covered at least between _____ (place of taking in charge or shipment) and _____ (place of discharge or final destination) showing claims payable at _____, in the currency of the draft, covering All risks, War risk ____.
    全套保险单/保险凭证，按[ ]发票金额/[ ]货物价值的_____%投保，空白背书，注明至少包括从_____（接管或发运地）到（卸货地或最终目的地）的风险，注明赔付_____，以汇票同种货币支付，投保一切险、战争险_____。
[ ] Packing List/Weight Memo in _____ original(s) and in __ copy(copies) indicating quantity, gross and net weight of each package.

（续表）

装运单/重量证明正本__份,副本__份,注明每一包装的数量、毛重和净重。
[ ] Certificate of Quantity/Weight in original(s) and in __ copy(copies) issued by _____.
数量/重量证明正本____份,副本__份,由_____出具。
[ ] Certificate of Quality in original(s) and in ____ copy(copies) issued by _____.
品质证正本__份,副本__份,由_____出具。
[ ] Certificate of Origin in _____ original(s) and in __ copy(copies) issued by _____.
产地证正本__份,副本__份,由_____出具。
[ ] Beneficiary's Certified copy of fax/telex dispatched to the applicant within _____ day(s) after shipment advising L/C No., name of Vessel/flight No., date of shipment, name of goods, quantity, weight and value of goods.
受益人传真/电传方式通知申请人装运证明副本。该证明须在装运后____天内发出,并注明该信用证号、船名/航班号、装运日以及货物的名称,货物的数量、重量和金额。
[ ] Other documents or see attachment(s), if any. 其他单据或详见附件。
(1) Beneficiary's certificate certifying that solid wood packing materials has been fumigated(MB) or heat treated (HT) and marked in accordance with regulations or shipment contains no solid wood packing material.
(2) Original beneficiary's certificate certifying that a non-negotiable set of documents has been faxed to the applicant by Fax ＋86(21) 69476967 Attn：Stephen Chang after shipment.
Additional instructions：附加条款
[ ] All banking charges outside the Issuing Bank andreimbursing charges [ ] and _____ charges are for account of Beneficiary.
开证行以外的所有银行费用(包括可能产生的偿付费用及_____费用)由受益人承担。
[ ] All document(s) must be made within _____ days after date of shipment but not later than the expiry date of Credit.
包含运输单据正本的单据,须在装运日后____天内提交,但不得迟于信用证有效期。
[ ] Both quantity and Credit amount ____% more or less are [×] allowed [ ] not allowed.
数量及信用证金额[ ]允许 [ ]不允许 有____%的增减。
[ ] Confirmation instruction：[ ] Without [ ] May add [ ] Confirm
保兑指示：[ ]不加保 [ ]可以加保 [ ]保兑
[ ] Other terms and conditions or see attachment(s), if any. 其他条款或详见附件。
(1) All document to be forwarded in one cover. Unless otherwise stated above.
(2) All documents presented under this credit must be expressed in theEnglish language.
(3) The number and date of the credit and name of bank must be quoted on all drafts required.
(4) Insurance certificate must be 1 originals plus 1 duplicate.
(5) Third Party documents are acceptable except invoice and draft.
本信用证为履行第_____号进口合同开立,开证前应存开证保证金为开证金额的_____%,即(币种及金额大写)_____,其余信用证金额申请减免保证金。本笔开证业务受理编号为_____的 □《进口开证合同》/□《进口开证额度合同》的约束。
申请人声明：贵行已依法向我方提示了本申请书及其背面承诺书相关条款(特别是黑体字条款),应我方要求对相关条款的概念、内容及法律效果做了说明,我方已经知悉并理解上述条款。

申请人(签章)
法定代表人
或授权代理人
年 月 日

ABCS(2009)3011b

开证申请人承诺书

我公司已依法办妥一切必要的进口手续，兹谨请贵行直接或通过贵行上级行为我公司依照本申请书所列条款开立不可撤销跟单信用证，并承诺如下：

一、遵守《开立不可撤销跟单信用证申请书》和《进口开证合同》/《进口开证额度合同》的约定。同意贵行依照国际商会第600号出版物《跟单信用证统一惯例》办理该信用证项下的一切事宜，并同意承担由此产生的一切责任。

二、及时提供贵行要求我公司提供的真实、有效的文件及资料，接受贵行的审查监督。

三、在贵行规定期限内支付该信用证项下的各种款项，包括货款及贵行和有关银行的各项手续费、杂费、利息以及国外受益人拒绝承担的有关银行费用等。

四、当实际存入保证金币种与开证币种不同时，愿意承担汇率变动风险。在信用证付款时，由于汇率变动导致所缴纳保证金不足的，我公司保证补交其中的差额。

五、在贵行《对外付款/承兑通知书》/《境内付款/承兑通知书》规定的期限内，书面通知贵行办理对外付款/承兑/确认延期付款/拒付手续。否则，贵行有权自行确定对外付款/承兑/确认延期付款/拒付，并由我公司承担全部责任。

六、我公司如因单证有不符之处而拟拒绝付款/承兑/确认延期付款时，将在贵行《对外付款/承兑通知书》/《境内付款/承兑通知书》规定期限内向贵行提出书面拒付请求，一次列明所有不符点。对单据存在的不符点，贵行有独立的终结认定权和处理权。经贵行根据国际惯例审核认为不属可据以拒付的不符点的，贵行有权主动对外付款/承兑/确认延期付款，我公司对此放弃抗辩权。

七、该信用证如需修改，由我公司向贵行提出书面申请，贵行可根据具体情况确定能否办理修改。我公司确认所有修改当受益人接受时才能生效。

八、经贵行承兑的远期汇票或确认的延期付款，我公司无权以任何理由要求贵行止付。

九、按上述承诺，贵行在对外付款时，有权主动借记我公司在贵行的账户款项。若发生任何形式的垫付，我公司将无条件承担由此而产生的债务、利息和费用等，并按贵行要求及时清偿。

十、在收到贵行开出信用证、修改书的副本之后，及时核对，如有不符之处，将在收到副本后的两个工作日内书面通知贵行。否则，视为正确无误。

十一、该信用证如因邮寄、电讯传递发生遗失、延误、错漏，贵行概不负责。

十二、本申请书及附件一律用英文填写。如用中文填写而引发的歧义，贵行概不负责。

十三、因信用证申请书及附件字迹不清或词意含混而引起的一切后果均由我公司负责。

十四、如发生争议需要诉讼或仲裁的，约束本笔开证业务的《进口开证合同》/《进口开证额度合同》，合同有约定的从其约定，无约定的由贵行住所地法院管辖。

任务二 审核结汇单据

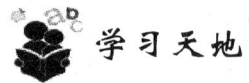

COMMERCIAL INVOICE	商业发票	BILLS OF LADING	海运提单
AIR WAYBILLS	空运单	INSURANCE POLICY	保险单
PACKING LIST	装箱单	WEIGHT MEMO	重量单
CERTIFICATE OF QUANTITY	数量证明		
CERTIFICATE OF QUALITY	品质证明		
BENEFICARY'S CERTIFICATE	受益人证明		
CERTIFICATE OF ORIGIN	原产地证明		

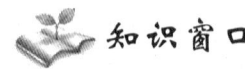

单据审核是对已经缮制、备妥或需付款的单据对照信用证(信用证支付项下)或合同(汇付、托收项下)的有关条款进行单证、单单、单同及时进行审核,发现问题可及时更正,顺利履行合约,同时可加强收付汇工作的有效性。

一、企业审单的基本要求

1. 正确

"相符交单"原则是安全收付汇的前提和基础,所以提交的单据要严格符合信用证或合同要求,同时参照《信用证统一惯例》和《国际标准银行实务》,保证单据不存在任何不符的小差错,避免造成难以挽回的损失。

2. 及时

从全面履行合同的要求出发,认真审核单据。不放过任何一个不符点,一旦发现,及时沟通、及时改正,在交单期内妥善处理问题单据,尽量不影响收汇的安全。

3. 全面审核

审核一般由制单员或审单员进行初审,必要时应当对有关单据进行复审。审核以商业发票为中心审核其他结汇单据,要求有关单据的内容严格符合信用证的规定,做到"单证相符""单单相符"。全面审核的要点有以下各项:

(1) 规定提交的单证是否齐全,包括所需单证的份数。
(2) 所提供的文件名称和类型是否符合信用证或合同条款的要求。
(3) 规定需认证的单证是否按信用证或合同规定进行了认证。
(4) 规定提交单证之间的收发货人名称、地址是否正确,是否符合信用证或合同规定。
(5) 货物描述、数量、金额、重量、体积、运输标志等是否一致,是否符合信用证或合同规定。

(6) 规定提交的单证出具日期是否符合信用证或合同条款要求。

(7) 应加背书的相关单据,须加背书。

二、银行审单

跟单信用证统一惯例规定,按指定行事的指定银行、保兑银行(如有)及开证行须审核交单,并仅基于单据本身确定其是否在表面上构成相符交单。

1. 按信用证规定的条款审单

信用证是根据交易双方签订的贸易合同而开立的,在其结算过程中,各有关当事人必须受其约束,按信用证所规定的条款,逐条对照,以确定单据是否满足信用证的要求。受益人提交的单据名称及其内容等表面上必须与信用证规定一致。

2. 按照国际惯例审单

《跟单信用证统一惯例》和《关于审核 UCP600 下单据的国际标准银行实务》是国际商会在信用证领域编纂的国际惯例,是各国银行、进出口公司信用证业务单据处理人员在工作中的必备工具。银行必须根据惯例要求,合理、谨慎地审核信用证要求的所有单据,以确保其表面上是否符合信用证条款。

三、对"单证不符"的处理

所谓"单证不符"是指信用证受益人向银行提交的结汇单据存在不符合信用证条款规定的内容。在国际贸易的履约过程中,由于制单过程的粗心大意,或者出口商发货备货时的意外,都有可能造成"单证不符""单单不符"的情况,此类情况,一方面会影响企业信誉,另一方面会影响企业安全收汇,所以对不符点应及时处理。

(1) 修改单证。如时间充裕,或货物尚未出运,应尽快修改单据。如有必要修改信用证,则应立即通知开证申请人改证,确保出口单据符合信用证要求。

(2) 表提结汇。如货物已装船,或虽未装船但须赶船期,令无法提出修改信用证,在这种情况下,受益人可向议付行出具担保书,要求凭担保议付货款。如果日后遭到开证行拒付,由受益人承担一切后果。

(3) 电提结汇。如果受益人交单金额较大,则由议付行先向开证行拍发电传、传真或电邮列明不符点,征求开证行同意。待开证行同意接受不符点,再将单据寄给开证行,否则立即将开证行拒付意见告知受益人,以便受益人采取相应措施,减少损失。

(4) 随证托收。在"单证不符"的情况下,如货物已发出,而议付行又不愿采用"表提"或"电提"方法时,出口商可采用托收方式,委托银行寄单收款。由于开证行对该笔业务比较熟悉,所以一般仍由原开证行作为代收行,代为收取款项。

在信用证业务中,如果单据中存在不符点,无论采用何种结汇方式,事实上原先信用证项下的银行信用已经变为商业信用,作为出口商要以积极、稳妥的方式处理相关单据,及时采取措施,以便有效控制货物所有权,掌握代表物权的运输单据,促使买方不能提取货物,以避免款、货两空情况的发生。作为出口商来说,出现不符单据是有很大风险的,对不符单据的接受与否完全取决于进口商。

项目十

不同结汇方式下单据的缮制

学习目的

◆ 会在信用证方式下根据信用证缮制相关单据
◆ 会在电汇方式下根据销售合同缮制相关单据
◆ 会在托收方式下根据销售合同缮制相关单据

任务一 在信用证方式下根据信用证缮制相关单据

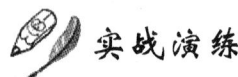 实战演练

一、信用证资料

SEQUENCE OF TOTAL	*27：	1/1
FORM OF DOC. CREDIT	40A：	IRREVOCABLE
DOC. CREDIT NUMBER	*20：	LC-410-046405
DATE OF ISSUE	31C：	141022
EXPIRY	*31D：	DATE150115 PLACE CHINA
APPLICANT	*50：	SUMITOMO CORPORATION
		3-5-8 ORBURA, MINATO-KU
		OSAKA105-8005 JAPAN
BENEFICIARY	*59：	GUANGDONG YUEFENG TRADING CO., LTD.
		NO. 31 ZHEN AN ROAD, GUANGZHOU, CHINA
AMOUNT	*32B：	CURRENCE USD AMOUNT 86 800.00
AVAILABLE WITH/BY	*41D：	ANY BANK IN CHINA BY NEGOTIATION
DRAFTS AT …	42C：	DRAFTS AT SIGHT FOR FULL INVOICE VALUE
DRAWEE	42A：	ASAHI BANK LTD, TOKYO
PARTIAL SHIPMENT	43P：	ALLOWED
TRANSHIPMENT	43T：	ALLOWED
LOADING IN CHARGE	44A：	CHINESE MAIN PORT
FOR TRANSPORT TO	44B：	OSAKA, JAPAN
LATEST DATE OF SHIP	44C：	111231
DESCRIPT OF GOODS	45A：	HALF DRIED PRUNE 2014 CROP

GRADE	SPEC		QNTY	UNIT PRICE (CASE)	SHIPMENT (USD/CASE)
B	L：800 CASE	M：800 CASE	1 600	28.0 CFR OSAKA	DEC., 2014
A	L：700 CASE	M：700 CASE	1 400	30.0 CFR OSAKA	DEC., 2014

PACKING: IN WOODEN CASE, 12KGS PER CASE
TRADE TERMS: CFR OSAKA

DOCUMENTS REQUIRED　　　46A

+ 2/3 SET OF CLEAN ON BOARD OCEAN BILLS OF LADING MADE OUT TO ORDER OF SHIPPER AND BLANK ENDORSED AND MARKED "FREIGHT PREPAID" AND NOTIFY "SUMITOMO CORPORATION OSAKA"
+ MANNUALLY SIGNED COMMERCIAL INVOICE IN TRIPLICATE (3) INDICATING APPLICANT'S REF. NO. SCL I-11-0474
+ PACKING LIST IN TRIPLICATE (3)
+ MANUALLY SIGNED CERTIFICATE OF ORIGIN IN TRIPLICATE (3)
+ BENEFICIARY'S CERTIFICATE STATING THAT CERTIFICATE OF MANUFACTURING PROCESS AND OF THE INGREDIENTS ISSUED BY GUANGDONG YUE FENG TRADING CO., LTD. SHOULD BE SENT TO SUMITOMO CORP. ESCLZ SECTION
+ CERTIFICATE OF WEIGHT AND QUALITY IN TRIPLICATE ISSUED BY THE AUTHORITY

ADDITIONAL COND. 47 A:
1. INSURANCE TO BE EFFECTED BY BUYER
2. TELEGRAPHIC REIMBURSEMENT CLAIM PROHIBITED
3. 1/3 ORIGINAL B/L AND OTHER SHIPPING DOCUMENTS MUST BE SENT DIRECTLY TO APPLICANT SUMITOMO CORP EXCLZ SECTION IN 3 DAYS AFTER B/L DATE AND SENT BY FAX

DETAILS OF CHARGES　　71B: ALL BANKING CHARGES OUTSIDE JAPAN ARE FOR ACCOUNT OF BENEFICIARY

PRESENTATION PERIOD　　48: DOCUMENTS TO BE PRESENTED WITHIN 15 DAYS AFTER THE DATE OF SHIPEMNT BUT WITHIN THE VALIDITY OF THE CREDIT

CONFIRMATION　　　　　*49: WITHOUT

INSTRUCTIONS　　　　　78: THE NEGOTIATING BANK MUST FORWARD THE DRAFTS AND ALL DOCUMENTS BY REGISTERED AIRMAIL DIRECT TO US (INT'L OPERATIONS OFFICE MAIL ADDRESS: C. P. O. BOX NO. 800 TOKYO 100-8691 JAPAN) IN TWO CONSECUTIVE LOTS UPON RECEIPT OF THE DRAFTS AND DOCUMENTS IN ORDER, WE WILL REMIT THE PROCEEDS AS INSTRUCTED BY THE NEGOTIATING BANK

二、有关资料

发票号码：11IN-C314　　　　　　　　发票日期：2014年11月18日
提单号码：GSOK30088　　　　　　　提单日期：2014年12月1日
船名：CHANG GANG　V.98097H　　装运港：广州港
集装箱：2×20′ FCL CY/CY　　　　　运费：USD 1 700.00
CN/SN：TRIU5167753/11133　　　　杂费：USD 120.00
CN/SN：KHLU2616718/11134　　　　原产地证号：891896998
外汇核销单号码：5446580　　　　　　商品编码：0813.2000
生产厂家：广州农垦丰华食品厂　　　　出口口岸：广州海关（5100）
货物装箱情况：木箱包装　　　　　　　H.S.：08132000
净重：12.00 KGS/CASE　　　　　　　毛重：14.00 KGS/CASE
尺码：(20×10×10)CM/CASE
唛头：GA/OSAKA/NOS1-3 000/MADE IN CHINA

根据资料完成以下练习:
(1) 分别回答此信用证的开证日、最后装运日、有效期、到期地点和交单期。
(2) 这份信用证要求提供哪些单据?
(3) 按信用证制作汇票、提单、发票、装箱单、报检单、产地证、通关单、报关单各一份。

商 业 发 票

COMMERCIAL INVOICE

To:

                                                                  Invoice No.: _____

                                                                  Invoice Date: _____

                                                                   S/C No.: _____

                                                                  S/C Date: _____

Letter of Credit No.: _____

Issued by: _____

Marks and Numbers	Number and kind of package Description of goods	Quantity	Unit Price	Amount

装 箱 单

PACKING LIST

To:

                                                   Invoice No.: _____

                                                   Invoice Date: _____

                                                 S/C No.: _____

From: _____ To: _____

Credit No.: _____ Dateof Shipment: _____

Marks and Numbers	C/No., Package	Quantity, Description of goods	G. Weight	N. Weight	Meas.

中华人民共和国出入境检验检疫

出境货物报检单

报检单位(加盖公章)　　　　　　　　　　　　　　＊编号_____

报检单位登记号：　　　联系人：　　　电话：　　　报检日期：

发货人	（中文）					
	（外文）					
收货人	（中文）					
	（外文）					
货物名称(中/外文)		H.S.编码	产地	数/重量	货物总值	包装种类及数量
运输工具名称号码			贸易方式		货物存放地点	
合同号			信用证号		用途	
发货日期			输往国家（地区）		许可证/审批号	
启运地			到达口岸		生产单位注册号	
集装箱规格、数量及号码						

合同、信用证订立的检验检疫条款或特殊要求	标记及号码	随附单据(划"√"或补填)	
		□ 合同	□ 包装性能结果单
		□ 信用证	□ 许可/审批文件
		□ 发票	□
		□ 换证凭单	□
		□ 装箱单	□
		□ 厂检单	□

需要证书名称(划"√"或补填)		＊检验检疫费	
□ 品质证书　__正__副	□ 植物检疫证书　__正__副	总金额（人民币）	
□ 重量证书　__正__副	□ 熏蒸/消毒证书　__正__副		
□ 数量证书　__正__副	□ 出境货物换证凭条	计费人	
□ 兽医卫生证书　__正__副	□ 出境货物通关单		
□ 健康证书　__正__副	□	收费人	
□ 卫生证书　__正__副	□		
□ 动物卫生证书　__正__副	□		

报检人郑重声明：	领取证书	
1. 本人被授权报检 2. 上列填写内容正确属实，货物无伪造或冒用他人的厂名、标志、认证标志，并承担货物质量责任	日期	
签名：_____	签名：	

注：有"＊"号栏由出入境检验检疫机关填写。　　　　　　　　　　　◆ 国家出入境检验检疫局制

一般原产地证明书/加工装配证明书
申 请 书

申请单位(盖章):　　　　　　　　　　　　　　　　　证书号:

注册号:

申请人郑重声明:

本人是被正式授权代表出口单位办理和签署本申请书的。

本申请书及普惠制产地证格式A所列内容正确无误,如发现弄虚作假,冒充格式A所列货物,擅改证书,自愿接受签证机关的处罚并负法律责任。现把有关情况申报如下:

企业名称		发票号	
商品名称		H.S.税目号(以八位数码计)	

商品(FOB)总值(以美元计)		最终目的港及所在国家	
拟出运日期(以提单日期为准)		转口国(地区)	

贸易方式和企业性质(请在适用处划"√")					
一般贸易 C		灵活贸易 L		其他贸易方式 Q	
国营企业	三资企业	国营企业	三资企业	国营企业	三资企业

毛重、包装数量或其他数量				

原产地标准 (划"√")	1. 本项商品完全国产,未使用任何进口原材料:_____ 2. 本项商品含进口成分:_____ (含进口成分的商品,须提交"含进口成分产品加工工序成本明细单")

现提交中国出口商业发票副本一份,一般原产地证明书/加工装配证明书一正三副,以及其他附件____份,请给予审核签证。

申请人说明:

　　　　　　　　　　　　　　　　　　　　　　　申请人(签名):
　　　　　　　　　　　　　　　　　　　　　　　电话:
　　　　　　　　　　　　　　　　　　　　　　　日期:　　年　　月　　日

1. Exporter	Certificate No.
	CERTIFICATE OF ORIGIN **OF** **THE PEOPLE'S REPUBLIC OF CHINA**
2. Consignee	
3. Means of transport and route	5. For certifying authority use only
4. Country/region of destination	

6. Marks and numbers	7. Number and kind of packages; description of goods	8. H. S. Code	9. Quantity	10. Number and date of invoices

11. Declaration by the exporter The undersigned hereby declares the above details and statements are correct, that all the goods were produced in China and that they comply with the Rules of Origin of the People's Republic of China	12. Certification It is herery certified that the declaration by the exporter is correct
Place and date, signature and stamp of authorized signatory	Place and date, signature and stamp of certifying authority

中华人民共和国出口货物报关单

预录入编号： 海关编号：

出口口岸		备案号		出口日期		申报日期	
经营单位		运输方式		运输工具名称		提运单号	
发货单位		贸易方式		征免性质		结汇方式	
许可证号	运抵国(地区)		指运港		境内货源地		
批准文号	成交方式		运费		保费	杂费	
合同协议号	件数		包装种类		毛重(千克)	净重(千克)	
集装箱号	随附单据				生产厂家		
标记唛码及备注							

项号	商品编号	商品名称、规格型号	数量及单位	最终目的国(地区)	单价	总价	币制	征免

税费征收情况

录入员	录入单位	兹声明以上申报无讹并承担法律责任	海关审单批注及放行日期(签章)	
报关员			审单	审价
单位地址		申报单位(签章)	征税	统计
邮编 电话 填制日期			查验	放行

Consignee	B/L NO.
	Port-to-Port or Combined Transport
	BILL OF LADING
Notify party	**RECEIVED** in external apparent good order and condition except as other-wise noted. The total number of packages or units stuffed in the container. The description of the goods and the weights shown in this Bill of Loading are furnished by the Merchants, and which the carrier has no reasonable means of checking and is not a part of this Bill of Loading contract. The carrier has issued the number of Bill of Loading stated below, all of this tenor and date. one of the original Bill of Loading must be surrendered and endorsed or signed against the delivery of the shipment and whereupon any other original Bill of Loading shall be void. The merchants agree to be bound by the terms and conditions of this B/L as if each had personally signed this B/L. See clause 4 on the back of this B/L. (Terms continued on the back hereof, please read carefully)

Pre-carriage by	Place of Receipt
Ocean Vessel Voy. No.	Port of loading
Port of Discharge	Place of delivery

Marks & Nos. Container/Seal No.	No. of Containers or Packages	Description of Goods (if Dangerous Goods, See clause 20)	Gross Weight	Measurement
		Description of Contents for Shipper's Use Only (Not Part of This B/L Contract)		
Total No. ofContainer and/or Packages (in words)				

Freight & Charges	Revenue Tons	Rate	Per	Prepaid	Collect
Ex rate	Prepaid at		Payable at	**Place and date ofIssue:**	
	Total prepaid		No. of Original B(s)/L	Signed by	

Ladenon Board the Vessel
Date　　　　　　　　**By**

BILL OF EXCHANGE

凭 Drawn Under	不可撤销信用证 Irrevocable L/C NO.
日期 Date	支取 按 息 付款 Payable With interest @ %
号码 No.	汇票金额 Exchange for 广州 Guangzhou
见票 at Being unpaid) Pay to the order of	日 后（本汇票之副本未付）付交 sight of this FIRST of Excgange (Second of Exchange
金额 the sum of	
此致 To	

任务二 在电汇方式下根据销售合同缮制相关单据

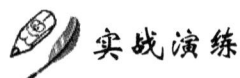
实战演练

一、合同资料

销售合同
SALES CONTRACT

卖方 SELLER	LESHENG TRADING CO., LTD. HUARONG MANSION RM2901 NO. 85 JINGLING ROAD, SHANGHAI 210005, CHINA TEL: 0086-21-4715004 FAX: 0086-21-4711363	编号 NO.: NEO2011026 日期 DATE: FEB. 28, 2011 地点 SIGNED IN: SHANGHAI, CHINA
买方 BUYER	NEO GENERAL TRADING CO. P.O. BOX 99552, RIYADH 22766, KSA TEL: 00966-1-4659220 FAX: 00966-1-4659213	

(续表)

买卖双方同意以下条款达成交易： This contract is made by and agreed between the BUYER and SELLER, in accordance with the terms and conditions stipulated below			
1. 品名及规格 Commodity & Specification	2. 数量 Quantity	3. 单价及价格条款 Unit Price & Trade Terms	4. 金额 Amount
		CIF DAMMAM PORT, SAUDI ARABIA	
ABOUT 1 700 CARTONS CANNED MUSRHOOMS PIECES & STEMS 24 TINS X 425 GRAMS NET WEIGHT (D. W. 227 GRAMS) AT USD 9.80 PER CARTON. ROSE BRAND. G. W. : 19074.44KGS	1 500CARTONS	USD 9.80	USD 14 700.00
Total：	1 500CARTONS		USD14 700.00

5. 总值

    Total Value USD FOURTEEN THOUSAND SEVEN HUNDRED ONLY.

6. 包装

    Packing EXPORTED BROWN CARTON

（续上）

7. 唛头

Shipping Marks ROSE BRAND

178/2011

RIYADH

C/NO 1-UP

8. 装运期及运输方式

Time of Shipment & means of Transportation NOT LATER THAN APR. 15, 2014 BY VESSEL

9. 装运港及目的地

Port of Loading & Destination From：SHANGHAI PORT, CHINA

To：DAMMAM PORT, SAUDI ARABIA

10. 保险

Insurance：TO BE EFFECTED BY THE SELLERS FOR 110% OF FULL INVOICE VALUE COVERING F. P. A. AND WAR RISKS UP TO SAUDI ARABIA

11. 付款方式

Terms of Payment T/T

12. 备注

Remarks

The Buyer	The Seller
NEO GENERAL TRADING CO.	LESHENG TRADING CO., LTD.
（signature）	（signature）

二、补充资料

H. S.：

发票号码：LS-NEO11026

提单号码：GSOK30088

船名：JINJIANG V.817J

集装箱：2×20' FCL CY/CY

　　CN/SN：COSU6751735/13142

原产地证号：321896557

外汇核销单号码：3266549

生产厂家：上海新华食品有限公司

发票日期：2015年3月20日

提单日期：2015年4月10日

装运港：上海

CN/SN：COSU6217186/13451

商品编码：2003.1019

出口口岸：外高桥港区海关

要求：根据合同完成以下练习。

（1）分别回答这份合同的日期、数量、包装、支付方式、价格。

（2）这份合同的装运期是什么时间？是否可以分批装运或转运？需要投保什么险？

（3）按信用证制作汇票、提单、发票、装箱单、报检单、产地证、通关单、报关单、保险单各一份。

商 业 发 票
COMMERCIAL INVOICE

To:

Invoice No.: _____

Invoice Date: _____

S/C No.: _____

S/C Date: _____

Letter of Credit No.: _____

Issued by: _____

Marks and Numbers	Number and kind of package Description of goods	Quantity	Unit Price	Amount

装 箱 单
PACKING LIST

To:

Invoice No.: _____

Invoice Date: _____

S/C No.: _____

From: _____   To: _____

Credit No.: _____   Dateof Shipment: _____

Marks and Numbers	C/No., Package	Quantity, Description of goods	G. Weight	N. Weight	Meas.

中华人民共和国出入境检验检疫

出境货物报检单

报检单位(加盖公章)   *编号_____

报检单位登记号：   联系人   电话   报检日期

发货人	(中文)			
	(外文)			
收货人	(中文)			
	(外文)			
货物名称(中/外文)		H.S.编码	产地	数/重量	货物总值	包装种类及数量

运输工具名称号码		贸易方式		货物存放地点	
合同号		信用证号		用途	
发货日期		输往国家(地区)		许可证/审批号	
启运地		到达口岸		生产单位注册号	
集装箱规格、数量及号码					

合同、信用证订立的检验检疫条款或特殊要求	标记及号码	随附单据(划"√"或补填)	
		□ 合同	□ 包装性能结果单
		□ 信用证	□ 许可/审批文件
		□ 发票	□
		□ 换证凭单	□
		□ 装箱单	□
		□ 厂检单	□

需要证书名称(划"√"或补填)			*检验检疫费	
□ 品质证书 __正__副	□ 植物检疫证书 __正__副	总金额（人民币）	
□ 重量证书 __正__副	□ 熏蒸/消毒证书 __正__副		
□ 数量证书 __正__副	□ 出境货物换证凭条	计费人	
□ 兽医卫生证书 __正__副	□ 出境货物通关单		
□ 健康证书 __正__副	□	收费人	
□ 卫生证书 __正__副	□		
□ 动物卫生证书 __正__副	□		

报检人郑重声明： 1. 本人被授权报检。 2. 上列填写内容正确属实，货物无伪造或冒用他人的厂名、标志、认证标志，并承担货物质量责任。 签名：	领取证书 日期 签名：

注："*"号栏由出入境检验检疫机关填写。   ◆ 国家出入境检验检疫局制

一般原产地证明书/加工装配证明书
申 请 书

申请单位(盖章):   证书号:

注册号:

申请人郑重声明:

  本人是被正式授权代表出口单位办理和签署本申请书的。

  本申请书及普惠制产地证格式 A 所列内容正确无误,如发现弄虚作假,冒充格式 A 所列货物,擅改证书,自愿接受签证机关的处罚并负法律责任。现将有关情况申报如下:

企业名称		发票号		
商品名称		H.S.税目号(以八位数码计)		
商品(FOB)总值(以美元计)		最终目的港及所在国家		
拟出运日期(以提单日期为准)		转口国(地区)		
贸易方式和企业性质(请在适用处划"√")				
一般贸易 C		灵活贸易 L		其他贸易方式 Q
国营企业	三资企业	国营企业	三资企业	国营企业	三资企业
毛重,包装数量或其他数量					
原产地标准(划"√")	1. 本项商品完全国产,未使用任何进口原材料:_____ 2. 本项商品含进口成分:_____ (含进口成分的商品,须提交"含进口成分产品加工工序成本明细单")				

现提交中国出口商业发票副本一份,一般原产地证明书/加工装配证明书一正三副,以及其他附件___份,请给予审核签证。

申请人说明:

                申请人(签名):
                电话:
                日期: 年 月 日

1. Exporter	Certificate No.
	CERTIFICATE OF ORIGIN **OF** **THE PEOPLE'S REPUBLIC OF CHINA**
2. Consignee	
3. Means of transport and route	5. For certifying authority use only
4. Country/region of destination	

6. Marks and numbers	7. Number and kind of packages; description of goods	8. H. S. Code	9. Quantity	10. Number and date of invoices

11. Declaration by the exporter The undersigned hereby declares the above details and statements are correct, that all the goods were produced in China and that they comply with the Rules of Origin of the People's Republic of China	12. Certification It is herery certified that the declaration by the exporter is correct
Place and date, signature and stamp of authorized signatory	Place and date, signature and stamp of certifying authority

中华人民共和国出口货物报关单

预录入编号：　　　　　　　　　　　　　　　　　　　　海关编号：

出口口岸	备案号		出口日期	申报日期
经营单位	运输方式	运输工具名称		提运单号
发货单位	贸易方式		征免性质	结汇方式
许可证号	运抵国(地区)		指运港	境内货源地
批准文号	成交方式	运费	保费	杂费
合同协议号	件数	包装种类	毛重(千克)	净重(千克)
集装箱号	随附单据		生产厂家	

标记唛码及备注

项号	商品编号	商品名称、规格型号	数量及单位	最终目的国(地区)	单价	总价	币制	征免

税费征收情况

录入员	录入单位	兹声明以上申报无讹并承担法律责任	海关审单批注及放行日期(签章)	
报关员			审单	审价
单位地址		申报单位(签章)	征税	统计
邮编　　　电话　　　填制日期			查验	放行

PICC 中国人民财产保险股份有限公司
PICC Property and Casualty Company Limited
总公司设于北京　一九四九年创立
Head Office Beijing　Established in 1949

货 物 运 输 保 险 单
CARGO TRANSPORTATION INSURANCE POLICY

发票号码 Invoice No.：

合同号码 Contract No.：　　　　　　　　　　　　　保单号次 Policy No.

信用证号码 Credit No.：

被保险人 Insured：_____

中保财产保险有限公司(以下简称本公司)根据被保险人的要求,及其所缴付约定的保险费,按照本保险单承担险别和背面所载条款与下列特别条款承保下列货物运输保险,特签发本保险单。

This policy of Insurance witnesses that The People Insurance (Property) Company of China, Ltd. (hereinafter called the Company) at the request of the Insured and in consideration of the agreed premium paid by the Insured, undertakes to insure the under mentioned goods in transportation subject to the conditions of this Policy as per the Clauses printed overleaf and other special clauses attached hereon.

标记 Marks & No.	包装及数量 Quantity	保险货物项目 Description of goods	保险金额 Amount Insured

总保险金额：
Total Amount Insured：_____

保险费　　　　　　　启运日期　　　　　　　　　装载运输工具
Premium　As arranged　Date of commencement _____　Per conveyance _____

自　　　　　　　　　经　　　　　　　　　　　　至
From _____　Via _____　To _____

承保险别 Conditions：

所保货物,如发生本保险单项下可能引起索赔的损失或损坏,应立即通知本公司下述代理人查勘。如有索赔,应向本公司提交保险单正本(本保险单共有 2 份正本)及有关文件。如一份正本已用于索赔,其余正本则自动失效。

In the event of damage which may result in a claim under this Policy, immediate notice be given to the Company Agent as mentioned hereunder. Claims, if any, one of the Original Policy which has been issued in TWO Original(s) together with the relevant documents shall be surrendered to the Company, if one of the Original Policy has been accomplished, the others to be void.

赔款偿付地点
Claim payable at _____

出单日期
Issuing date _____

地址：中国上海中山东一路321号
Address：321 Zhongshanyi Road E. Shanghai, China

中国人保财险股份有限公司上海市分公司
PICC Property & Casualty Co Ltd,
Shanghai Branch
钱水凤
Authorized Signature

Consignee	B/L No.
	中远集装箱运输有限公司 **COSCO CONTAINER LINES** Port-to-Port or Combined Transport **BILL OF LADING**
Notify party	**RECEIVED** in external apparent good order and condition except as other-wise noted. The total number of packages or units stuffed in the container. The description of the goods and the weights shown in this Bill of Loading are furnished by the Merchants, and which the carrier has no reasonable means of checking and is not a part of this Bill of Loading contract. The carrier has issued the number of Bill of Loading stated below, all of this tenor and date. one of the original Bill of Loading must be surrendered and endorsed or signed against the delivery of the shipment and whereupon any other original Bill of Loading shall be void. The merchants agree to be bound by the terms and conditions of this B/L as if each had personally signed this B/L. See clause 4 on the back of this B/L. (Terms continued on the back hereof, please read carefully)

Pre-carriage by	Place of Receipt
Ocean Vessel Voy. No.	Port of loading
Port of Discharge	Place of delivery

Marks & Nos. Container/Seal No.	No. of Containers or Packages	Description of Goods (if Dangerous Goods, See clause 20)	Gross Weight	Measurement
		Description of Contents for Shipper's Use Only (Not Part of This B/L Contract)		
Total No. of Container and/or Packages (in words)				

Freight & Charges	Revenue Tons	Rate	Per	Prepaid	Collect
Ex rate	Prepaid at		Payable at	Place and date of Issue	
Total prepaid			No. of Original B(s)/L	Signed by	

Laden on Board the Vessel   Date   By

```
                        BILL OF EXCHANGE

凭                                          不可撤销信用证
Drawn Under                                 Irrevocable L/C NO.
日期                             支取    按    息    付款
Date                          Payable  With  interest  @   %
号码            汇 票 金 额                        上海
No.             Exchange for                     Shanghai
见票                        日后(本汇票之副本未付)付交
at                    sight of this FIRST of Excgange (Second of Exchange
Being unpaid) Pay to the order of

金额
the sum of

此致
To
```

任务三 在托收方式下根据销售合同缮制相关单据

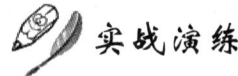
实战演练

一、销售合同资料

HUAMEI GLOVES CO., LTD.
2810, Shanghai International Trade Center 2201 Yan An Road(W), SHANGHAI 200336
TEL:+86 21 6278 9099   FAX:+86 21 6278 9569

销 售 合 同
SALES CONTRACT

Contract No.: 01JB05271
Date: Sep. 20, 2014

The Buyer: JAMES B ROWN&SONS.
♯304-310 JaJa Street,
Toronto, Canada
TEL: (1)7709910, FAX: (1)7701100

This contract is made by and between the Buyer and Seller, whereby the buyer agrees to buy and the saller agrees to sell the goods according to the under-mentioned and conditions.

Art. No.	Description	Size	Color	QTY	Price	Amounts
5121A	Latex Full Coated Cotton Woven, Knit Wrist Liner	10 1/2	Natural	1 000 DOZ. PER	FOB.SHANGHAI USD 4.47	USD 4 470
5294B	PVC Dipped Gloves, Interlock Liner, Rough Chip Finish, Gauntlet	10 1/2		1 200 DOZ. PER	USD 6.70	USD 8 040 =USD 12 510

Packaging: 1 DOZ IN A POLYBAG, 25 DOZS IN A EXPORT CARTON
Time of Delivery: NOV. 25, 2014
Payment: D/P IN ADVANCE
Remark:

    THE SELLER   THE BUYER
 HUAMEI GLOVES CO., LTD.   JAMES BROWN&SONS.
  （出口商签字和盖章）   （进口商签字和盖章）

二、该合同的相关其他资料

发票号码：HM03225   发票日期：NOV. 15, 2014

货名	毛重(KGS)	净重(KGS)	体积(CBM)
STYLE:1521A Latex Full Coated Cotton Woven, Knit Wrist Liner	1 665	1 583	10.80
STYLE:2954C PVC Dipped Gloves, Interlock Liner, Rough Chip Finish, Gauntlet	2 430	1 827	13.40

船名航次：CMA CGM V.216
起运港：SHANGHAI
目的港：MONTREAL

三、根据以上资料填制单据

商 业 发 票

COMMERCIAL INVOICE

To:

                   Invoice No.: _____

                   Invoice Date: _____

                   S/C No.: _____

                   S/C Date: _____

Letter of Credit No. _____

Issued by: _____

Marks and Numbers	Number and kind of package Description of goods	Quantity	Unit Price	Amount

装 箱 单

PACKING LIST

To:

                   Invoice No.: _____

                   Invoice Date: _____

                   S/C No.: _____

From: _____ **To:** _____

Credit No.: _____ **Date of Shipment:** _____

Marks and Numbers	C/No., Package	Quantity, Description of goods	G. Weight	N. Weight	Meas.

(续表)

Shipper			B/L No.		
			中远集装箱运输有限公司 COSCO CONTAINER LINES		
Consignee			Port-to-Port or Combined Transport **BILL OF LADING**		
			RECEIVED in external apparent good order and condition except as other-wise noted. The total number of packages or units stuffed in the container. The description of the goods and the weights shown in this Bill of Loading are furnished by the Merchants, and which the carrier has no reasonable means of checking and is not a part of this Bill of Loading contract. The carrier has issued the number of Bill of Loading stated below, all of this tenor and date. one of the original Bill of Loading must be surrendered and endorsed or signed against the delivery of the shipment and whereupon any other original Bill of Loading shall be void. The merchants agree to be bound by the terms and conditions of this B/L as if each had personally signed this B/L. See clause 4 on the back of this B/L. (Terms continued on the back hereof, please read carefully)		
Notify party					
* Pre-carriage by	* Place of Receipt				
Ocean Vessel Voy. No.	Port of loading				
Port of Discharge	* Place of delivery				
Marks & Nos. Container/Seal No.	No. of Containers or Packages	Description of Goods (if Dangerous Goods, See clause 20)	Gross Weight		Measurement
		Description of Contents for Shipper's Use Only (Not Part of This B/L Contract)			
Total No. of Container and/or Packages (in words)					
Freight & Charges	Revenue Tons	Rate	Per	Prepaid	Collect
Ex rate	Prepaid at		Payable at	Place and date of Issue	
Total prepaid			No. of Original B(s)/L	Signed by	
Ladenon Board the Vessel			Date	By	

SHIPMENT ADVICE

TO： DATE：

RE： S/C NO.

INVOICE NO.

WE HEREBY INFORMED YOU THAT THE GOODS UNDER THE ABOVE MENTIONED SALES CONTRACT HAVE BEEN SHIPPED. THE DETAILS OF SHIPMENT ARE STATED BELOW. PLEASE COVER INSURANCE.

COMMODITY：

QUANTITY：

INVOICE VALUE：

OCEAN VESSEL：

DATE OF SHIPMENT：

PORT OF LOADING：

PORT OF DESTINATION：

MARKS：

·····································
Authorized Signature

BILL OF EXCHANGE

凭		不可撤销信用证
Drawn Under		Irrevocable L/C NO.

日期　　　　　　　　　　支取　　按　息　　付款
Date　　　　　　　　Payable　With　interest　　@　　%

号码　　　　汇 票 金 额 ══════════ 上海
No.　　　　Exchange for ══════════ Shanghai

见票　　　　　　　　日 后（本汇票之副本未付）付交
at　　　　　　　sight of this FIRST of Excgange (Second of Exchange Being unpaid) Pay to the order of

金额
the sum of ═══════════════════════════════

此致
To

附件

附件1 常用国际贸易术语

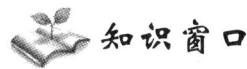

(一) 贸易术语的涵义和作用

贸易术语(Trade Terms)也称价格术语(Price Terms)。它用英文缩写字母(如CIF)或简短的概念(Cost, Insurance and freight)来表示商品价格的构成和买卖双方在货物交接过程中有关手续、风险、费用、责任的划分、所有权转移的界限等问题,它是国际贸易中单价的一个重要组成部分。

其作用主要体现在以下几个方面:

(1) 可以简化交易内容,缩短谈判时间,促进成交,有利于国际贸易的发展。

(2) 可以表示商品价格的构成,有利于买卖双方核算价格和成本。

(3) 可以表明商品风险和所有权转移的界线,有利于解决履约当中的争议。

(二) 贸易术语的国际贸易惯例

目前,有关贸易术语的成文国际贸易惯例主要有三种:

(1)《1932年华沙—牛津规则》。

(2)《美国对外贸易定义1941年修正本》。

(3)《国际贸易术语解释通则》

《国际贸易术语解释通则》(International Rules for the Interpretation of Trade Terms,以下简称通则)是当前应用范围最广,影响最大的一种惯例,已被国际上多数国家接受。

2010年通则内容如附表1所示。

附表1 《2010年国际贸易术语解释通则》(INCOTERMS 2010)(简称2010通则)

适用于海上和内河运输的术语(sea or inland waterway)	FAS: Free Alongside ship FOB: Free On Board CFR: Cost and Freight CIF: Cost Insurance and freight	装运港船边交货 装运港船上交货 成本加运费 成本加保险费加运费
适用于任何运输方式的术语(any mode)	CPT: Carriage paid to CIP: Carriage and Insurance Paid to DDP: Delivered Duty Paid DAT: Delivered at Termina DAP: Delivered at Placel EXW(Ex Works) FCA: Free Carrier	运费付至 运费/保险费付至 完税后交货 目的地的集散站交货 目的地交货 工厂交货 货交承运人

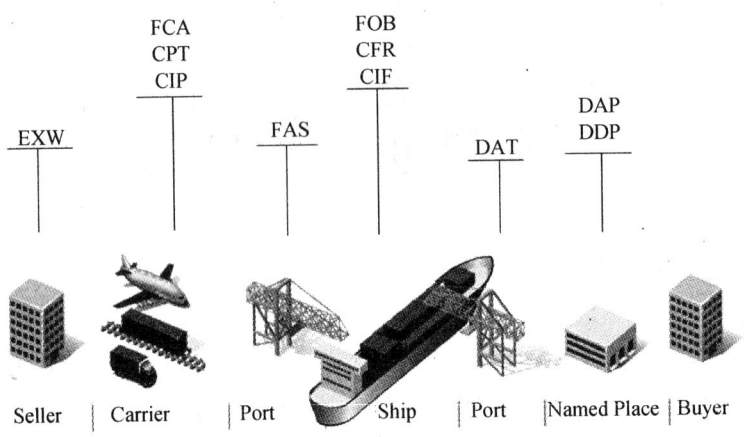

附图1 贸易术语示意图

(三) 常用的贸易术语

《2010年通则》的11种贸易术语按其适用运输方式的不同,主要分为两大类,其中FOB、CFR、CIF为适用海运方式的常用贸易术语。其异同点见附表2。

附表2 FOB、CFR、CIF术语的异同点

术语	不同点			相同点
	国外运输及运费	投保及保险费	价格构成	
FOB	买方	买方	出口销售成本价	1. 适用于海运或内河航运 2. 装运港完成交货 3. 风险转移在装运港船上
CFR	卖方	买方	FOB价+国外运费	
CIF	卖方	卖方	FOB价+国外运费+保险费	

(四) 贸易术语的选择方法

在进出口贸易中,FOB、CIF、CFR三种贸易术语使用最多。通常情况,出口时尽量采用CIF和CFR术语,进口时尽量采用FOB术语。随着集装箱运输和多式联运的发展,FCA、CPT和CIP三种术语的使用也越来越频繁,因为FCA、CPT和CIP不仅适用于各种运输方式,而且在海运和多式联运中比前三个贸易术语有更多的优越性:首先,可以提前获得运输单据,节省了卖方交单收汇的时间,有利卖方的资金周转;其次,减少了卖方承担的风险。

(五) 选用贸易术语应注意事项

1. 考虑运输条件

考虑使用何种运输方式,有无足够的运输能力。若能力许可且经济合理,按FOB、FCA或FAS术语进口,这样,可以节省运费和保险费,出口则按CIF、CFR或CIP术语,它有利于我国运输业和保险业的发展。否则,可考虑按FOB、FCA或FAS出口,按CIF、CFR或CIP进口。

2. 考虑运费因素

运费是货价的组成部分,货物经由不同的线路收取的运费也会各不相同。另外,运费还会受航运市场整体运价变动的影响。因此,在选用贸易术语时应考虑运费因素。一般情况,运价上涨时,出售货物采用 FOB 术语,进口货物采用 CFR 或 CIF 术语,可以避免承担运价上涨的风险。

3. 考虑货物情况

首先,进出口贸易中涉及各类货种,不同的货物在运输方面有各自不同的要求,其运费开支的大小也各有不同;其次,货物运量大的,运费较便宜。因此,在选用贸易术语时,都应予以考虑。

(六)考虑海运风险

在国际贸易中,货物一般都需经过长途运输,其中,海运过程中的风险较大。在采用贸易术语时,应考虑不同环境和时期、不同运输路线和运输方式的海上风险情况。

此外,选择贸易术语时,还应考虑当地的地理环境、港口条件、政治制度、货款支付方式、本国的船舶情况以及办理进出口货物结关手续有无困难等。总之,在选择贸易术语时,应综合各种因素,权衡利弊,综合考虑。

附件2 常用支付方式

出口贸易中常用的货款支付方式有三种:汇付、托收和信用证。

(一)汇付

汇付(Remittance)又称汇款,是进口方将货款交由银行汇给出口方。其基本做法如下:

由汇款人向汇出行递交"汇出汇款申请书"一式两联(包括申请书和汇款回执),委托汇出行办理汇款业务。汇出行按照申请书的指示,使用某种结算工具通知汇入行,汇入行按照双方银行事先订立代理协议的规定,向收款人解付汇款。结算工具主要包括以下三种。

1. 信汇

信汇(M/T)是指进口方将货款交给本地银行,请该行用信件手段委托出口方所在地的分行或代理行付款给进口方。

2. 票汇

票汇(D/D)是指进口方向本地银行购买银行汇票,自行寄给出口方,出口方凭以向汇票上指定的银行取款。

3. 电汇

电汇(T/T)是应付款人的申请,由汇出行拍发电报或电传给其在国外的分行或代理行,指示其解付一定金额给收款人的一种方式。

(二)托收

托收(Collection)是出口方委托银行代为向进口方收款的一种支付方式。

托收方式的信用基础仍是商业信用,与汇付方式相比,出口商收款的安全性有所加强。

国际贸易中开出的汇票多是跟单汇票,因此常用的托收方式是跟单托收。跟单托收包括付款交单(Documents against Payment,D/P)和承兑交单(Documents against Acceptance,D/A)。

付款交单是指出口方的交单是以进口方的付款为条件,即进口方付款后才能向代收行领取单据。

承兑交单是指出口方(或代收行)向进口方以承兑为条件交付单据的一种方式。我国外贸企业一般不采用承兑交单方式出口。

(三) 信用证

信用证(LETTER OF CREDIT,L/C)是银行(即开证行)依照进口商(即开证申请人)的要求和指示,对出口商(即受益人)发出的、授权出口商签发、以银行或进口商为付款人的汇票,保证在交来符合信用证条款规定的汇票和单据时,必定承兑和付款的保证文件。

信用证项下付款是一种单据的买卖,出口商交货后提交的单据,只要做到与信用证条款相符,"单证一致,单单一致",银行就保证向出口商支付货款。一般提交的单据有:汇票、商业发票、装箱单或重量单、海运提单、保险单、产地证和检验证书等。

(四) 各种支付方式的结合使用

在国际贸易中,一笔交易的货款结算可以只使用一种结算方式,也可以根据需要将两种或两种以上的结算方式结合使用,或有利于促成交易,或有利于安全、及时收汇,或有利于妥善处理付汇。常见的不同结算方式结合使用的形式有:信用证与汇付结合、信用证与托收结合、汇付与银行保函或信用证结合、汇付与银行保函结合等。

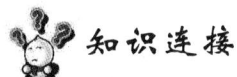

知识连接

(1) T/T,虽然有一定的风险,但是费用低,在全世界范围内的外贸付款方式中很流行。

(2) 100%前T/T,这种方式很少见,如果你的客人在下单的时候给你100%T/T过来,那么你走运了。一般来说,应该是老客人或者金额比较小才会这么做。

(3) 100%后T/T,这个有一定的风险性,除非是老客户,否则就太被动了,随时都有可能钱货两空,付不付款全靠客人的信用。

(4) 30%前T/T(作定金),70%后T/T,见提单后再付余款,这种方式是最为常见的。

参 考 文 献

[1] 童宏祥.常用国际商务单证制作[M].上海:华东师范大学出版社,2013.
[2] 王莉,等.进出口业务单证操作手册[M].广州:广东经济出版社,2005.
[3] 陈文培.国际贸易实务认证考试辅导精编[M].上海:上海财经大学出版社,2014.
[4] 杨金玲.国际商务单证实务[M].北京:首都经济贸易大学出版社,2014.
[5] 胡俊文.国际贸易实战操作教程[M].北京:清华大学出版社,2009.